# The Dynamics of Influencer Marketing

YouTube, Instagram, Facebook, Vimeo, Twitter, and so on, have their own logics, dynamics and different audiences. This book analyses how the users of these social networks, especially those of YouTube and Instagram, become content prescribers, opinion leaders and, by extension, people of influence.

What influence capacity do they have? Why are intimate or personal aspects shared with unknown people? Who are the big beneficiaries? How much is vanity and how much altruism? What business is behind these social networks? What dangers do they contain? What volume of business can we estimate they generate? How are they transforming cultural industries? What legislation is applied? How does the legislation affect these communications when they are sponsored? Is the privacy of users violated with the data obtained? Who is the owner of the content? Are they to blame for "fake news"? In this changing, challenging and intriguing environment, *The Dynamics of Influencer Marketing* discusses all of these questions and more.

Considering this complexity from different perspectives: technological, economic, sociological, psychological and legal, the book combines the visions of several experts from the academic world and provides a structured framework with a wide approach to understand the new era of influencing, including the dark sides of it. It will be of direct interest to marketing scholars and researchers while also relevant to many other areas affected by the phenomenon of social media influence.

**José M. Álvarez-Monzoncillo** (PhD, Complutense University of Madrid) is full-time Professor of Audiovisual Communications at Rey Juan Carlos University in Madrid. He is currently the Course Director of a Master's degree in Television Journalism and Director of the Infocent research group. His research and teaching interests include international media strategies, media branding, media business models, media and cultural policy, social media and media industries/cultural industries.

# Routledge Studies in Marketing

This series welcomes proposals for original research projects that are either single or multi-authored or an edited collection from both established and emerging scholars working on any aspect of marketing theory and practice and provides an outlet for studies dealing with elements of marketing theory, thought, pedagogy and practice.

It aims to reflect the evolving role of marketing and bring together the most innovative work across all aspects of the marketing 'mix' – from product development, consumer behaviour, marketing analysis, branding and customer relationships, to sustainability, ethics and the new opportunities and challenges presented by digital and online marketing.

For more information about this series, please visit: www.routledge.com/ Routledge-Studies-in-Marketing/book-series/RMKT

# The Dynamics of Influencer Marketing

A Multidisciplinary Approach

**Edited by José M. Álvarez-Monzoncillo**

Routledge
Taylor & Francis Group

LONDON AND NEW YORK

First published 2023
by Routledge
4 Park Square, Milton Park, Abingdon, Oxon OX14 4RN

and by Routledge
605 Third Avenue, New York, NY 10158

*Routledge is an imprint of the Taylor & Francis Group, an informa business*

© 2023 selection and editorial matter, José M. Álvarez-Monzoncillo;
individual chapters, the contributors

The right of José M. Álvarez-Monzoncillo to be identified as the author of
the editorial material, and of the authors for their individual chapters, has
been asserted in accordance with sections 77 and 78 of the Copyright,
Designs and Patents Act 1988.

*Trademark notice*: Product or corporate names may be trademarks or
registered trademarks, and are used only for identification and explanation
without intent to infringe.

*British Library Cataloguing-in-Publication Data*
A catalogue record for this book is available from the British Library

*Library of Congress Cataloging-in-Publication Data*
A catalog record has been requested for this book

ISBN: 978-0-367-67890-6 (hbk)
ISBN: 978-0-367-68091-6 (pbk)
ISBN: 978-1-003-13417-6 (ebk)

DOI: 10.4324/9781003134176

Typeset in Bembo
by SPi Technologies India Pvt Ltd (Straive)

# Contents

# Contributors

**Antonio Baraybar Fernández** is Associate Professor of Audiovisual Communication and Advertising at the Rey Juan Carlos University, Madrid and has a PhD in Information Sciences from the Universidad Complutense de Madrid. His research and teaching interests are in the area of the economics of communication, specifically marketing, communication management in organizations, new, emerging business models fostered by new technologies, and the effects of persuasive communication from the perspective of neuroscience. For more than a decade he worked in private television, as head of corporate marketing management at Antena 3 Television.

**Adele Berndt** is Associate Professor at Jönköping International Business School (JIBS), Sweden and an affiliated researcher at Gordon Institute of Business Science (GIBS) at the University of Pretoria. Her research focuses on the intersection of consumers and branding in diverse product and service contexts, lecturing and publishing in a range of journals in these areas. She is a member of the Academy of Marketing Science and serves on the boards of various academic journals.

**Toon Brouwers** is Teacher of TV-Journalism, HU University of Applied Science. He is passionate about audiovisual media, and entrepreneurship education related to journalism. He has extensive experience about being a journalist and producing for different kinds of media, such as TV, radio, video, and photography. He is the owner of a startup called "Toon op TV", which centers on tv production. He aims to share his knowledge about how to become a media entrepreneur with his students. In his free time, he develops podcasts about innovative topics, and is very hard to beat in gaming.

**Dr. Sylvia Chan-Olmsted** is the Director of Media Consumer Research in the College of Journalism and Communications at the University of Florida. A Professor of Media Management, Dr. Chan-Olmsted's research expertise includes emerging media consumption behavior, brand and media engagement, brand trust, marketing strategy of media firms, and AI applications in media and marketing communications.

**Tiffany Chee**, Undergraduate Student, Wee Kim Wee School of Communication and Information, Nanyang Technological University, TIFF0015@e.ntu.edu.sg

**Tim Dwyer** is the author of several books including *Sharing News Online: Commendary Cultures and Social Media News Ecologies* (with Fiona Martin) and *Convergent Media and Privacy*. He researches media and communications industries, algorithmic mediatisation, and pluralism in news media platform transformations.

**José Esteves** is full-time Professor of Information Systems at IE Business School, and Associate Dean of full-time MBA programs. He holds a PhD in software and information systems from Universidad Politecnica de Catalunya, Barcelona, Spain. He is also a master in information systems, Universidade do Minho, Braga, Portugal, and he has a Diploma in Business Administration (DBA) and a minor in financial management from Instituto Superior de Tecnologia Empresarial, Porto, Portugal. In addition to his research and teaching, he continues to act as a consultant to a number of companies.

**Emilio Fernández Peña** is founding Director of the Sport Research Institute at the Universitat Autònoma de Barcelona. He is Head of the Olympic Studies Centre at the university and a research collaborator of the International Olympic Committee. He is a member of the Development Working Group set up to design the educational offering of the new International Olympic Academy.

**Sven–Ove Horst** is Assistant Professor for Media and Creative Industries at Erasmus University Rotterdam, and Visiting Professor at Universidad de Navarra, Pamplona. His research centers on strategic media management, media entrepreneurship, and organization theory, and has been published in, for example, the *International Journal on Media Management*, the *Journal of Media Business Studies*, and the *Journal of Media Management and Entrepreneurship*. He likes exploring emergent phenomena, and is currently taking a deep dive into cryptocurrencies, social media and investing.

**Jonathon Hutchinson** is Senior Lecturer in Online Communication and Media at the University of Sydney and a Chief Investigator on the Australian Research Council Discovery Project, *Media Pluralism and Online News*. His research explores Public Service Media, cultural intermediation, everyday social media, automated media, and algorithms in media. He is Editor of the *Policy & Internet* journal, and the Treasurer for the Australian and New Zealand Communication Association (ANZCA).

**Prince Chacko Johnson** is PhD Candidate at Jönköping International Business School. Johnson is interested in artificial intelligence and its effects on firms. He makes use of digital media databases, social media data, and a combination of analytics and web scraping techniques.

**Hyehyun Julia Kim** is a PhD student in the Department of Advertising at the University of Florida. She received her M.A. in Mass Communications from Korea University and B.A. in English Literature from University of British

Columbia. Her research interests include consumer perceptions of influencer marketing and consumer brand relationships. Prior to joining the University of Florida, she worked as a media planner at Mindshare Korea.

**Chen Lou** (PhD, Michigan State University) is Assistant Professor of Integrated Marketing Communication, Wee Kim Wee School of Communication and Information, Nanyang Technological University, chenlou@ntu.edu.sg

**Anne Morawietz** is a doctoral student in marketing at Jönköping University, Sweden. Her research focuses on consumer engagement, experiences, and transformation in branded communities of practice. She has a particular interest in fitness communities, for example CrossFit.

**Tomas Müllern** is Professor in Business Administration at Jönköping International Business School. His research in marketing is focused on sustainable marketing, with a special focus on marketing communication practices, promoting sustainability messages and how consumers react to those.

**Adolfo Nieto** is a junior researcher in the Sport Research Institute at the Universitat Autònoma de Barcelona. He has been a guest researcher at Monash University (Melbourne, Australia) and he is currently conducting his doctoral research on sports personal brand management on social media.

**Natividad Ramajo** is Senior Lecturer in, and Director of, the Department of Audiovisual Communication and Advertising at the Universitat Autònoma de Barcelona. Her research activity focuses on social media and sport, media gender studies, and teenagers' interaction with audiovisual media.

**Christian Sandström** is Senior Associate Professor at Jönköping International Business School and the Ratio Institute. His research concerns the interplay between technological and institutional change along with the related strategic challenges for firms and policymakers. Sandström has made use of both social media data and digital archives in his research.

**Marina Santín** is Associate Professor and Researcher at the Department of Communication Science and Sociology at the Rey Juan Carlos University. She has a doctorate in Communication and a degree in Journalism and Law from the Universidad Complutense of Madrid. She specializes in the study of the production and distribution of media content. Her main line of research focuses on the analysis of the journalistic profession and the application of professional deontology therein.

**Xuan Zhou** (M.S., University of Edinburgh), PhD Candidate, Wee Kim Wee School of Communication and Information, 05-13, Nanyang Technological University, ZHOU0352@e.ntu.edu.sg

# Introduction[1]

*José M. Álvarez-Monzoncillo*

The time we spend connected to social networks is growing more and more. The phenomenon of social media entertainment (SME) is capturing the attention of the traditional media audience and of the entertainment industry in general. In many countries, the average amount of time dedicated to social networks per day is in excess of one hour. The study of this new style of consumption is complex because during that time users also share content from the media and entertainment industry: news, video-clips, and so on. A large number of television companies and many newspapers have also opened channels on platforms such as YouTube in a search for visibility and, consequently, possible revenue.

However, those professional contents live alongside amateur ones. This has been the key element of change in communication this century: users can create their own content and distribute it freely on exchange platforms, thus giving them considerable visibility. The "sharing economy", the idea that certain products should be free (the common goods), and the free playing of digital products (zero marginal cost) have transformed the current ecosystem of communication and digital leisure.

At the same time, something which is transcendental for understanding this transformation has changed: the personal information which search engines or social networks obtain is being sold to others in order to optimize marketing. The digital footprint has economic value – something which clashes with the right to privacy and intimacy.

In a scenario dominated by platforms such as YouTube, Instagram, Facebook, Twitch, Snapchat, Twitter, and so on, many users have appeared and are actively participating with each of them: vloggers, streamers, YouTubers, influencers, Instagrammers, gameplayers, TikTokers, and so on. Each platform has its own features and its own specialization and users take advantage of them in different ways with different profiles and different aims. Some create content for fun, others for altruistic motives and others to make money – often involving their hobbies.

In the context of this mixture, the book focuses on the phenomenon of influencers. It is a blurred concept with a lot of stereotypes. Most of the population would associate it with femininity and fashion & beauty. However, it is obvious that the business of influence goes beyond that and can affect any industry, as has been the case historically. In recent years, new ways of influencing have appeared,

DOI: 10.4324/9781003134176-1

rendering the traditional ones obsolete. There are many examples but the Twitter accounts of Donald Trump or Elon Musk are paradigms of how, by using a platform, you can reach a greater level of influence than via conventional media, as the so-called "fourth estate". Lobby groups are regulated by states. Advertising and public relations agencies have also attempted to gain influence over consumers' purchasing decisions. Companies themselves have always developed strategies and campaigns to influence buyer behaviour. That's why the term "influencer", as a concept and business, is so broad and has had a long history, as can be seen in Chapter 5 on the evolution of the influence business.

When influencers reach a critical mass of followers, companies appear which are willing to invest in many channels to promote their products in such a way that the production of content is becoming professional as production costs rise. This phenomenon would not be possible without platforms which bring one and the other together. They are intermediaries in the value chain and, consequently, they receive a percentage of the income – the figure is normally around 20 per cent. Followers tend to participate actively with comments or likes, creating certain community links. Platforms have personal information about the digital footprint so they can market and advertise programmatically. At the same time some companies have an interest in sponsoring content creators to link the brand image to some influencers. Normally contents are produced professionally to capture more attention and increase influence. On many occasions that poses ethical problems and causes a fall in the ability to influence.

The logic of brand communities is also very interesting since marketing has several peculiarities which are linked to exchanges and the participation of community members.

The relationships which are established are emotional as what brings people together is a common idea, taste or hobby. Feelings of belonging are, therefore, generated which is why people share and collaborate. Personal information from search engines and internet activity plus the feelings of belonging to a group which develop around an influential person is all of interest to organizations because they can target their marketing. These are new ways of functioning. Years ago a large manufacturer of sportswear would sign up a leading sportsperson so that their adverts would appear all over the media whereas today they contract them so that on their blog or Instagram profile they give an opinion, make comments or post photos to influence their followers. These are new opportunities which firms are working to optimize and, at the same time, there are new features which are less well known such as the factors which determine the engagement between followers and influencers.

On the other hand, intermediaries must give influencers a financial reward and manage advertising spending in exchange for a percentage. These control the information in the process in an automated way. The true power lies in the control of algorithms.

No-one doubts that this opens up an interesting field of academic and applied research into the marketing of influencers. Many studies have already been carried out and research results published. This book contains ten chapters which analyse the marketing of influencers with a multi-disciplinary and complementary approach.

The first chapter, "Making use of digital methods to study influencer market-ing" by Prince Chacko Johnson, Christofer Laurell and Christian Sandström, dis-cusses how digital media and specifically social media open up new opportunities for scholars, describing and discussing them in further detail. We also address the possibilities of making use of AI and machine learning in order to analyse large amounts of data present in social media.

At the same time, media industries are looking for a subscription model which allows them to work with higher costs to adapt to the new digital environment with its numerous competitors. In Chapter 2, Professor Santín and I analyse this new ecosystem made up of platforms, traditional media and UGC. The chapter also explains the codes used in the marketing of influencers as well as the problems derived from aspirational work in the middle of a wave of narcissism. We believe that the power of the hydra of platforms may be changed by the power of the people, technological innovation itself and the powerful level of entrepreneurship which exists in the current ecosystem.

José Esteves, in Chapter 3 of the book analyses the use of algorithms in social media. Social media services are the kings of algorithm usage, namely for content curation, user data collection and content creation. First, we describe these main applications of algorithms. Then, we outline challenges of using algorithms in social media, in particular transparency and objectivity.

In Chapter 4, considering the large social capital of social media influencers, we believe that there is much untapped potential beyond the commercial sphere. Therefore, a systematic literature review that aims to uncover the greater impact of social media influencers – both commercially and socially – is conducted by Chen Lou, Tiffany Chee and Xuan Zhou. The chapter also describes the methodology and framework that form the basis of the literature review. This is followed by a synthesis of the findings gathered, before concluding with the future direction for research and practical implications.

In western culture, the concept of influence has been linked from the very beginning to the power of persuasion. Influence seeks to confirm or change the behaviour of others, either to prevent other coercive methods or to justify their use. The development of mass media communication facilitated the appearance of a whole new industry of persuasion and the surge in advertising activity and public relations. Many of these practices have adapted to (or are trying to) the current digital environment; but new opportunities are also appearing, there are modifications of the players who make up the market and new business formulas are being explored. This path can be seen in Chapter 5 by Antonio Baraybar Fernández.

The basis of Chapter 6, by Sylvia Chan-Olmsted and Julia H. Kim, is the true potential of influencers. Their aim is to analyse the marketing dynamic of influ-encers and discuss the roles of four emotion-laden factors: engagement, trust, authenticity and relationship, as well as how they might collectively influence the effectiveness of influencer marketing.

In Chapter 7, Jonathon Hutchinson and Tim Dwyer explore the complexities of news production and distribution across the highly popular social media plat-forms, YouTube and Instagram. They argue that amidst unprecedented calls to make platform providers accountable for the content that is created, distributed and consumed within our societies, there is an urgent need to better understand their business models in terms of their platform affordances. In this chapter, Hutchinson and Dwyer outline how the constraints surrounding digital intermediation, specifically those that determine and manage the content monetization process, are shaping how content creators produce and publish their work on these platforms. They provide details of this dynamic digital intermediation process, contextualizing it through the lens of South Korean *Mukbang* content producers before then examining three international YouTube news providers.

In Chapter 8 Emilio Fernández Peña, Natividad Ramajo and Adolfo Nieto analyse the interactions on Instagram of sports stars and famous people. Their work deals with Instagram in the context of the system of social and digital media which contributes to the creation of a personal brand and they explore what they refer to as "cross-pollination". In other words, they study in depth the complementary action and feedback between the different participations of the personality on social networks and their activity on Instagram.

Chapter 9 by Anne Morawietz, Adele Berndt and Tomas Müllern builds on the fact that there has been limited published research into the community as well as the form and types of influence that exist within and between the various members of the CrossFit community. Their work aims to provide a conceptual model that seeks to develop and illustrate the nature of these dynamic influences based on the CrossFit context. In this chapter we use the CrossFit example to describe the phenomena of crowd influencing (moving within and between online and offline communities and its members and the range of brands), and how it has contributed to make CrossFit a global success story.

In the final chapter, Sven-Ove Horst and Toon Brouwers dive into the process and practices of early career journalists who are building their identity as freelancers and early-stage entrepreneurs in the media field. Based on recent interview data with Dutch journalism students, they explored what kind of practices related to social media are important and found that storytelling about themselves, responsive networking and managing social media mindfully are key for image building.

All that remains is to express our gratitude to all those who have taken part in the book, and for all the excellent work they have carried out.

## Note

1   This publication sets forth the results of research carried out as part of the R&D project CSO2012-37976 of the Spanish Ministry of Economy and Competitiveness.

# 1 Making use of digital methods to study influencer marketing

*Prince Chacko Johnson and Christian Sandström*

## 1.1 Introduction

Digitalization and the emergence of social media has fundamentally altered the media landscape. The growth of these communication channels has spawned the rise of influencers, influencer marketing and the related phenomena of social media celebrities, a.k.a. Instafamous (Khamis et al., 2016). Relatedly, big data and various approaches that make use of analytics are still in the process of transforming media in terms of customer experiences and the underlying competitive dynamics.

Navigating and understanding the new era of influencer marketing can be a daunting task. The rise of digital and computational methods that facilitate large-scale data collection and analysis to be performed automatically (Flaounas, Ilias, Omar et al., 2013) open up novel opportunities to study influencer marketing. These methods could be classified as digital methods, as they tend to capture developments, while approaching the web as a data set (Rogers, 2015).

At present, little is known regarding how these novel sources of data and related methodological approaches can be applied in order to study influencers and influencer marketing. While a couple of contributions have been made discussing how digital advances can inform management research more generally (e.g. Eriksson et al., 2019), there is presently a need for more research addressing how this can be done. In a broader sense, digitalization is creating new opportunities to conduct research with potentially significant effects across the social sciences (Kosinski et al., 2016), but little is presently known regarding how these advances can be applied in order to study influencer marketing.

In this chapter, we describe how digital data and digital methods can be used in order to study influencer marketing, media management and business administration. We begin by providing a background to influencer marketing. Next, we describe a collection of challenges that have historically been hard to deal with in academic research. Then, we describe two methodological approaches and discuss how they can be applied to study influencer marketing. We subsequently discuss some of the potential benefits of these approaches. Last, a concluding remark is provided.

DOI: 10.4324/9781003134176-2

## 1.2 Background: influencer marketing

We begin this background by describing the current state of research in influencer marketing. Social media celebrities are usually perceived as distinct from real-world celebrities and can be referred to as micro celebrities (Abidin, 2016; Brown and Hayes, 2008). Influencer celebrities can be defined as "people who built a large network of followers and are regarded as trusted tastemakers in one or several niches" (De Veirman et al., 2016, p. 1). As these celebrities are interpreted as more real and accessible than conventional celebrities, consumers tend to identify more with them and imitate them to a greater extent (Tran and Strutton, 2014).

Research on influencers and influencer marketing has been highlighted recently by scholars as an important research area to study further (Taylor, 2020). Market research also points at influencer marketing as an important and growing phenomenon. A study written by the Association of National Advertisers (ANA) (2018), observed that 75% of consumers were reached by influencer marketing, and 36% of them regarded it as effective. Data on youth consumer behavior also suggest that influencers are becoming increasingly important as a marketing channel. YPulse (2020) reports that the likelihood of 13–18-year-olds to follow influencers online has increased by 54 to 70% in only one year. Below, we turn to a couple of topics that need further investigation.

### 1.2.1 Influencers as opinion leaders

Literature on diffusion and adoption of innovations has highlighted the critical role opinion leaders play in the introduction of new products, behaviors and services (Rogers, 2010). An opinion leader can be defined as an actor that others within a social system listen to and follow. Sport stars, celebrities and models often take on the role of opinion leaders as crowds tend to pay attention to them. A lot of marketing activities such as advertising is built on the critical role of influencers in order to convince adopters.

Influencers can almost by definition be conceptualized as a form of opinion leaders. With a large base of followers, they have obtained a high status, are a form of semi-celebrities that can introduce novel products or trends and reach a wider audience. Plenty of research has been done by now concerning opinion leaders online, but most of it has so far concerned bloggers and covered a range of different methods for detecting opinion leadership (Deng et al., 2013; Li et al., 2013; Feng, 2014). Relatedly, we also see some research on opinion leadership on social media platforms such as Twitter (Dubois and Gaffney, 2014) particularly concerning political issues (Park and Kaye, 2017). As of now, however, these issues remain largely unexplored within the area of influencer marketing.

### 1.2.2 The practices of influencers

A key question concerning influencer marketing concerns what influencers actually do. In, for example, strategic management, practice-oriented perspectives have emerged over the past decades (Whittington, 1996; Whittington, 2006), arguing that strategy should be understood as an activity rather than a hard science. Gosling and Mintzberg (2004) state that:

> management is neither a science nor a profession, neither a function nor a combination of functions. Management is a practice – it has to be appreciated through experience, in context.
>
> (p. 19)

Practice-oriented perspectives in management may be further enabled to grow and gain acceptance due to the emergence of both digital research methods and digital sources of data (Eriksson et al., 2019) as this approach has previously been constrained by access to data and the relatively labor-intense nature of this form of research.

Likewise, we would argue that development of digital data sources and methods make it possible to study influencers and influencer marketing in new ways, potentially opening up more practice-oriented perspectives as such data sources can show what influencers actually do. While previous research has shown that influencers who are likeable and popular are more effective brand promoters (De Veirman et al., 2016) and that influencers with higher levels of trust are more likely to successfully promote a product (Chen and Yuan, 2019), more knowledge is presently required in order to show and illustrate how this can be done in practice. Specifically, we need a better understanding of what practices that actually create this trust and credibility. As pointed out by Taylor (2020):

> academic research on measurement accuracy, effectiveness of various measures, impact of influencers taking on multiple sponsors, and impact on disclosures can clearly be helpful and the time is ripe for a focus on these issues. Addressing these issues will be an important driver of the growth of influencer marketing post-pandemic.
>
> (p. 890)

### 1.2.3 Internal and external validity

Broadly speaking, the social sciences have faced a tradeoff between internal and external validity. High degrees of internal validity can be seen in some subjects such as economic history and business history. Parts of management research and media management scholarship has employed the case study method, which tends to be suitable for theory development and for the exploration of new topics rather than for testing hypotheses (Eisenhardt, 1989; Yin, 1994).

Conversely, quantitative approaches prevailing in for instance economics and areas of business administration such as strategic management may be suitable for testing hypotheses. Aggregated data may, however, be less useful when the scholar wishes to disentangle various complex causal relations.

We would argue that the social sciences more broadly have been trapped in a tradeoff between internal and external validity. Attempts at generalization have often been made at the expense of internal validity, and vice versa.

### 1.2.4 Differences between across media platforms

We currently see and experience the rapid rise and growth of social media and the media landscape is, as a consequence, being transformed. At present social media and traditional media are partially overlapping, partially complements and partially substitutes.

There are presently few studies systematically comparing social and traditional media. One early contribution pointed out that social media may be more simplistic and less critical towards new phenomena (Laurell and Sandström, 2018), but generally, more knowledge is needed concerning differences between these two forms of media. Here, the role of influencers and influencer marketing needs to be better understood, especially concerning how they are portrayed in social media and in traditional media differently.

Little is also presently known concerning differences across social media platforms. How do social media platforms differ in terms of the practices employed by influencers? Below, we describe two digital methodological approaches that can be applied in order to study influencer marketing. We begin with Social Media Analytics and then turn to digital media databases.

## 1.3 Digital data and digital methods

Usage of digital data and digital methods has increased over the past decades. In the early days of internet penetration, netnographic approaches were popular (Kozinets, 1997, 1998, 2010). The systematic collection and coding of digital data was employed in fashion blogging and the study of their practices in a number of studies (Laurell, 2014; Pihl and Sandström, 2013).

As netnography turned out to be rather labor intense, it has been increasingly displaced by Social Media Analytics (SMA), which can be regarded as an interdisciplinary combination of data collection and analysis that systematically makes use of social media (Stieglitz et al., 2014). As data can be gathered without intrusion and in real-time, SMA has been described it as *"a kind of living lab, which enables academics to collect large amounts of data generated in a real-world environment"* by some of the pioneering academics in this field (Stieglitz et al., 2014, p. 90).

An SMA study begins with the choosing of a subject to study. The researcher decides upon what or who to study, that is, a certain innovation, an influencer, a firm, or a keyword. In recent times, increasing efforts have neem taken to collect data by using publicly accessible information from online sources either by using application programming interfaces (APIs) or scrapping techniques and at the same time the trend of compiling original datasets of archival data, as well as other media sources, has gained popularity (Garz, 2020). Here, it is important to choose keywords that generate sufficient amounts of activity. Next, a researcher can either decide to make use of databases, software services or develop scrapping techniques for data collection.

### 1.3.1 Tracking and data collection

An SMA study begins with the choosing of a subject to study. The researcher decides upon what or who to study, that is, a certain innovation, an influencer, a firm or a keyword. Here, it is important to choose keywords that generate sufficient amounts of activity. Next, a researcher can either decide to make use of software services or develop scrapping techniques for data collection.

### 1.3.1.1 Database approach

The use of academic databases to conduct research on specific topics has become the new normal of scholarly investigations, where journal articles and other publications are catalogued which further eliminates the need to manually go through them (Driedger and Weimer, 2015). While there are multiple curated databases that compile data from various sources *ProQuest* and *Factiva* are two of the major providers. Both *ProQuest* and *Factiva* require subscriptions which are generally made available by most universities and libraries (Garz, 2020). Articles and publications from most leading media houses around the globe can be obtained from these two databases.

### 1.3.1.2 Data collection software

Next, data collection commences. Here, the researcher can make use of either APIs or RSS/HTML as ways to access and collect the data. There are several software services available for doing this, for example, Notified that has been used for many SMA studies in management (e.g. Laurell and Sandström, 2017, 2018; Geissinger et al., 2019). Making use of software services has several benefits. Specific filters can be applied in order to look for users in specific languages, or with certain user origins such as countries. Also, the fact that social media and the internet is still comparatively fragmented means that standardized ways to gather data hold considerable potential.

### 1.3.1.3 Web scrapping techniques

An alternative to making use of software would be to develop and employ scrapping techniques. Scrapping is a technique that is used for automated data collection of online data ranging from media from news outlets, social media, app reviews, websites, and so on (Marres and Weltevrede, 2013). It is a great approach to extract unstructured and cluttered data from the internet and further transform that data into structured, organized, and uncluttered data that can be stored and further analysed in a database (Sirisuriya, 2015).

Mitchell (2018) defines web scrapping as a practice of gathering data through any means other than a program interacting with an API; this could be done by writing an automated program that queries a web server, requests data, and then passes the data to extract needed information. The idea behind scrapping is to collect data from unstructured websites and outlets and bring it together in structured formats such as spreadsheets, comma-separated values (CSV) files, etc. (Figure 1.1).

There are various tools and techniques that can be used for web scrapping. Web data is generally scrapped using hypertext transfer protocol (HTTP) programming, hypertext markup language (HTML) parsing, through a web browser along with an automatic bot or web crawler (Zhao, 2017). Previous studies such as (Johnson

*Figure 1.1* Basic flowchart of web scrapping derived from Mitchell 2018.

et al., 2022) has used python to scrap large amounts of data from online newspaper outlets. Owing to the large amount of data that is continuously generated on the world wide web, web scraping is accepted and acknowledged widely as an efficient and powerful tool in collecting data (Mooney et al., 2015; Bar-Ilan, 2001; Zhao, 2017). One of the tools called scrapy is an open-source application that has gained traction for web scrapping over the last few years which can be written in python (Thomas and Mathur, 2019).

While web scrapping is a powerful tool which ideally helps us to collect large amounts of data, there have been ethical debates around it such as copy right concerns (O'Reilly, 2006) and terms of service (Fisher et al., 2010; Zhao, 2017).

### *1.3.2 Data analysis*

Having finished data collection, different forms of content analysis techniques can subsequently be employed (Silverman, 2006). Here, both structured data such as account details and unstructured data such as text can be used. First, data sets are studied by looking at how the data is spread across different social media platforms. Next, different techniques for data analysis can be employed, including manual coding, statistical and computational methods and more sociological approaches such as Social Network Analysis (SNA).

Below, we expand further on different techniques for data collection and analysis.

#### *1.3.2.1 Manual coding techniques*

Coding of material can be done manually. In the first step, the researcher needs to remove material that concerns other issues. Next, a coding scheme can be employed. What scheme to use ultimately depends on the research objective at hand. In previous literature, there are examples of applications of institutional theory to track and measure practices (e.g., Laurell and Sandström, 2017). Other examples include studies of entrepreneurs and how they position themselves on Twitter (e.g., Obschonka, 2017). As manual coding schemes can be quite laborious, we next describe some software-based techniques that can be employed.

#### *1.3.2.2 Software-based analysis*

There are various reasons why one would want to opt for an automated system for content analysis of text, as it is known that human decision makers are potentially subject to influence that can't be reported (Nisbett and Wilson, 1977). The usage of software to assist and support researcher in the analysis of data has been very important over the years, such as statistical package for the social sciences and NVivo has been the most commonly used software for analysis (Sotiriadou et al., 2014). There is an extensive requirement of time and effort in the process of human content analysis where the code books or dictionaries must be validated, coders must be rained, intercoder reliabilities must be tested, and so on (e.g., Weber, 1990), whereas automating the analysis process would reduce the time and effort but also simultaneously allow more rapid and frequent analysis and reanalysis of text (Smith and Humphreys, 2006). Content analysis has been applied in different ways and techniques such as Hyperspace Analog to Language (HAL) (Lund, 1997), Latent Semantic Analysis (LSA) (Landauer et al., 1998), Leximancer (Smith, 2000) are common algorithms used to take text and extract concepts for analysis.

Over the years AI techniques such as data mining (Liu, 2007), natural language processing (NLP) (Manning and Schutze, 1999; Yi et al., 2003), computer visual analytics (Butler, 2008), and machine learning (ML) (Shawe-Taylor and Cristianini, 2004) can be used for analysis. Text mining tools and concept maps are techniques and tools that are well established methods for extracting key concepts from a textual corpus and further displaying them in a graphical representation (Stockwell et al., 2009). Automated content analysis (ACA) is referred to as a suite of algorithms that uses models such as topic models or concept mapping models (Blei, 2012) to explain and understand hidden composition of a body of text or literature (Nunez-Mir et al., 2016). Many tools have been developed to facilitate the use of topic modelling and concept mapping for ACA over time which included R packages, python libraries and various software solutions. Some tools such as Mallet, Standord TMT, topic models, and so on, require coding skills while on the other hand Leximancer, Gavagai and Google TMT feature user-friendly graphic user interfaces (Nunez-Mir et al., 2016). These automated analysis techniques can be either utilized by individual researchers or by service providers that use these techniques and help with scientific research. Leximancer and Gavagai are two of the many services that have been leading automated analysis and which are described below.

1.3.2.2.1 LEXIMANCER

Leximancer is a relatively new software that can perform ACA which transforms lexical co-occurrence information from free text and natural language into semantic patterns in an unsupervised manner with no pre-conceptions while the analysis emerges from the data (Cheng and Edwards, 2019). It is semi-automated content analysis tool that can be used to analyse either a single document or even a collection of documents by identifying the key terms by using word frequency and co-occurrence usage (Smith, 2000). It goes beyond keyword searching but discovers and extracts thesaurus-based concepts from the text data; an external dictionary can be used however it is not mandatory. Based on the data concept, maps and themes are generated in steps as seen in Figure 1.2. It analyses text data while using statistics-based algorithms to automatically analyse text and then derives visual representations (Smith and Humphreys, 2006). The concepts are then streamlined into different themes and then representational figures are generated.

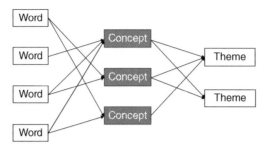

*Figure 1.2* Adapted from Crofts and Bisman 2010.

1.3.2.2.2 GAVAGAI

Gavagai Explorer analyses texts in 47 different languages which is commercially available for users and they provide end-to-end analysis of unstructured data while dealing with various components such as topic clustering, sentiment analysis, and concept modelling (Espinoza et al., 2018). Topic clustering is done based on lexical cues and is used to detect prevalent themes and topics within the dataset, followed by concept modelling and sentiment analysis (Afsarmanesh et al., 2019). After the topic clustering, Gavagai also offers an extension where seed words can be entered and the user is presented with similar terms acquired from an online distortional semantic model which is constantly updated within data from various data sources such as trendiction, twingly, gnip, notified, and so on (Sahlgren et al., 2016). While Gavagai Explorer helps with analysis, it also offers data scrapping opportunities from various public sources.

The whole motive of these automated analysis techniques is to empower research, analysts, and data scientists rather than replacing them. These approaches and techniques help to increase coverage and consistency throughout the analysis process, making it more reliable. They could also be used as an approach to analyse free text responses within surveys which would otherwise be a tedious task (Espinoza et al., 2018).

## 1.4  Discussion

Having outlined above how social media data, media data, SMA and some related software services can be applied for the study of influencer marketing, we now describe some of the benefits of doing so.

### 1.4.1  Uncovering influencers as opinion leaders

How do influencers become opinion leaders? What characterizes those that successfully become opinion leaders as opposed to those who don't? How does word of mouth spread across social media? We see ample opportunities to integrate research on diffusion of innovations and opinion leadership with influencer marketing by making use of digital methods and digital data.

As data is digital and available online on various accounts, the emergence and growth of successful influencers can be tracked and studied in greater detail. Their followership, their activities and marketing efforts can both be studied historically and in real-time. Within the applied sciences, methods have been developed to make use of expert systems in order to detect and identify opinion leaders (Bamakan et al., 2019). Others have studied the role of blogs in shaping word of mouth marketing activities. Li and Du (2011) state that previous research highlighted the importance of social networks, but struggled to identify opinion leaders. They develop a framework to find opinion leaders based on their blog contents, relationships and activities. We see ample opportunities to develop a similar approach for studying influencers as opinion leaders and welcome such efforts in the coming years.

### 1.4.2 Exploring practices of influencers

By making use of SMA and related software services, we would argue that it is possible to study the practices of influencers. Previous scholarly work has done so with fashion bloggers and the blogosphere, being able to disentangle the share of private messages, commercial messages and how bloggers integrate brands into their daily lives (Pihl and Sandström, 2013). Similar studies can be employed on influencers in the social media landscape, potentially with less effort regarding data collection and analysis as this can be done by making use of software. We would also suggest that computational approaches can decipher what forms of entries result in more or less likes, shares and so on.

### 1.4.3 Comparisons across media platforms

As stated previously, little is presently known regarding how influencer practices differ across platforms. Access to, and systematic data collection across media platforms enable such studies to be pursued. Previous research has measured and documented how social media differs from traditional media (Laurell and Sandström, 2018). Portrayal of influencers and differences between these two forms of media can be studied in a similar fashion. We also see that it has been possible to compare different social media platforms such as Twitter, Facebook, Instagram, Forums and Blogs with regard to their contents (Laurell and Sandström, 2021). As SMA enables the systematic collection of data across platforms, we see that this approach holds considerable potential for the study of influencer marketing and how it differs across platforms.

### 1.4.4 Increasing internal and external validity

Social sciences have broadly faced a tradeoff between internal and external validity (Eisenhardt, 1989). The emergence and growth of digital data and digital methods makes it possible to partially transcend this tradeoff. Detailed ethnographic approaches can be combined with aggregated studies of patterns across media platforms, across different influencers and different sectors of the economy.

The application of software techniques and programmes such as Gavagai and Leximancer described above is likely to enable increased internal and external validity.

### 1.4.5 A need for new skill sets among researchers

Having identified several directions of future research that are enabled by digital data and digital methods, we also see a need for further skill development among scholars in order to realize this potential.

An increased need for digital skills is likely to manifest in several ways. First, we expect that scholars to a greater extent need to master programming languages such as Python or Java. Beyond this, a command of several digital tools and software services will be needed as well as different techniques for both manual and automatic coding techniques.

A shift to more digital scholarship is therefore likely to induce a process of skill renewal within academia. Doctoral education needs to a greater extent to integrate digital data usage and methods in order to foster competitive researchers for the future.

This ongoing and coming transition may also potentially alter the role of researchers. When a scholar relies upon software to conduct an analysis, productivity might increase substantially. At the same time, a scholar effectively relies upon the work of programmers and developers, who are unknown and whose biases or preferences cannot be known, but may nevertheless influence the outcome of such work. Effects on internal and external validity may be positive in the long term, yet need to be analysed. We welcome further discussions of how the role of researchers may be affected by digitalization in the coming years.

## 1.5 Conclusion

In this chapter, we have described how some digital data sources and methods can be used in order to study influencers and influencer marketing. Our contribution is twofold: we provide some tangible guidelines for how to apply digital methods and, relatedly, we highlight some of the potential benefits of doing so.

As influencers are digital in their operations, it makes sense to study them by making use of digital data and digital methods. Digital data can be collected in an unobtrusive manner. The use of various software services for data collection can make it possible to gather large datasets in real-time with little effort. In this chapter, we also mention and describe some of these services and how they can be applied to the subsequent analysis.

We identify several benefits of making use of digital data when studying influencer marketing. First, we note that by doing so, it is possible to study the practices of influencers, highlighting what they actually do. In doing so, we would expect that research on opinion leaders and diffusion of innovations can be further developed. Second, we note that larger datasets can be collected and analysed, thereby transcending some of the tradeoffs between internal and external validity. Third, we would also suggest that differences across social media platforms as well as traditional media platforms can be studied in greater detail by making use of these methods.

These digital research methods can be very effective and utilized while research-ing within the space of influencer marketing and social media. Automated concept mapping, analysis software, text mining tools, and so on are proven effective for research, to identify trends within the collected data (Stockwell et al., 2009; Garz, 2020). However, as mentioned above, none of these techniques are meant to replace humans but rather empower them while replacing the frustrating tasks alone. While working with digital methods for research and analysis, detailed grammatical information cannot be obtained, but there is an abundance of infor-mation that is both rich and complex that can be obtained from commercial ser-vices such as Gavagai or Leximacer (Smith and Humphreys, 2006).

As the adoption of digital tools and methods continues to grow, we argue that the skill sets of scholars need to change and that competence renewal will become a source of competitive advantage for researchers in the coming years.

# References

Abidin, C. (2016). 'Aren't these just young, rich women doing vain things online?' Influencer selfies as subversive frivolity. *Social Media + Society*, 2(2), 1–17.

Afsarmanesh, Nazanin, Jussi Karlgren, Peter Sumbler, and Nina Viereckel 2019. Team Harry Friberg at SemEval-2019 Task 4: Identifying Hyperpartisan News through Editorially Defined Metatopics. In *Proceedings of the 13th International Workshop on Semantic Evaluation*, pp. 1004–1006

Association of National Advertisers. (2018). Advertisers love influencer marketing: ANA study. https://www.ana.net/content/show/id/48437 (accessed September 1, 2020).

Bamakan, S. M. H., I. Nurgaliev, and Q. Qu (2019). Opinion leader detection: A method-ological review. *Expert Systems with Applications*, 115, 200–222.

Bar-Ilan, Judit (2001). Data collection methods on the web for infometric purposes—A review and analysis. *Scientometrics* 50(1), 7–32.

Blei, D. M. (2012). Probabilistic topic models. *Communications of the ACM*, 55(4), 77–84.

Brown, D., and N. Hayes (2008). *Influencer marketing*. London: Routledge.

Butler, John. (2008). Visual web page analytics. U.S. Patent Application 11/841,397 filed February 21.

Chen, L., and S. Yuan (2019). Influencer marketing: How message value and credibility affect consumer trust of branded content on social media. *Journal of Interactive Advertising* 19(1), 58–73. [Taylor & Francis Online], [Google Scholar]

Cheng, Mingming, and Deborah Edwards (2019). A comparative automated content anal-ysis approach on the review of the sharing economy discourse in tourism and hospitality. *Current Issues in Tourism*, 22(1), 35–49.

Crofts, Ken, and Jayne Bisman (2010). Interrogating accountability: An illustration of the use of Leximancer software for qualitative data analysis. *Qualitative Research in Accounting & Management*, 7(2), 180–207.

De Veirman, M., V. Cauberghe, and L. Hudders (2016). Marketing through Instagram influencers: Impact of number of followers and product divergence on brand attitude. *International Journal of Advertising*, 36(5), 798–828.

Deng, X., Y. Li, and S. Lin (2013). Parallel micro blog crawler construction for effective opinion leader approximation. *AASRI Procedia*, 5, 170–176.

Driedger, S. M., and Weimer, J. (2015). Factiva and Canadian newsstand major dailies: Comparing retrieval reliability between academic institutions. *Online Information Review*, 39(3), 346–356.

Dubois, E., and Gaffney, D. (2014). The multiple facets of influence: Identifying political influentials and opinion leaders on Twitter. *American Behavioral Scientist, 58*(10), 1260–1277.

Eisenhardt, K. M. (1989). Building theories from case study research. *Academy of Management Review,* 14(4), 532–550.

Eriksson, K., Ernkvist, M., Laurell, C., Moodysson, J., Nykvist, R., & Sandström, C. (2019). A revised perspective on innovation policy for renewal of mature economies–Historical evidence from finance and telecommunications in Sweden 1980–1990. *Technological Forecasting and Social Change,* 147, 152–162.

Espinoza, Fredrik, Ola Hamfors, Jussi Karlgren, Fredrik Olsson, Per Persson, Lars Hamberg, and Magnus Sahlgren. Analysis of open answers to survey questions through interactive clustering and theme extraction. In *Proceedings of the 2018 Conference on Human Information Interaction & Retrieval,* pp. 317–320, 2018.

Feng, X. I. A. O. (2014). A study on formation of grass root opinion leader in micro-blog. *Journal of Gannan Normal University,* 2014(5), 85–88.

Fisher, Danyel, David W. McDonald, Andrew L. Brooks, and Elizabeth F. Churchill (2010). Terms of service, ethics, and bias: Tapping the social web for CSCW research. In *Computer Supported Cooperative Work (CSCW),* Panel Discussion, February 6–10, 2010, Savannah, Georgia: 603–606. ACM 978-1-60558-795-0/10/02.

Flaounas, Ilias, Omar Ali, Thomas Lansdall-Welfare, Tijl De Bie, Nick Mosdell, Justin Lewis, and Nello Cristianini (2013). Research methods in the age of digital journalism: Massive-scale automated analysis of news-content—topics, style and gender. *Digital Journalism* 1(1), 102–116.

Garz, M. (2020). 6 Quantitative methods. In M. Bjørn von Rimscha *Management and economics of communication* (pp. 109–128). De Gruyter Mouton.

Geissinger, A., Laurell, C., Sandström, C., Eriksson, K., and Nykvist, R. (2019). Digital entrepreneurship and field conditions for institutional change–Investigating the enabling role of cities. *Technological Forecasting and Social Change,* 146, 877–886.

Gosling, J., & Mintzberg, H. (2004). The education of practicing managers. *MIT Sloan Management Review,* 45(4), 19.

Johnson, P. C., Laurell, C., Ots, M., and Sandström, C. (2022). Digital innovation and the effects of artificial intelligence on firms' research and development–Automation or augmentation, exploration or exploitation? *Technological Forecasting and Social Change,* 179, 121636.

Khamis, S., L. Ang, and R. Welling (2016). Self-branding, 'micro-celebrity' and the rise of social media influencers. *Celebrity Studies,* 8(2), 191–208.

Kosinski, M., Wang, Y., Lakkaraju, H., and Leskovec, J. (2016). Mining big data to extract patterns and predict real-life outcomes. *Psychological Methods,* 21(4), 493.

Kozinets, R. V. (1997). "I want to believe": A netnography of the X-Philes' subculture of consumption. *Advances in Consumer Research,* 24, 470–475.

Kozinets, R. V. (1998). On netnography: Initial reflections on consumer research investigations of cyberculture. *ACR North American Advances.*

Kozinets, R. V. (2010). *Netnography: Doing ethnographic research online.* London, UK: Sage Publications.

Landauer, T. K., P. W. Foltz, and D. Laham (1998). An introduction to latent semantic analysis. *Discourse processes,* 25(2–3), 259–284.

Laurell, C. (2014). *Commercialising social media: a study of fashion (blogo) spheres* (Doctoral dissertation, School of Business, Stockholm University).

Laurell, C., and Sandström, C. (2017). The sharing economy in social media: Analyzing tensions between market and non-market logics. *Technological Forecasting and Social Change,* 125, 58–65.

Laurell, C., and Sandström, C. (2018). Comparing coverage of disruptive change in social and traditional media: Evidence from the sharing economy. *Technological Forecasting and Social Change*, 129, 339–344.

Li, F., and T. C. Du (2011). Who is talking? An ontology-based opinion leader identification framework for word-of-mouth marketing in online social blogs. *Decision support systems*, 51(1), 190–197.

Li, Y., S. Ma, Y. Zhang, and R. Huang (2013). An improved mix framework for opinion leader identification in online learning communities. *Knowledge-Based Systems*, 43, 43–51.

Liu, Bing. (2007). *Web data mining: Exploring hyperlinks, contents, and usage data*. Springer Science & Business Media.

Lund, C. B. A. K. (1997). Modelling parsing constraints with high-dimensional context space. *Language and Cognitive Processes*, 12(2–3), 177–210.

Manning, Christopher, and Hinrich Schutze (1999). *Foundations of statistical natural language processing*. MIT Press.

Marres, Noortje, and Esther Weltevrede (2013). Scraping the social? Issues in live social research. *Journal of Cultural Economy* 6(3), 313–335.

Mitchell, Ryan (2018). *Web scraping with Python: Collecting more data from the modern web*. O'Reilly Media, Inc.

Mooney, Stephen J., Daniel J. Westreich, and Abdulrahman M. El-Sayed (2015). Epidemiology in the era of big data. *Epidemiology (Cambridge, Mass.)* 26(3), 390.

Nisbett, R. E., and T. D. Wilson (1977). Telling more than we can know: Verbal reports on mental processes. *Psychological Review*, 84(3), 231.

Nunez-Mir, G. C., B. V. Iannone III, B. C. Pijanowski, N. Kong, and S. Fei (2016). Automated content analysis: addressing the big literature challenge in ecology and evolution. *Methods in Ecology and Evolution*, 7(11), 1262–1272.

O'Reilly, Sean (2006). Nominative fair use and Internet aggregators: Copyright and trademark challenges posed by bots, web crawlers and screen-scraping technologies. *Loyola Consumer Law Review* 19, 273.

Park, C. S., and B. K. Kaye (2017). The tweet goes on: Interconnection of Twitter opinion leadership, network size, and civic engagement. *Computers in Human Behavior*, 69, 174–180.

Pihl, C., and C. Sandström (2013). Value creation and appropriation in social media – The case of fashion bloggers in Sweden. *International Journal of Technology Management*, 61(3/4), 309–323.

Rogers, E. M. (2010). *Diffusion of innovations*. Simon and Schuster.

Rogers, Richard (2015). Digital methods for web research. In Robert A Scott and Stephen M. Kosslyn (Eds), *Emerging trends in the social and behavioral sciences: An interdisciplinary, searchable, and linkable resource*, 1–22. Hoboken: Wiley Online.

Sahlgren, Magnus, Amaru Cuba Gyllensten, Fredrik Espinoza, Ola Hamfors, Jussi Karlgren, Fredrik Olsson, Per Persson, Akshay Viswanathan, and Anders Holst (2016). The Gavagai living lexicon. In *Proceedings of the 10th International Conference on Language Resources and Evaluation (LREC'16)*, pp. 344–350.

Shawe-Taylor, John, and Nello Cristianini (2004). *Kernel methods for pattern analysis*. Cambridge: Cambridge University Press.

Silverman (2006). *Interpreting Qualitative Data* (3rd Ed.), London, UK: SAGE Publications.

Sirisuriya, De S. 2015. A comparative study on web scraping. In *Proceedings of 8th International Research Conference, KDU*.

Smith, A. E. (2000 December). Machine mapping of document collections: The Leximancer system. In *Proceedings of the fifth Australasian Document Computing Symposium* (pp. 39–43). DSTC Sunshine Coast, Australia.

Smith, Andrew E., and Michael S. Humphreys (2006). Evaluation of unsupervised semantic mapping of natural language with Leximancer concept mapping. *Behavior Research Methods*, 38(2), 262–279.

Sotiriadou, Popi, Jessie Brouwers, and Tuan-Anh Le (2014). Choosing a qualitative data analysis tool: A comparison of NVivo and Leximancer. *Annals of Leisure Research* 17(2), 218–234.

Stieglitz, S., Dang-Xuan, L., Bruns, A., and Neuberger, C. (2014). Social media analytics. *Business & Information Systems Engineering*, 6(2), 89–96.

Stockwell, P., R. M. Colomb, A. E. Smith, and J. Wiles (2009). Use of an automatic content analysis tool: A technique for seeing both local and global scope. *International Journal of Human-Computer Studies*, 67(5), 424–436.

Thomas, David Mathew, and Sandeep Mathur (2019). Data analysis by web scraping using python. In *2019 3rd International conference on Electronics, Communication and Aerospace Technology (ICECA)*, pp. 450–454. IEEE.

Tran, G. A. and D. Strutton (2014). Has reality television come of age as a promotional platform? Modeling the endorsement effectiveness of celebreality and reality stars. *Psychology & Marketing*, 31(4), 294–305.

Weber, R. P. 1990. *Basic content analysis* (No. 49). Beverly Hills, CA: Sage.

Whittington, R. 1996. Strategy as practice. *Long range planning*, 29(5), 731–735.

Whittington, R. (2006). Completing the practice turn in strategy research. *Organization studies*, 27(5), 613–634.

Taylor, Charles R. (2020). The urgent need for more research on influencer marketing. *International Journal of Advertising*, 39(7), 889–891, DOI: 10.1080/02650487.2020.1822104

Yi, Jeonghee, Tetsuya Nasukawa, Razvan Bunescu, and Wayne Niblack (2003). Sentiment analyzer: Extracting sentiments about a given topic using natural language processing techniques. In *Third IEEE International Conference on Data Mining*, pp. 427–434. IEEE.

Yin, R. K., (1994). *Case Study Research Design and Methods: Applied Social Research and Methods Series* (2nd edn). Thousand Oaks, CA: Sage Publications Inc.

YPulse 2020. 3 stats that show influencers are as influential as ever. *YPulse daily*. New York: YPulse.

Zhao, Bo (2017). Web scraping. *Encyclopedia of Big Data*, 1–3.

# 2 The marketing of UGC, media industries and business influence

## The Hydra of Lerna and the sword of Heracles

*José M. Álvarez-Monzoncillo and Marina Santín*

## 2.1 Introduction

The transformation, as brought about by the development of the Internet and digitalization of production and post-production in the media industry, has triggered the rupture of the value chain, forcing the industry to reinvent itself. This transformation has empowered users and even allowed them, on occasion, to become content creators who dare question the traditional power of large media players. "In recent decades there has been a marked shift from consumer electronics to information technology as the most powerful sectoral force shaping how media content gets produced, distributed, and experienced" (Deuze & Prenger, 2019: 14). These new means of production, distribution and consumption have affected the whole of the media industry at different levels.

Some media have had to reinvent their business model drastically, redefining their engagement with their audience, favoring multi-platform distribution. This has been a difficult process which not only seeks to capture audiences on a one-off basis but, especially, to generate new opportunities by interacting and creating a community. This is an uncertain process of adaptation to the digital media environment in which competition among all players is tough.

The new ways of communicating which have emerged on the net have made it possible not only to produce and distribute, but also to interact emotionally with followers. This empowerment has, perhaps, been one of the most important innovations in the field of communication. User activity not only adds traffic – which is beneficial to telecommunication companies – but the fact that it also allows them to empathize with a large public is of great interest to brands. This ability to work with a community of fans of cultural products, with a mix of genres and reinterpreting a new "acquisition" of others' work, has been studied thoroughly (Jenkins, 2006; Jenkins, Ford & Green, 2018). The value is not solely in the production and distribution of the product but in the consumption, itself, given that valuable information is obtained from the interaction.

The apparent ease for creating content has encouraged many to opt for content creation and the use of different platforms when it comes to distribution. That is a reference to user-generated content (UGC), with its different labels: vloggers, streamers, YouTubers, influencers, Instagramers, gameplayers, Tiktokers and so on. Each one has their own motivation: altruism, fun, the search for social recognition

DOI: 10.4324/9781003134176-3

or the possibility of making money. All of them have taken advantage of platforms such as YouTube, Instagram, Facebook, Twitch, Snapchat, Twitter … to share content and, in the case of some of them, they have achieved a commercial value for their creations, monetizing the relationship which they have established with their followers or subscribers. In addition, this phenomenon of cultural creation has often been sprinkled with a considerable dosage of entrepreneurship, innovation, creativity and sound management which is, in turn, encouraging the so-called "traditional" media to renew themselves.

The millennials and generation Z have embraced this phenomenon because they too want to play an active role in the process: new spectators interacting with other spectators and even with the new idols who have emerged on the net. The idea of Hollywood vs Silicon Valley is becoming more and more apparent (Cunningham & Craig, 2019a). As consumption is of great importance and, consequently, attracting advertising, its social importance is also a determining factor as more and more users take part on social networks.

The close relationship which these creators establish with their followers makes them of particular importance for brands. They can take advantage of content to improve their interaction in the area of marketing. The trend is unstoppable and, day after day, influencers are having more sway in the purchasing decisions and opinions of many followers. Having said that, this potential brings with it certain problems as there are fake followers and influencers who lose their efficiency when they promote too many brands. In addition, we must bear in mind the lack of any legal control over advertising in these spaces. It is a new phenomenon which requires a much more in-depth study due to its constantly changing nature (Taylor, 2020).

In such a context, the growing power – and not only in economic terms – which the platforms that make up new digital capitalism have obtained, is a concern. The contemporary platforms "are reconfiguring the production, distribution, and monetization of cultural content in staggeringly complex ways" (Duffy, Poell & Nieborg, 2019: 1).

Consequently, we are faced with a paradox: on the one hand, the important phenomenon of the empowerment of audiences that can create and distribute content and assess products, and, on the other, the control in the hands of very few platforms which are the ones who reap the benefit. Audiences may co-create value, but it is not easy for media companies to monetize that value, which is clearly shifting towards global platforms.

Paradoxically, technological development is destroying the old model of entertainment and media industries. Internet, which, initially, generated too many utopias, has placed the media companies under the control of a small number of global companies who can define the future rules governing how power and citizens relate. That means we are living at a very exciting time as reasons for concern and reasons for hope still co-exist (Hesmondhalgh, 2019).

The dream of long queues was shattered (Napoli, 2016), the dominion of the blockbuster (Elberse, 2013) and the omnipresent power of the hydra FAANG (Facebook, Amazon, Apple, Netflix and Google) were confirmed. Just as with the Hydra of Lerna from Greek mythology – an enormous aquatic snake with venomous breath and many terrifying heads, which lived in the depths – the hydra

FAANG conditions the underworld of the planet's information, culture and entertainment, using algorithms, big data, artificial intelligence and virtual reality (VR). But, as with Heracles, who used a mask to combat the venomous stench, managed to strike in just the right place with his sword so that no more heads grew back, technology itself can break the FAANG curse because it can generate new opportunities and uncertainties. For that reason, we can say that we are living in exciting times with many empowered Heracles who are experiencing a new golden age of creativity. The hydra no longer holds all the aces as users can co-create and make important decisions, taking advantage of the monster's contradictions.

Entrepreneurship is also considerable, with new initiatives appearing which question the status quo. It would also be fair to acknowledge that the monster has some amicable heads which satisfy important user needs and allow progress in that direction.

This chapter focuses on the change which is taking place in media industries and the empowerment of people on different content-sharing platforms in the context of digital marketing and the change in consumption habits.

## 2.2  Media industries: a future with co-creation?

The feeling that the media industry has collapsed is around at present, and not only because its business models are wobbling – something which is clear and particularly troublesome for the press. The regulation of the media has also become more flexible, facilitating concentration, and technology firms have overcome the power of large media conglomerates, taking on a key role when it comes to what news story we read or which film/series we watch.

The appearance of new ways of communicating, such as Twitter, have triggered a concern in media industries, making media, "particularly with regard to the role of news and information that is essential to ideals of public access, shared narratives, and the democratic principles of quality, diversity, and plurality in content and services offered" (Faustino & Noam, 2019: 177). It should be added that radio and public television channels have lost their legitimacy and there has been a cut in subsidies to help cultural industries, these being reduced to a fake support for entrepreneurship, and innovation using the label of "creative industries". The problem has worsened because, in addition, the power of states has been limited in the face of the new digital capitalism which functions as an oligopoly. There is talk of a platform-state. The change in media industries has been so stark that "many of the effects of a post-television system of content creation and distribution remain unknown" (Strangelove, 2015: 228). An environment of decadence is envisioned and an uncertain future with the growth of globalization. However, this collapse, at the same time, opens new opportunities in the new environment "that is characterized by the fragmentation of media options, competition for attention, and empowered audiences" (Chan-Olmsted & Wang, 2019: 133).

Many studies (Álvarez-Monzoncillo & López-Villanueva, 2014; Holt & Perren, 2009; Mayer, Banks & Caldwell, 2009; Maxwell & Miller, 2012; Albarran, 2013; Doyle, 2013, Flew, 2013; Starks, 2013; Strangelove, 2015; Picard & Wildman, 2015; Athique, 2016; Chalaby, 2015; Smith & Telang, 2016; Lotz, 2017;

McRobbie, 2016; Evens & Donders, 2018; Deuze & Prenger, 2019; Hesmondhalgh, 2019; Kawashima, 2020; Kim, 2021) have tackled this collapse, revealing its consequences at all levels.

Not only are the business models being questioned, but the digital disruption has also upset the analogical status quo. Technological innovation has modified the media-making sector, facilitating new support and new ways to produce content, as well as the change in consumption habits. In this disruptive context, new economic agents of significant importance in the media market have appeared: Internet providers, Internet companies, OTT platforms and social networks. Media industries have been forced to adapt their business models to this new context in which these new operators, which make inter-connectivity possible, have joined the market. This new development, as Negroponte had already foreseen, has led to the integration of computer science, telecommunications and audiovisual industries, a phenomenon which has been called "convergence".

This process meant the expansion of the information, communication and technology (ICT) sectors with the borders becoming blurred. In addition, it has made it possible for media content to be produced, distributed and experienced very differently. Convergence has brought with it the debate about net neutrality to the degree that Internet service providers (ISP) have joined up with the Internet giants to discriminate content and services by price, bringing into question Internet access as a public service in line with democratic principles (Pickard & Berman, 2019).

The new communication market has been made up of new intermediaries who, in principle, barely add value to content, but seem to be the ones who are taking most advantage. As Franklin Foer (2017) points out, they have managed to dominate the media, but without actually contracting editors or doing much of anything. They are the champions of the so-called digital capitalism: Samsung, Apple, Microsoft, Facebook, Google, YouTube, Netflix, Amazon, and so on. The group of new operators has broken the strategy of interaction – as was the traditional case – between audiences and advertisers, with a proliferation of side effects and high complexity (Gabszewicz, Resende & Sonnac, 2015).

Consequently, the digital disruption and these corporations

> have nestled themselves firmly in-between media users and producers, making each of them co-dependent on their products and platforms for formatting, distributing, accessing, and sharing media content … adapt to this new reality, the values, expectations, and structures of the digital economy come to co-determine creative decisions and processes.
>
> (Deuze & Prenger, 2019:14)

This control is clearly market-orientated and reduces the pluralism and cultural diversity which, in the past, were guaranteed by states: the same states which today, and as a result of globalization, have less efficient maneuverability from that point of view.

This situation has led to a transcendental change in media industries. The essential features which had traditionally characterized the sector, such as the mixture of state and private ownership, and the rise of corporations; the importance of copyright; poor compensation and inequalities for media workers; media production by the few, distributed to the many and overproduction and blockbusters (Hesmondhalgh, 2019), have begun to crumble. There was a model which tended towards concentration and commercialization, but which also boasted some advantages since there was a certain democratic control (public operators, fees, etc.) which has been relaxed.

The aforementioned transformation means we are at a crucial stage of great change. The media face great uncertainty since the classic models are crumbling and audiences, which are often empowered, show less and less support for historical media to the point of daring to challenge them. Amateur, professional and corporate USC of all types are posting content on social networks. It is very possible that this empowerment of users will lead to frustration with the inherent difficulties in any creative process, but there are opportunities for democratizing the so-called Social Media Entertainment (SME) and, to an extent, communication. Everything will depend upon users' ability to innovate, the boosting of co-creation by media industries, and the possibility of using legislation to limit the power of platforms.

In the face of the boom of individuals creating and sharing content on different platforms, some authors have coined the phrase "SME" for "the emerging industry of native online cultural producers together with the platforms, intermediaries, and fan communities operating interdependently, and disruptively, alongside legacy media industries and across global media cultures" (Cunningham & Craig, 2019b: 1). Clearly, the phenomenon goes beyond entertainment and considers information, education, external innovation of companies, and so on.

SME brings with it large quantities of innovation from which conventional media are also feeding. This innovation is complex to understand since it is transversal and affects the whole process of production and distribution (Krumsvik et al., 2019).

In this new ecosystem, platforms exercise a strong control and there is a clear decline of media business but there is also a great empowering of individuals and considerable technological development, meaning that this system is a promising, albeit unstable, one. In addition, the change has also come about with the arrival of technological companies in the media sector and the entertainment industry for example, with the merger of ATT and Discovery or Amazon purchasing the catalogue of MGM. One of the most important drivers of this change is the integration of media and life and tech-media content creation, aggregation and distribution (Chan-Olmsted & Wang, 2019: 139).

The future for media companies is uncertain. They need managers with experience in different fields, media products segments and who are able to monetize the collaboration with their audiences. The power of platforms may also change and the status quo of media industries and entertainment industries may be altered. Technology advances, entrepreneurship is constant, business models are changing and users want to innovate to modify the ecosystem of communication and entertainment. Technology could also change the landscape and threaten the establishment of today's operators (Smith & Telang, 2016). Many companies have disappeared, many mergers have failed and small innovation projects have had the effect of breaking up. That has been the story of the last two decades. The pathway to success is "the adoption of business model and strategies that utilize data, engage audiences, and co-create value through content" (Chan-Olmsted & Wang, 2019: 144). The power of UGCs is such that the sword of Heracles may influence the future of the media and entertainment industries. Perhaps we are being naive, but we believe there is still hope for the democratization of technology. There are new opportunities for old TV channels and newspapers, for the weakest cinema companies, but they must work in a different way and with different targets. States' public policies also need to be redirected to favour quality in information and guarantee pluralism and diversity at the same time.

## 2.3 Advertising and influencers: the different context of platforms

The potential sector of UGCs and their capacity to distribute content, generate a lot of visits and empathize with their followers has not gone unnoticed with the media and brands. The advertising industry has undergone a great change due to the upheaval caused by the Internet and the rise of UGCs. Classical ways of working have been destroyed although, by contrast, new opportunities have opened up (Auletta, 2018). Independent artists from the creative sector have more options than ever before to get themselves noticed. Having said that, they have to do it in a scenario dominated by platforms and a loss of income in media industries. The phenomenon of influencers shows us how the logic behind digital marketing and the opportunities for creators, organizations and firms works.

All the opportunities for collaboration, as offered by social networks and other spaces in which users share their opinion about different services or products, are having an influence on digital marketing. Organizations are more and more keen to increase the participation of their clients and build a greater engagement with their brands. To do so, they seek to reap the maximum benefit from the opportunities given to them by the net. Not only do they advertise in the different ways available to them on social networks, but they also try to create communities of like-minded people or fans, centered on the brand. They want these groups of consumers to actively take part in boosting the sales and opportunities of each brand. They even create emotional bonds with them. It is clear that users are equipped to have an influence on brands on networking sites (Tajvidi et al., 2020) and that is why brands are trying to improve their reputation with them and to strengthen the links of the community.

Brands influence these communities which are organized on conventional social networks so that people take part not only by commenting on content, but also by sharing their experience of the brand and diminishing the critical comments of unsatisfied customers. These followers are, at times, a source of inspiration for the brands – so much so that we could even speak of an outsourcing of creativity and innovation. In both directions, these followers become opinion leaders who help enhance the reputation of brands. At the same time, the companies who use celebrities to promote their brand have also boosted the so-called "influencers". These are people who have many followers and whose comments, photos or videos can influence the marketing of products and services of different brands, or improve their reputation against the competition. In the words of Enke and Borchers (2019), the social media influencers (SMI) are "like third-party actors who have established a significant number of relevant relationships with a specific quality to and influence on organizational stakeholders through content production, content distribution, interaction, and personal appearance on the social web" (Enke & Borchers, 2019: 261).

The phenomenon and rise of influencers has been spectacular in recent years, but, essentially, and from the point of view of marketing, their role is closely related to what media companies used to do. The relationship between traditional marketing and digital marketing is very close nowadays because they have some common features, although they also have notable differences too. The economy which requires the analysis of cost per mile (CPM) in advertising campaigns has been overcome by these new relationships which are created in communities of followers. The advertising model has been turned on its head. SMIs can "cross traditional boundaries in many ways and oscillate between intimacy and publicity, authenticity and commercialization, ingratiation and critical distance … potentially combine different roles, which, have traditionally been occupied by separate actors" (Borchers, 2019: 255).

It is a challenge for organizations to know how to mix these functions in order to improve their targets, since the effectiveness of increasing promotional expenditure has been proved beyond any shadow of doubt in virtually all countries.

Until recently, the conventional consumer was known thanks to the corporate complexity made up of advertisers, advertising agencies, traditional media and below the line strategies. Today, new consumer behavior in a scenario with new social networks is more complex and requires more multidisciplinary empirical information. Audiences have shifted from the role of content receivers to content creators, distributors, and commentators. Consumers of one specific brand "exhibit enhanced consumer loyalty, satisfaction, empowerment, connection, emotional bonding, trust and commitment" (Brodie et al., 2013: 105). The change is such that the fact that the advice may be mixed with endorsement in a way that is indiscernible to the follower is being questioned and a regulation of the relationship between the influencer and the follower may be considered to benefit followers (Mitchell, 2021).

Studies into SMIs and social media engagement with brands, organizations, consumers in the area of marketing, advertising and public relations has been important in recent years and that is reflected in some chapters of this book. Research into the figure of the SMI has been analyzed from many enriching perspectives as revealed by different pieces of work (Abidin, 2016; Duffy, 2017; Khamis, Ang & Welling, 2017; Phua, Jin & Kim, 2017; Voorveld et al., 2018; Himelboim & Golan, 2019; Jiménez-Castillo & Sánchez-Fernández, 2019; Jin, Muqaddam & Ryu, 2019; Firat, 2019; Lee & Kim, 2020; Fumagalli, 2020; Schouten, Janssen & Verspaget, 2020; Tuten, 2020; Guoquan et al., 2021).

The different approaches of the aforementioned studies facilitate an understanding of how digital marketing is changing. The fact that consumers are, at the same time, "prosumers" has altered the playing field of digital marketing. These exchanges, for example, between guests (consumers) and hosts (providers) and Airbnb has already been studied (Lang et al., 2020). In sharing economy platforms (SEPs) the role of so-called "influencers" on social networks is key. The economic growth of these platforms in the coming years is expected to be spectacular with the coming together of artificial intelligence, big data and sharing economy (Sundararajan, 2016; McAfee & Brynjolfsson, 2017; Srnicek, 2017; Nambisan, Wright, Feldman, 2019; Van Dijck, Poell & De Waal, 2018; Van Dijk, 2020). Digital marketing will build on these new advances to improve the strategic communication of organizations.

The power of SMI has increased the commitment of the general public with brands and influences the future behavior of its followers. Although it may seem like a contradiction in terms, conflict and rivalry are one of the main reasons why humans form groups centered on brands to exchange comments which are either comical or hostile about the products of the competition. From that point of view, identifying with a brand may generate hatred towards other brands (Ewing, Wagstaff & Powell, 2013; Ramírez, Veloutsou & Morgan-Thomas, 2019 and Itani, 2020).

Companies often empower their consumers on the net so that they can take part in the search for solutions for themselves or for other consumers of the same product or service, thus enhancing even more the community effect of a brand (Hajli, 2018). There remains a lot to be studied about the workings of active and passive participation of users on social networks and spaces on the net of shared economies and how the actions of influencers generate possible effects related to information, entertainment and money-making and these are issues which are being studied by different authors (Dolan et al., 2019).

The act of sharing with a community is nothing new. In fact, it was the revolution brought about by homo sapiens, according to Harari. However, the term "sharing economy" has become very common due to its zero marginal cost and collaborative commons (Rifkin, 2014). The general idea is that by sharing between companies and user value is created (Tajvidi et al., 2017), even though we cannot be 100 percent sure about consumers' intentions when it comes to the co-creation of value in SEPs. Some models have been set out to explain these intentions using three approaches that offer the following concepts: social support theory, consumer's ethical perceptions and relationship quality theory (Nadeem et al., 2020).

Even though the effectiveness of digital marketing on social networks has been demonstrated, these networks also throw up risks for companies since the advertising value of these spaces may be affected by many variables.

For example, there is great concern among the heads of marketing of companies surrounding advertising on social networks and, in particular, YouTube: on the one hand, there is great potential since interactive videos appear on platforms where people spend a lot of time but, on the other, it is considered content of a lower value as it is generated by users. For that reason, studies have already been carried out to assess the effectiveness of advertising on YouTube, identifying factors affecting it in the context of online video advertising (Djafarova & Kramer,

2019) or in the context of vlogs (Munnukka et al., 2019). Context is very important in advertising and it is not enough to simply measure CPM.

A conventional TV advert is not the same as watching a video of your favourite influencer or a video from a channel which you subscribe to, because you have a specific interest, almost as if it were a hobby. As consumers are becoming more and more omnivorous and nomadic, so, the place where they connect is a factor: away from home, on public transport, in a waiting room, and so on. Quantitative metrics are not so good at measuring the influence of different types of advertising. There are, in this hybrid environment, more and more emotional bonds, related to reception. Brands want to develop ties with the community of fans and have great interest in their comments and in the logic which leads them to share. There remains work to be done in this area for the sector of academic research.

The credibility of influencers is a determining factor since it is hoped that they will empathize with their followers and that their behavior will be ethical when informing about or assessing brands rather than just being someone who is a consumer of one product or another. There have been many studies which analyse the effectiveness of adverts from the discipline of marketing, but what is missing is more analysis from the perspective of the communication of emotional relationships between followers and influencers. In many cases, for example with electronic products, users are influenced in their purchasing decision-making by an expert influencer more than an attractive celebrity influencer (Trivedi & Sama, 2020).

All that leads us to conclude that the efficiency of influencers depends on their level of empathy and the know-how of whoever is giving their opinion. In line with that statement, there are studies which emphasize not only the relationship as referred to the consumption of followers but also the relationship between influencers and their followers (parasocial relationship) and the concept of organizational justice/fairness (Yuan & Lou, 2020).

The experience on each platform is unique and, from the point of view of brands, not all social networks are equally efficient as far as reaching targets is concerned. For that reason, there are authors (Voorveld et al., 2018) who state that the concept of social networks is too wide to be studied without distinctions since each platform has a unique advertising profile. "Engagement and advertising evaluations are related in a highly context-specific way because the relationship is highly contingent on the platform" (Voorveld et al., 2018: 50). That implies that a consumer´s engagement must also be assessed individually. Identifying and assessing influencers requires a consideration not only of the content of messages but also the context. Personality, style and the chosen platform will determine the engagement of influencers and, consequently, its assessment from the point of view of the influence business.

The possibilities offered to users by social networks such as YouTube or Instagram for sharing, commenting on and assessing different content with a like/dislike facilitates the interaction, togetherness and sense of community. This boosts the value of social networks, as, with certain profiles, it is easier for advertising and marketing to identify where its target public may be. The diversity of contents about which the user community interacts makes it possible to construct profiles, not only from the point of view of entertainment, hobbies, journalistic interest, but also that of brands. Digital platforms increase the value of the brand and are used on occasions not only as just another promotional strategy but, at times, this space is its main promotional strategy. The trend reveals, according to Schouten, Janssen & Verspaget (2020), a shift of the patronage from celebrities to influencers. The stories, photographs and videos which they share, although their aim may be advertising, are not necessarily seen as such by the consumer and that helps their persuasive power.

From the analysis of digital marketing and the role of influencers, the following ideas are worth pointing out:

- That brands with a great reputation appear on social networks "has a positive impact on message credibility, attitude toward the ad, purchase intention, and eWOM intention" (Lee & Kim, 2020);
- "The influencer narratives impair the effectiveness of sponsorship disclosure by analyzing the disclosure language in each post as well as the engagement performances" (Feng, Chen & Kong, 2020:1);
- The identification of the desires and confidence by means of the relationship between type of endorser and advertising effectiveness (Schouten, Janssen and Verspaget, 2020);
- The negative spiral when it comes to sharing and commenting on content on social networks is stronger than positiveness (Dhaoui & Webster, 2021);
- The business models evolve in a complex way, with a mixture and hybrid nature for the types of monetization very similar to what is happening with Twitch (Johnson & Woodcock, 2019; Sjöblom et al. 2019 and Diwanji et al., 2020);
- The popularity of the influencer has an influence on their leadership but if their followers have very few accounts, this can have a negative effect on how likeable they are (De Veirman, Cauberghe & Hudders, 2017);
- There is a trend to not take followers into account and to pay only for views as Snapchat has announced;
- In advertising on social networks, the context triumphs over content and, consequently, "content is not king" (Voorveld et al., 2018);
- "a high degree of congruence between the image of a social media influencer and the consumer's ideal self-image leads to effective endorsement outcomes" (Shan, Chen & Lin, 2020: 590).

No-one doubts the potential of digital marketing in social networks, but there are also problems derived from the fact that user data has become merchandise. Understanding the term influencers in the broadest sense, we accept that the marketing which uses it has a great future and will be integrated little by little into traditional media and gradually advertising will shift towards UGC.

## 2.4  The risks of "platformization" and "datafication"

The network which was born from the social and supportive economy, at the same time promising a democratization of the media, is in the hands of powerful global companies which act in a market with little regulation, and not without accusations of monopolistic and scandalous practices such as that of Cambridge Analytics. Benkler's idea of the wealth of networks has given way to a savage new capitalism with virtually no control. It is clear that the existing concern about the great global power of platforms, which are go-betweens who reap the most benefit and the total control of distribution without actually generating any content, is clear. This question was dealt with in the above text where we talk about the great hydra marketing information about users which was obtained during their experience.

The marketing of personal information on social networks happens a lot, but the real danger in the control of this hydra is in the power that it exerts over production, distribution and consumption of all types of content. Its power is not limited to entertainment. Rather, its tentacles reach journalistic information. This increasing power of the group over the value chain is having an influence on the future of media industries, making media and cultural production. In addition, personal information has become a commodity, a good to be traded. Platforms have turned into a paradox by not truly facilitating social, cultural and socioeconomic interaction (Gillespie, 2017). Its algorithms seek the maximum monetization of these processes. Behind it all, there hides the power of intermediation and the idea of a market characterized by "disappearing products" (Bilton, 2017). Platforms are technological companies and not media ones, since they barely finance content producers (Napoli & Caplan, 2017). However, they control an industry which is becoming more and more important and represented by the UGC or influencers. They have become the epicenter of digital marketing in as much as they manage the contents created by users, the advertisers who want to promote their products and services and the data of users who play an active role on social networks.

The control of platforms is based on the process of datafication, taken as a "form of mediation" (Powell, 2019). The reality is that true control does not lie in the content but rather in big data. This great analysis of data is not neutral since it affects our social relationships, our wishes and our reputation. Big data also creates digital gaps. The management of data is affecting possible cultural experiences, exposure to advertising and how we socialize depending on demographic and sociocultural levels. It is also changing how we work, get information and enjoy ourselves.

Platforms have also paved the way for new professions which are considered "creative": social media entertainers, influencers (Abidin, 2016) and many others who work for free. They all adapt their work to platform algorithms in order to monetize their work (Duffy, Poell & Nieborg, 2019). Platformization renders cultural commodities contingent (Nieborg & Poell, 2018). The social media platforms' business models are "increasingly more interdependent with creator culture" (Cunningham & Craig, 2019b: 2). These authors also point out the internal contradictions and tensions inherent in the main commercial platforms centered on the value of content which was, originally, amateur.

Platforms are, apparently, neutral and distribute plural content in an attempt to satisfy the demand for content by everybody; however they determine "the strategies, routines, experiences, and expressions of creativity, labor, and citizenship that shape cultural production through platforms" (Duffy, Poell & Nieborg, 2019:

2). This side effect of platforms takes away from the cultural diversity and plural-ism, all the more so in countries with very weak cultural industries which depend on imports. Governments are already beginning to demand investment quotas and the provision of a catalogue, as is the case with the European Union. This control may bring with it many threats for diversity, pluralism or even democracy (Allocca, 2018 and Kyncl & Peyvan, 2017). Obviously, they are not "neutral carriers of content" (Cunningham & Craig, 2019b), and, although it may seem paradoxical, platforms aim their strategies more towards the spectator than the community (Van Dijk, 2020). All of this is very difficult to analyse because algorithms work like a black box which is mutating constantly.

This is not a debate between Utopians and Marxists or pessimists and optimists, but platforms offer both sides of the coin: it is obvious that they are also providing many people with opportunities. Platforms also promote the creation of content, innovation, communication, the interests of groups of people, and so on. It has made changes in creative work possible, and allowed many people to monetize some of their passions and share them with others. We are not only talking about the false equality of influencers with the female world linked to the stereotypes of health and beauty, but many other influencers who comment on and assess the news, give their opinion about products and services and, in particular, share hobbies. There still remains a lot of work to be done in the area of marketing for UGCs to be more active and improve their relationship with platforms and audiences.

Despite the incredible control and power of platforms, we feel that the status quo may change because of the high level of innovation of users and the technol-ogy itself. The level of entrepreneurship and the constant appearance of new start-ups are destabilizing the platforms' power ecosystem. Governments are also becoming aware of the need to regulate the process of social interaction via plat-forms inasmuch as citizens' rights are in play. There is considerable uncertainty but the power of the hydra will not be eternal and absolute. Technological innovation and the power of users counteracts it. New competitors will also appear, even from among them. In addition, of course many pirates will serve to destabilize too. Let's hope that the voice of the people will be recognized not only by Alexa, Siri or Cortana, or represented by their favourite influencers.

## 2.5  Pandemic narcissism and aspirational labor

Creative work has traditionally been considered very cool since it empowered the workers of the cultural and creative industries. However, being an influencer, hav-ing a lot of followers and making a lot of money in any of the social network platforms is the "crème de la crème". It portrays an image of modernness and exclusivity with an aura of freedom and know-how beyond any shadow of doubt. The subjects of the content created by influencers is very diverse, but the most successful ones are gaming, gossip and beauty. The concept of happiness could be studied, using the images of people on Instagram. If we add the varnish of entre-preneurship, we are witnessing a phenomenon which is changing traditional marketing. In the same way as with influencers, their followers work together to create a fake image of themselves. For that reason, it could be said that we are living in a pandemic of narcissism (Twenge & Campbell, 2009). However, these social networks distort our identities, empower status-seeking extremists, and render moderates all but invisible (Bail, 2021).

The problem is that there are many who are left behind, even those who market their intimacy. In the same way as making media, there is a lot of precariousness and too many regrettable situations. Many people use platforms as aspirational labor – a job which has all the advantages and inconveniences of any other temporary job (Duffy, 2015). Undoubtedly, "the valorization of creative work normalizes forms of precarious, individualized employment alongside a reduction in workers' rights and social protections" (Bishop, 2021:10). Precarious employment not only occurs in the area of media making but also on social media and in the traditional employment of cultural industries (Curtin & Sanson, 2016 and McRobbie, 2016).

It is obvious that few amateur users who post content on networks manage to become professionals and make a good living. In addition, many of them end up monetizing their intimacy. Their followers and the brands that sponsor them turn into a boss with no regard for their rights: the algorithm of the platform. If things do not work out, the boss recommends a change. So, for example, when the content created by YouTube members is demonetized, they must change to adapt to the algorithm strategy and recover income. Very often this situation may lead to conflict between both parties (Caplan & Gillespie, 2020). That's why YouTube represents itself as "legislator, judge, and executive authority" (Kopf, 2020: 1). The contemporary model of digital capitalism with the idea of accumulation of wealth based on the exploitation of users is well known (Fuchs, 2014). Obviously, many users find themselves in a position of inferiority and must direct their creativity and content production to be in line with the principles of platforms. However, many influencers in addition to reinterpreting the algorithm of Instagram, for example, play at visibility, and influence the platforms in such a way that they have a certain room for maneuver for "gaming the system" (Cotter, 2019). In other words, "influencers play by the rules, but not always by the spirit of the rule" (Cotter, 2019: 908).

The algorithm redesigns itself in favour of the interests of the platform and companies. It learns, little by little, in order to optimize those interests. That is known as "experience technologies" (Cotter & Reisdorf, 2020). This form of learning uses many applications and also artificial intelligence (AI). At the same time it produces a dynamic which destroys many dreams of the influencers themselves and their followers who tend to confuse reality with desire. All of that leads to "value-laded algorithmic judgments map onto well-worn hierarchies of desirability and employability that originate from systemic bias along the lines of class, race, and gender" (Bishop, 2021: 1).

The creative process of influencers cannot be free as it must adapt to an algorithm which is continually changing. There is a big brother who is watching all the time in order to improve digital marketing: a job under observation, as Abidin

(2016) calls it. This permanent adaptation leads to a questioning of the false autonomy without commercial pressure and a fake collaborative experience of a commercial community.

Many highly motivated users carry out unpaid work for personal reasons. Indeed, "aspirational laborers expect that they will one day be compensated for their productivity – be it through material rewards or social capital. But in the meantime, they remain suspended in the consumption and promotion of branded commodities" (Duffy, 2017: 6). Behind the wishes of "self-branding" there lies a situation of exploitation. The same as in real life, some make it and others don't. Social relevance and monetary income most of the time go hand in hand, but not always. Many manage to reach a level of empowerment, doing a job and making a living from something they find fulfilling.

Digital capitalism, which tends to maximize profits and increase share value, also makes it possible for many influencers to do a job which is of interest to their followers, although some profit is also made for platforms. They are the two sides of the same coin: a few winners who work for their sponsors have a special relationship with their followers but there are many who try but don't make it.

It is a phenomenon which has gone beyond entertainment, and the subjects it deals with are often more relevant and useful for people looking for information about health, learning languages or mathematics, or solving complex problems such as what to do with a pension plan, and so on. The subjects are numerous and varied, using video, podcast and text. They are UGCs whose activity combines with that of influencers, which, basically, is that of a recommender of products. This new phenomenon is not only changing digital marketing but also the ways in which people receive information, training and have fun with a certain degree of freedom.

## 2.6  Conclusion

There is a struggle to control the attention of users involving the media and the content on offer created by both amateurs and professionals on social networks. This level of competition paves the way for new business opportunities, leading organizations to redefine their strategies and users to modify their consumption styles in such a way that there has to be permanent innovation. This new information and entertainment ecosystem has caused a large-scale fragmentation of audiences and the apparition of diverse business models.

In the new scenario, the gathering of data about users' experiences is of great value for digital marketing and programmatic advertising. In this process, the media lose presence in the life of the general public to the users who share content on different platforms. This shift takes place in the context of rampant globalization and retreat, and there is a certain sense of impotence among states regarding the ability to regulate and reinforce the quality of information and guarantee diversity, cultural pluralism and equal opportunities.

Audiences have become empowered, now that they can create all types of content and distribute it on different platforms. The sensation that all media industries and media making is going to be a business in which the process rather than the product is controlled, is now appearing. It is the power of powerful platforms and the context is more important than the content and may in fact be more lucrative. Each platform is specializing in something and advertisers know the advantages that each one offers. There is a clear difference between, for example, Facebook, YouTube or Instagram.

Vloggers, streamers, YouTubers, influencers, Instagramers, gameplayers, TikTokers attract more and more of people's time. Brands aim their advertising towards those platforms by generating a feeling of community and certain emotional bonds. Audiences are more and more fragmented and, paradoxically, between fewer operators. New opportunities and success depend on control of data, engagement and the co-creation of content.

However, platforms act like a hydra which mutates permanently and reinvents itself constantly by means of algorithms, big data and artificial intelligence. It is very efficient as it mechanizes many processes in order to market information about users more effectively. These platforms have taken over by controlling the intermediation between creators and they cannot be considered neutral since they determine the type of content and influence the tastes of the general public. The trend in the digital environment is towards a monopoly of the control of user data. They have the capacity for feedback, almost all their innovation is outsourced and they barely help creators. The latter are subject to the problems of aspirational labor as is unpaid work, in the middle of a pandemic of global narcissism. However, we feel that technological innovation, itself, entrepreneurship and the empowerment of people may be the sword of Heracles to finish with the overarching power of the hydra. We are aware that states must also help to limit this power by guaranteeing many rights and improving democracy.

## References

Abidin, C. (2016). Visibility labour: Engaging with Influencers' fashion brands and# OOTD advertorial campaigns on Instagram. *Media International Australia*, 161(1), 86–100.

Albarran, A. B. (Ed.). (2013). *The social media industries*. London: Routledge.

Allocca, K. (2018). *Videocracy: How YouTube is changing the world … with double rainbows, singing foxes, and other trends we can't stop watching*. New York, NY: Bloomsbury.

Álvarez-Monzoncillo, J.M. & López-Villanueva, J. (2014). El audiovisual español: evolución en curso. In E. Bustamante & F. Rueda (Eds.), *Informe sobre el Estado de la Cultura en España. La salida digital* (pp. 65–72). Madrid: Fundación Alternativas.

Athique, A. (2016). *Transnational audiences: Media reception on a global scale. Malden.* MA: Polity.

Auletta, K. (2018). *Frenemies: The epic disruption of the advertising industry (and why this Matters)*. London: Harper Collins Publishers.

Bail, C. (2021). *Breaking the social media prism: How to make our platforms less polarizing*. Princeton: Princeton University Press.

Bilton, C. (2017). *The disappearing product: Marketing and markets in the creative industries*. Cheltenham: Edward Elgar Publishing.

Bishop S. (2021). Influencer management tools: Algorithmic cultures, brand safety, and bias. *Social Media + Society*. DOI:10.1177/20563051211003066

Borchers, N.S. (2019). Social media influencers in strategic communication. *International Journal of Strategic Communication*, 13, 255–260.

Brodie, R., Ilic, A., Juric, A. & Hollebeek, L. (2013). Consumer engagement in a virtual brand community: An exploratory analysis, *Journal of Business Research*, 66(1), 105–114.

Caplan, R., & Gillespie, T. (2020). Tiered governance and demonetization: The shifting terms of labor and compensation in the platform economy. *Social Media + Society*. https://doi.org/10.1177/2056305120936636

Chalaby, J. K. (2015). *The format age: Television's entertainment revolution*. Malden: Polity.

Chan-Olmsted, S. & Wang, R. (2019). Shifts in consumer engagement and media business models. In M. Deuze & M. Prenger (Eds.), *Making media: Production, practices, and professions* (pp. 133–146). Amsterdam: Amsterdam University Press.

Cotter, K. (2019). Playing the visibility game: How digital influencers and algorithms negotiate influence on Instagram. *New Media & Society*, 21(4), 895–913.

Cotter, K., & Reisdorf, B. (2020). Algorithmic knowledge gaps: A new horizon of (digital) inequality. *International Journal of Communication*, 14, 745–765.

Cunningham, S. & Craig, D. (2019a). *Social media entertainment: The new intersection of Hollywood and Silicon Valley*. New York: New York University Press.

Cunningham, S. & Craig, D. (2019b). Creator governance in social media entertainment. *Social Media + Society*. https://doi.org/10.1177/2056305119883428

Curtin, M. & Sanson, K. (Eds.) (2016). *Precarious creativity: Global media, local labor*. Oakland, CA: University of California Press.

De Veirman, M.; Cauberghe, V. & Hudders, L. (2017). Marketing through Instagram influencers: The impact of number of followers and product divergence on brand attitude, *International Journal of Advertising*, 36 (5), 798–828, DOI: 10.1080/02650487.2017.1348035

Deuze, M. & Prenger, M. (Eds.) (2019). *Making media: Production, practices, and professions*. Amsterdam: Amsterdam University Press.

Dhaoui, C., & Webster, C. M. (2021). Brand and consumer engagement behaviors on Facebook brand pages: Let's have a (positive) conversation. *International Journal of Research in Marketing*, 38(1), 155–175. https://doi.org/10.1016/j.ijresmar.2020.06.005

Diwanji, V., Reed, A., Ferchaud, A., Seibert, J., Weinbrecht, V., & Sellers, N. (2020). Don't just watch, join in: Exploring information behavior and copresence on Twitch. *Computers in Human Behavior*, 105, 106221.

Djafarova, E. & Kramer, K. (2019). YouTube advertising: Exploring its effectiveness. *The Marketing Review*, 19(1–2), 127–145.

Dolan, R., Conduit, J., Frethey-Bentham, C., Fahy, J. & Goodman, S. (2019). Social media engagement behavior: A framework for engaging customers through social media content. *European Journal of Marketing*, 10, 2213–2243.

Doyle, G. (2013). *Understanding media economics*. London. Sage.

Duffy, B. (2015). Amateur, autonomous, and collaborative: Myths of aspiring female cultural producers in Web 2.0. *Critical Studies in Media Communication*, 32, 48–64.

Duffy, B. E. (2017). *(Not) getting paid to do what you love: Gender, social media, and aspirational work*. New Haven: Yale University Press.

Duffy, B. E., Poell, T., & Nieborg, D. B. (2019). Platform practices in the cultural industries: Creativity, labor, and citizenship. *Social Media+ Society*, 5(4), 1.

Elberse, A. (2013). *Blockbusters: Hit-making, risk-taking and the big business of entertainment*. New York: Henry Holt.

Enke, N & Borchers, N. S. (2019). Social media influencers in strategic communication: A conceptual framework for strategic social media influencer communication. *International Journal of Strategic Communication.* 13, 261–277.

Evens, T., & Donders, K. (2018). *Platform power and policy in transforming television markets.* London: Palgrave Macmillan.

Ewing, M. T., Wagstaff, P. E., & Powell, I. H. (2013). Brand rivalry and community conflict. *Journal of Business Research* 66(1), 4–12.

Faustino, P. & Noam, E. (2019). Media Industries management Characteristics and Challenges in a Converging Digital World. In M. Prenger and M. Deuze (Eds.), *Making media: Production, practices, and professions* (pp. 147–159). Amsterdam: Amsterdam University Press.

Feng, Y., Chen, H. & Kong, Q. (2020). An expert with whom I can identify: The role of narratives in influencer marketing, *International Journal of Advertising,* doi.org/10.1080/02 650487.2020.1824751

Firat, D. (2019). YouTube advertising value and its effects on purchase intention. *Journal of Global Business Insights,* 4(2), 141–155.

Flew, T. (2013). *Global creative industries.* MA, Malden: Polity Press.

Foer, F. (2017). *World without mind.* New York. Random House.

Fuchs, C. (2014). *Digital labour and Karl Marx.* London: Routledge.

Fumagalli, E., (2020). Tough love: When social media influencers' digital detox goes wrong. In *SAGE Business Cases.* SAGE Publications, Ltd., https://www.doi.org/10.4135/9781526496638

Gabszewicz, J. J., Resende, J., & Sonnac, N. (2015). Media as multi-sided platforms. In R. G. Picard and S.S. Wildman (Eds.), *Handbook on the economics of the media* (pp. 3–35). Northampton, US: Edward Elgar Publishing.

Gillespie, T. (2017). Algorithmically recognizable: Santorum's Google problem and Google's Santorum problem. *Information, Communication & Society,* 1, 63–80.

Guoquan Y, Hudders, L; De Jans, S & De Veirman, M. (2021). The value of influencer marketing for business: A bibliometric analysis and managerial implications, *Journal of Advertising.* DOI: 10.1080/00913367.2020.1857888

Hajli, N. (2018). Ethical environment in the online communities by information credibility: A social media perspective. *Journal of Business Ethics,* 149(4), 799–810.

Hesmondhalgh, D. (2019). Have digital communication technologies democratized the media industries? In Curran, J. and D. Hesmondhalgh (Eds.), *Media and society* (6th edition). London: Bloomsbury Academic.

Himelboim, I., & Golan, G. J. (2019). A social networks approach to viral advertising: The role of primary, contextual, and low influencers. *Social Media+ Society,* 5(3). DOI: 10.1177/2056305119847516

Holt, J., & Perren, A., (Eds.) (2009). *Media industries: History, method, and theory.* Malden, MA: Blackwell.

Itani, O. S. (2020). "Us" to co-create value and hate "them": Examining the interplay of consumer-brand identification, peer identification, value co-creation among consumers, competitor brand hate and individualism. *European Journal of Marketing,* 55(4), 1023–1066.

Jenkins, H. (2006). *Convergence culture. Where old and new media collide.* New York: New York University Press.

Jenkins, H., Ford, S., & Green, J. (2018). *Spreadable media: Creating value and meaning in a networked culture.* New York: New York University Press.

Jiménez-Castillo, D. & Sánchez-Fernández, R. (2019). The role of digital influencers in brand recommendation: Examining their impact on engagement, expected value and purchase intention. *International Journal of Information Management,* 49, 366–376.

Jin, S. V., Muqaddam, A. & Ryu, E. (2019). Instafamous and social media influencer marketing. *Marketing Intelligence & Planning*, 5, 567–579.

Johnson, M. R. & Woodcock, J. (2019). And today's top donator is: How live streamers on Twitch. Tv monetize and gamify their broadcasts. *Social Media+ Society*, 5(4).

Kawashima, N. (2020). Changing business models in the media industries. *Media Industries Journal*, 7(1).

Khamis, S., Ang, L., & Welling, R. (2017). Self-branding, 'micro-celebrity' and the rise of social media influencers. *Celebrity Studies*, 8, 191–208.

Kim, T. (2021). Critical interpretations of global-local co-productions in subscription video-on-demand platforms: A case study of Netflix's YG future strategy office. *Television & New Media*. https://doi.org/10.1177/1527476421999437

Kopf, S. (2020). "Rewarding Good Creators": Corporate social media discourse on monetization schemes for content creators. *Social Media + Society*. https://doi.org/10.1177/2056305120969877

Krumsvik, A. H., Milan, S., Bhroin, N. N., & Storsul, T. (2019). 14. Making (sense of) media innovations. In M. Prenger and M. Deuze (Eds.), *Making media: Production, practices, and professions* (pp. 193–205). Amsterdam: Amsterdam University Press.

Kyncl, K. & Peyvan, M. (2017). *Streampunks: How YouTube and the new creators are transforming our lives*. London, England: Virgin Books.

Lang, B., Botha, E., Robertson, J., Kemper, J. A., Dolan, R., & Kietzmann, J. (2020). How to grow the sharing economy? Create Prosumers! *Australasian Marketing Journal*, 28, 58–66.

Lee, S. & Kim, E. (2020) Influencer marketing on Instagram: How sponsorship disclosure, influencer credibility, and brand credibility impact the effectiveness of Instagram promotional post, *Journal of Global Fashion Marketing*, 11(3), 232–249. DOI: 10.1080/20932685.2020.1752766

Lotz, A. D. (2017). *Portals: A treatise on internet-distributed television*. Ann Arbor: Michigan Publishing.

Maxwell, R., & Miller, T. (2012). *Greening the media*. Oxford: Oxford University Press.

Mayer, V., Banks, M. J., & Caldwell, J. T. (Eds.) (2009). *Production studies: Cultural studies of media industries*. London: Routledge.

McAfee, A. & Brynjolfsson, E. (2017). *Machine, platform, crowd: Harnessing our digital future*. New York: WW Norton & Company.

McRobbie, A. (2016). *Be creative: Making a living in the new culture industries*. Cambridge, UK: Polity Press.

Mitchell, M. (2021). Free ad (vice): Internet influencers and disclosure regulation. *The RAND Journal of Economics*, 52(1), 3–21.

Munnukka, J., Maity, D., Reinikainen, H. & Luoma-Aho, V. (2019). "Thanks for watching". The effectiveness of YouTube vlogendorsements. *Computers in human behavior*, 93, 226–234.

Nadeem, W., Juntunen, M.; Shirazi, F.& Hajli N. (2020). Consumers' value co-creation in sharing economy: The role of social support, consumers' ethical perceptions and relationship quality. *Technological Forecasting and Social Change*, 151, 1–13.

Nambisan, S., Wright, M., & Feldman, M. (2019). The digital transformation of innovation and entrepreneurship: Progress, challenges and key themes. *Research Policy*, 48, 103773.

Napoli, P. M. (2016). Requiem for the long tail: Towards a political economy of content aggregation and fragmentation. *International Journal of Media & Cultural Politics*, 12(3), 341–356.

Napoli, P. M. & Caplan, R. (2017). Why media companies insist they're not media companies, why they're wrong, and why it matters. First Monday, 22(5). Retrieved from https://firstmonday.org/ojs/index.php/fm/article/view/7051/6124

Nieborg, D. B., & Poell, T. (2018). The platformization of cultural production: Theorizing the contingent cultural commodity. *New Media & Society*, 20, 4275–4292.

Phua, J., Jin, S. V. & Kim, J. J. (2017). Gratifications of using Facebook, Twitter, Instagram, or Snapchat to follow brands: The moderating effect of social comparison, trust, tie strength, and network homophily on brand identification, brand engagement, brand commitment, and membership intention. *Telematics and Informatics*, 34(1), 412–424.

Picard, R. G. & Wildman, S. S. (Eds.) (2015). *Handbook on the economics of the media.* Northampton: Edward Elgar Publishing.

Pickard, V. & Berman, D. (2019). *After net neutrality: A new deal for the digital age.* New Haven: Yale University Press. DOI:10.2307/j.ctvqc6h2t

Powell, A. (2019). The mediations of data. In Curran, J. & Hesmondhalgh, D. (Eds.), *Media and society*, (6th ed.) (pp. 121–138). London: Bloomsbury Academic.

Ramírez, S. A. O., Veloutsou, C., & Morgan-Thomas, A. (2019). I hate what you love: brand polarization and negativity towards brands as an opportunity for brand management. *Journal of Product & Brand Management.*

Rifkin, J. (2014). *The zero marginal cost society: The internet of things, the collaborative commons, and the eclipse of capitalism.* New York: Palgrave Mcmillan.

Schouten, A., Janssen, L. & Verspaget, M. (2020). Celebrity vs. Influencer endorsements in advertising: the role of identification, credibility, and Product-Endorser fit. *International Journal of Advertising*, 39, 258–281.

Shan, Y., Chen, K. & Lin, J. S. (2020). When social media influencers endorse brands: The effects of self-influencer congruence, parasocial identification, and perceived endorser motive, *International Journal of Advertising*, 39(5), 590–610, DOI:10.1080/02650487.2019. 1678322

Sjöblom, M., Törhönen, M., Hamari, J., & Macey, J. (2019). The ingredients of Twitch streaming: Affordances of game streams. *Computers in Human Behavior*, 92, 20–28.

Smith, M. D., & Telang, R. (2016).*Streaming, sharing, stealing: Big data and the future of entertainment.* Boston: MIT Press.

Srnicek, N. (2017). *Platform capitalism.* New York: John Wiley & Sons.

Starks, M. (2013). *The digital television revolution: Origins to outcomes.* Basingstoke: Palgrave Macmillan.

Strangelove, M. (2015). *Post-TV: Piracy, cord-cutting, and the future of television.* Toronto: University of Toronto Press.

Sundararajan, A. (2016). *The sharing economy. The end of employment and the rise of crowd-based capitalism.* Cambridge: MIT Press.

Tajvidi, M., Richard, M-O., Wang, Y., Hajli, N. (2020). Brand co-creation through social commerce information sharing: The role of social media. *Journal of Business Research*, 121, 476–486.

Tajvidi, M., Wang, Y., Hajli, N., & Love, P. E. (2017). Brand value Co-creation in social commerce: The role of interactivity, social support, and relationship quality. *Computers in Human Behavior*, 105238.

Taylor, C. (2020). The urgent need for more research on influencer marketing. *International Journal of Advertising*, 39(7), 889–891.

Trivedi, J. & Sama, R. (2020). The effect of influencer marketing on consumers' brand admiration and online purchase intentions: An emerging market perspective, *Journal of Internet Commerce*, 19, 103–124.

Tuten, T. L. (2020). *Social media marketing.* London: Sage.

Twenge, J. M., & Campbell, W. K. (2009). *The narcissism epidemic: Living in the age of entitlement.* New York, Simon and Schuster.

Van Dijck, J., Poell, T., & De Waal, M. (2018). *The platform society: Public values in a connective world.* Oxford: Oxford University Press.

Van Dijk, J. (2020). *The network society.* London: Sage.

Voorveld, H.A.M.; Van Noort, G.; Muntinga D.G. & Bronner, F. (2018). Engagement with social media and social media advertising: The differentiating role of platform type, *Journal of Advertising*, 47(1), 38–54, DOI:10.1080/00913367.2017.1405754

Yuan, S & Lou, C. (2020). How social media influencers foster relationships with followers: The roles of source credibility and fairness in parasocial relationship and product interest, *Journal of Interactive Advertising*, 20, 2, 133–147, DOI: 10.1080/15252019.2020.1769514

# 3 The power of algorithms and keys of participation

*José Esteves*

## 3.1 Introduction

We live in the era of algorithms. Some even called it a new economy, the algorithm economy. They are the building blocks of any software application. Every day we are increasingly exposed to algorithmically curated information. Algorithms dictate everything users see online. From news to search information, to entertainment (Netflix) and shopping (Amazon), algorithms increasingly impact how we make decisions, how we consume information and how we understand the world around us. Web users increasingly enjoy more access to information more speedily and in an accessible manner as the media landscape shifts more towards digital and mobile domains (Levordashka & Utz, 2016; Boczkowski et al., 2018). The general belief that algorithmic use has a significant impact on daily life in this digital world is reflected in the high level of interest in public and scholarly debates (Gillespie, 2014; Willson, 2017).

What is an algorithm? Essentially, algorithms are a step-by-step list of instructions that are executed, in a certain order, for solving a problem or performing a task (Gillespie, 2014; Introna, 2016). For example, a cake recipe is an algorithm for making a cake. We use algorithms every day. A computer program is an implemented set of algorithms. Furthermore, algorithms are used to run the Internet and all Web services, including Web searches.

The use of algorithms will continue to proliferate everywhere as huge amounts of data are being generated, collected, analysed and managed by companies, public administrations and governments. Additionally, the exponential growth of Internet users makes it impossible to manage certain tasks manually. There are just not enough moderators to thoroughly review each piece of content due to the volume of content submitted on a daily basis. Moreover, the complexity and subtleties of language present significant obstacles. Artificial Intelligence (AI) and techniques like Machine Learning (ML), Deep Learning (DL) and Natural Language Processing (NLP) are at the forefront of this new era of algorithms. Moreover, AI-based algorithms, particularly the ones based on deep learning, are challenging the notion of transparency and objectivity (Zerilli et al., 2018).

One of the Web services that uses intensive algorithms is social media. Social media (and the Web) has grown exponentially in the last decade, and it has forever changed the way we interact, work and do business (Sterrett et al., 2019). Social

DOI: 10.4324/9781003134176-4

media is defined as "a group of Internet-based applications that build on the ideological and technological foundations of Web 2.0, and that allow the creation and exchange of User Generated Content" (Kaplan & Haenlein, 2010, p. 61). It includes, among other tools, weblogs (e.g. TechCrunch, Gary Vaynerchuk Blog, and TMZ), microblogging (e.g. Twitter, Tumblr and Weibo), social networking platforms (e.g. LinkedIn and Xing), platforms for sharing videos and images (e.g. TikTok, YouTube, Dailymotion, Pinterest, and Instagram), instant messaging (e.g. WhatsApp, Snapchat, WeChat and QQ), news aggregators (e.g. Reddit, Hacker News and BizSugar) and social live streaming services (e.g. Socialive and Periscope).

All these social media services use algorithms to perform different tasks and different personalization mechanisms. The adoption of social media algorithmic tools serves as a helpful way to avoid becoming overwhelmed with the amount of information. For example, Facebook and Twitter show to the user posts from his/her closest friends and in the user feed because those are the people that the user interacts with most often. However, it transfers human decision-making power towards social media algorithms (Diakopoulos & Koliska, 2016). Often, users do not know how these algorithms make decisions for them. The control of advertising that appears on YouTube videos is an example. This is done automatically by algorithms that pick which advertisements the user will see during a YouTube video in real time. These decisions may have strong implications related to the risk of discriminating those affected (Coeckelbergh, 2020; Cowgill & Tucker, 2020). This content bias issue and the potential discrimination effect can occur intentionally (Speicher et al., 2018), or even unintentionally through their respective choice of criteria (Diakopoulos, 2013).

Yet, there has been scant attention to the different effects of the social, organizational, cultural and political dynamics related to the process of algorithm development and implementation (Diakopoulos, 2016; Ettlinger, 2018). One of the big issues is the potential risk of algorithmic bias and, in certain situations, ethical concerns (Tsamados et al., 2021). Although the term bias differs based on the context (Narayanan, 2018), in general, tt refers to errors that are systematic and repeats that result in unfair consequences, like favouring one arbitrary user community over another.

This chapter outlines the challenges of using algorithms in social media, in particular transparency and objectivity. First, I describe the main areas of algorithm usage in social media. Then, I discuss the challenges associated with that use.

## 3.2 Social media and algorithms

As mentioned before, social media services are the kings of algorithm usage. This section delves into the three most common uses of algorithms on social media: content curation, user data collecting and content production.

### 3.2.1 *Content curation*

Curation is the act of selecting, classifying, filtering, prioritizing and presenting content. Algorithmic curation and filtering is one of the most used tools on social media (and digital media in general), and it is a great challenge in hyper-technological and digital society (Thurman et al., 2019; Jussupow et al., 2020). Essentially, filtering algorithms automatically select and filter data that the user sees based on the extrapolation of viewing or usage preference of the user's previous behaviour, or many other users, to predict what that user might like too (Messing & Westwood, 2014; Bakshy et al., 2015; Rader and Gray, 2015; Mothes & Ohme, 2019). Algorithmic filtering has the potential to improve users' experience (Bozdag, 2013; Ricci et al., 2015, Zarouali et al., 2021). Recommender algorithms which are quite common in online retailing platforms like Amazon or streaming platforms like Netflix are a type of curation algorithms.

A good example of algorithmic curation on social media is Facebook. In 2011, algorithms were incorporated in the news feed feature. One of the key goals was to decrease content hypersaturation on social media. Then, in 2018, the platform decided to prioritize posts from family members and friends over public content. According to Facebook, the company wants users to get the content they care about and from the friends they care about. Most of social media companies argue that the introduction of curation algorithms is to offer a user-centered solution for managing vast amounts of content, allowing the users to quickly "see what matters" on their social feeds.

The three most frequently used filtering algorithms are content-based filtering, demographic filtering and collaborative filtering (Ryngksai & Chameikho, 2014; Thorat, 2015). Content-based filtering analyzes user preferences related to similarities in products, services or content features to make recommendations for the user. The demographic filtering approach employs the social-demographic data (e.g. age, gender, job) of a user to select the content that might be suitable for recommendation. Finally, collaborative filtering algorithms make suggestions for an individual user by collecting data and preferences from many other users. This perspective relies on the premise that social media users who accepted specific content are likely to accept it again in the future.

There are different types of curation personalization approaches on social media. The most common differentiation is between explicit and implicit personalization (Thurman & Schifferes, 2012; Kaptein et al., 2015; Borgesius et al., 2016; Haim et al., 2017; Yeung, 2018; Reviglio & Agosti, 2020). Explicit personalization relies on data that the social media user proactively disclosed, and implicit personalization uses data that the social media user has not directly volunteered; in some cases, the user does not require a user to create an account. Basically, it tracks user behaviour. Some algorithms use a combination of both types of personalization. More recently, a new type of personalization is emerging – contextual personalization – which is based on the user's current location and time.

Although curation algorithms have the potential to increase user experience and satisfaction, this had not always been the result. In the last years, curation algorithms have been criticized for creating "filter bubbles" and other phenomena on social media (for a critical review see: Dahlgren, 2021; Cinelli et al., 2021). The term filter bubbles, also called echo chambers (Sunstein, 2009) was coined by Eli Pariser (2011), is related with the filtering algorithms mechanism that dictates the information and opinions that the user can see based on the user's own beliefs. Some studies suggest that filter bubble state limits diversity of content, and it can increase user polarization (Flaxman et al., 2016; Dubois & Blank, 2018; Chitra & Musco, 2020). Some recent studies investigated whether the YouTube video recommendation system contributes to social media polarization by promoting sensitive content (e.g. Hussein et al., 2020; Roth et al., 2020). Hussein et al. (2020) discovered a filter bubble effect in top recommendations for all topics, excluding vaccine controversy, after examining more than 56,000 videos across five topics. They also found that for users with brand-new accounts, demographic factors like gender, age, and geolocation have no effect on amplifying disinformation in returned search results.

Despite the potential filter bubble risk, other studies do not support this viewpoint (e.g., Hosanagar et al., 2014; Bakshy et al., 2015; Borgesius et al., 2016; Fletcher and Nielsen, 2018; Boxell et al., 2020; Levy, 2021). A study conducted by Hosanagar et al. (2014) found that algorithm filtering can build commonality, not fragmentation, in online music preferences. Similar studies have found the YouTube recommendation algorithm may foster the creation of highly homophilous communities (e.g. Hussein et al., 2020; Kaiser & Rauchfleisch, 2020; Tang et al., 2021). A recent study by Boxell et al. (2020) found that although affective polarization has grown faster in the United States, it is decreasing in other countries with high Internet usage. Also, the authors found that U.S. polarization was highest for the older age groups (75+).

### 3.2.2  User data collection

Social media algorithms are also collecting vast amounts of data from social media users, and using that data for different purposes, such as advertising, promotions, business intelligence, data analytics, and personalization. As we mentioned before, one of the most relevant aspects is how data collection tools affect how users find social media content (Mittelstadt et al., 2016).

Social media firms collect enormous amounts of data about social media users, allowing them to create advanced psychometric profiles of users (Schirch, 2021). This data has proven to be immensely valuable for many social media firms because their business model based on advertising revenues depends on this sort of data. Social media data-centric business models focus on collecting as much data as possible and link it to individual users, and create psychometric profiles of those users which will let the firms better target their advertising strategies. This data-centric approach affects the design of social media profiles, which is continuously reviewed and updated.

Profile making has become omnipresent in social media platforms and digital world. Users are frequently invited (most of the times it is mandatory) to create profiles for using most of the Web services. Combining algorithms with profiling approaches might be troublesome since the profiling criteria can provide controversial categories and adverse effects, allowing discrimination or questionable user targeting. For example, some years ago, Facebook allowed to target "anti-Semites" (Angwin et al., 2017). Also, some social media platforms (e.g. Google, YouTube or Facebook) allegedly used racial profiling (Angwin & Parris Jr., 2016; Gardner, 2020).

The rise of data analytics and emerging technologies like machine learning and AI are expanding the ability of social media firms to contextualize data and draw on insights gained from this data analysis. Overall, social media platforms based their design, operations and business model on a datafication strategy. Social data collected by social media firms can be categorized into four main categories:

- Personal data. It includes data that can be used to identify a person. Beyond the common information like name, phone number, and addresses, it also includes data of national IDs, passport number, social security numbers, gender, photos, and financial data, as well as non-personally identifiable information (Non-PII) such as Web browser type, Web browser cookies, language preference, IP address, and device types and IDs.
- Engagement data. Also called interaction data, it includes data that describes how consumers interact with the social media platforms, mobile apps, text messages, emails, paid adverts.
- Behavioral data. It includes data generated or in response to the user experience with a social media platform and it encompasses the transactional details such as product usage, purchase history, and gathering qualitative data (e.g., click tracking, scrolling, and mouse movement).
- Attitudinal data. It helps to understand that social media users think about the platform and the content provided. Examples include online reviews, user satisfaction surveys and content desirability.

### 3.2.3 Content creation

New emerging technologies are allowing social media firms, businesses and certain users to create content automatically. Content creation automation is a growing area, especially in the digital marketing arena. Certain AI tools like NLP are quickly expanding content creation automation in social media (Farzindar &Inkpen, 2017; Khan et al., 2020).

NLP, sometimes referred to as computational linguistics, is a branch of computer science, AI and linguistics, that uses different machine learning techniques to build algorithms that process and analyze natural language data. NLP comprises two main areas: Natural Language Understanding (NLU) and Natural Language Generation (NLG). While NLU concentrates on machine reading comprehension through grammar and context, NLG concentrates on text generation.

The benefits of adopting NLP comprise the large volume of textual and speech data that can be managed, the velocity of analysis (tens of thousands of documents in seconds) and the capacity to detect tiny patterns that would be indecipherable to human analysts otherwise. Further are the large number of data sets (known as corpuses) and the time required to train some NLP models, and the challenge of converting the NLP model analysis outcomes into a human-readable format are all disadvantages.

Another example of algorithm application within content creation is the use of "chatbots", software programs based on AI to conduct online conversations via audio or text (Shevat, 2017). Essentially, chatbots are algorithmically automated users that are programmed to establish a conversation with a human agent (Følstad & Brandtzæg, 2017; Prasetya et al., 2018). The main purposes for chatbots adoption include informational support, social-emotional support or entertainment (Gehl and Bakardjieva, 2017; Meng & Dai, 2021).

Also, chatbots have been investigated from several dimensions (Adamopoulou and Moussiades, 2020). The most investigated dimension is related to the technical aspects such as speech conversation systems (Masche & Le, 2018), and programming techniques for chatbots (Long et al., 2019). Another relevant dimension is related to human-chatbot interactions, for example chatbots and customer purchase intentions (Luo et al., 2019), customer service and satisfaction (Kang & Kim, 2017; Chung et al., 2020) and collaboration and interaction with chatbots (Araújo & Casais, 2020; De Cosmo et al., 2021; Li et al., 2021). The adoption of chatbots is growing rapidly in instant messaging platforms and social media sites (e.g. Kahiga, 2019; Assenmacher et al., 2020), and also some industries are at the forefront of chatbots adoption such as: healthcare (Safi et al., 2020), tourism (Melián-González et al., 2019; Calvaresi et al., 2021; Li et al., 2021) and finance (Hwang & Kim, 2021; Jang et al., 2021).

Social chatbots, also referred to as "emotional chatting machines" (Zhou et al., 2018), are becoming popular. They are designed to be humanlike, with the potential to perceive, integrate, understand and express emotions (Stieglitz et al., 2017; Zhou et al., 2018). Usually, users feel chatbots as friendly digital colleague (or even co-worker) and not just as basic digital assistants (Costa, 2018; Ciechanowski et al., 2019; Adamopoulou & Moussiades, 2020). Using an artificial conversational system on Twitter, Xu et al. (2017) discovered that over 40 percent of user requests are emotional rather than informative. Over time, chatbots have become more sophisticated and based on new AI features such as sentiment analysis, machine learning and deep learning, and they are able to detect emotional situations and respond to the emotions appropriately during the conversation (Xu et al., 2017).

A big issue in content creation is the problem of fake content (Di Domenico et al., 2021). Fake content is many times created and shared using social media algorithms. In the case of fake news, this is especially crucial (Zimmer et al., 2019; Abu Arqoub et al., 2020; Di Domenico & Visentin, 2020; Preston et al., 2021). Marx et al. (2020) discovered that social bots interfered with COVID conversations on social media, spread misinformation, and interspersed news from reputable sources.

The sharing habits of social media users are equally important. On Twitter, tweets that include images and videos are more likely to be retweeted than only text tweets (Goel et al., 2015; Vosoughi et al., 2018). Moreover, tweets with videos are six times more likely to be retweeted than images (Farkas, 2016). For example, during the 2016 United States Presidential election, tweets from Hillary Clinton and Donald Trump with photos or videos obtained more favourites and retweets than those without (Pancer & Poole, 2016; Lee & Xu, 2018). Vosoughi et al. (2018) mention that real Twitter users are still 70 percent more likely to retweet fake news than real news. In addition, the authors found that it is highly possible that human users fake content than social media bots.

The problem is just starting and it is getting worse with the evolution of deepfake technology (Westerlund, 2019). This term is a combination of the words "deep learning" (AI technique) and "fake" (not real). Deepfakes are AI-generated content that are created by manipulating real-life images or videos of people to create fictitious circumstances. (Ferreira et al., 2021). Deepfake videos by Barack Obama and Mark Zuckerberg, for example, have gone viral on social media.

## 3.3 Algorithm challenges

If social media firms want to use algorithms in different tasks in social media, then then they must confront the present challenges of using algorithms. Below, we discuss some of the main challenges, particularly transparency and objectivity.

### 3.3.1 Transparency

The lack of transparency of social media algorithms is often cited by users (Burrell, 2016; Leetaru, 2018; Kim & Moon, 2021). Algorithmic solutions are becoming progressively complex and heterogeneous, and substantially opaque. One of the big concerns of social media algorithms is that they appear like a black box (Pasquale, 2015; Burrell, 2016; Buhmann et al., 2020). Basically, there is an input, something happens in the black box and an output comes out.

Some algorithms are designed to be deliberately opaque. In most of the cases (with the exception of open-source platforms), it is nearly impossible to view the internal algorithm operation. The reason is because most algorithms are proprietary in nature (Kitchin, 2017). Some online firms are built around algorithms such as online travel, search engines, social media and recommendation services, and most of them are protected under intellectual property and patent regulations. As more algorithm business models are emerging, more firms possess the incentive to protect their algorithms like trade secrets, releasing minimal details but never fully divulging the inner workings of their systems to the public. This opacity also affects researchers and the analysis of transparency in algorithmic environments. Some techniques like reverse-engineering help to study algorithms, but they are complex and time-consuming (Kitchin, 2017).

Social media firms are sometimes open about what helps users and businesses to understand how to improve their content rank and qualify as high-quality on these social platforms. Consider the recent adjustments to Facebook's algorithms: prioritize posts from friends that spark meaningful conversations and interactions over transactions, and post more authentic and genuine video content. Recently, some researchers have started proposing new mechanisms to improve algorithm awareness. For example, Fouquaert and Mechant (2021) created the "Instawareness" visual feedback tool to reduce illiteracy about the Instagram curation algorithm. As the usage of algorithms increases, so does algorithmic illiteracy. An increasing number of experts, researchers and institutions are requesting to teach algorithmic literacy to Web users, especially younger generations. Sometimes, even AI experts who build algorithms are unable to fully comprehend the machine learning techniques that allow decisions to be made (Rainie & Anderson, 2017).

Another critical issue with transparency is not alerting the user that he or she is communicating with a chatbot or that the information is being shared by a bot.

Bots created roughly 19 percent of all tweets connected to the 2016 United States elections, according to a study by Bessi and Ferrara (2016). The combination of technological advancement and usage of social cues bears the challenge for consumers to accurately differentiate between algorithmic or human conversational agents. This development is highlighted by an empirical study on Google's chatbot Meena, in which its conversation quality was rated nearly as highly as the quality of real human conversations, leaving previously appraised chatbots such as Cleverbot or Mitsuku far behind (Adiwardana et al., 2020)

### 3.3.2  Objectivity

Algorithm adoption has frequently been questioned due to concerns about algorithmic bias, objectivity and trustworthiness (Lee, 2018; Shin, 2021). To maintain various judgements and a democratic society, it is vital to keep the audience informed without persuading them toward a single viewpoint. Algorithms are more than just tools; they also act as trust builders and stabilizers, guaranteeing users that their judgments are fair and objective, unbiased, inaccurate, or showing skewed results (Gillespie, 2014). As mentioned by Gillespie (2014), the algorithm's technological nature is positioned as a guarantee of objectivity. Yet, because what we search for and read feeds directly into what algorithms play back to us, the objectivity and impartiality of information sources is constrained by our own preconceptions and pretensions. To put it another way, we develop our own filter bubbles, and algorithms assist us in staying within them.

According to Ward (2009), the real recording of an event defines objectivity, and it's critical to keep the public informed without swaying them toward a certain point of view in order to maintain a democratic society and a diverse range of judgments. An example of lack of objectivity is the Robert Mercer scandal that was highlighted in the documentary *Trumping Democracy*. Trump appointed Steve Bannon as his campaign manager and recruited Breitbart News, a data firm headed by Steve Bannon and funded by Robert Mercer. Using AI and data analytics, this firm analyzed data from Google, Facebook, banks and other sources to determine who would support Trump and who would not. Breitbart News also exploited a Facebook feature known as "dark post," which allowed them to send out persuasive and tailored messages to millions of individuals before they vanished. All these messages were managed using algorithms.

Another good example is the usage of social media bots during the United States presidential election campaign of 2016, which demonstrated how influential and persuasive social media bots can be in influencing political debate, distorting communication and raising doubts about their future role (Howard et al., 2018; Grinberg et al., 2019). Social media bots can increase the prominence of a topic or ruin people's reputations by flooding social media with fake news and manipulating social media's currency: likes, shares, follows, and retweets. Although some researchers (e.g. Yang et al., 2019; Pastor-Galindo et al., 2020; Schuchard & Crooks, 2021) have proposed metrics to detect social bots, spot a social bot is not a simple task. The number of social media bots has exploded in recent years, and their impact on online conversations is quickly becoming a major issue on social media.

On a positive side, some experts mention that social media have helped society overcome the bias in legacy media. It encourages the minority groups to have a voice and to interact with different types of communities. Nevertheless, algorithmic social media may be frightening for many users because it takes information and transforms it into another piece of information based on calculations. There is evidence that when social media platforms moderate user-posted content, they consider freedom of expression and press considerations (Klonick, 2018). However, there is evidence that they attempt to reconcile these decisions with their own corporate objectives, and that these objectives may be prioritized (Citron, 2014; Klonick, 2018).

The filter bubble perspective proposed by Pariser (2011) suggests that, rather than maintaining diversity, algorithms attempt to maximize economic advantage by increasing content consumption. In consonance with this viewpoint, social media algorithms remove content that is deemed to be irrelevant to specific users while supplying them with more social media content that they are more likely to consume. Additionally, when faced with scenarios with high polarization, misinformation can quickly spread (Vicario et al., 2019), like in the coronavirus health crisis (Cinelli et al., 2020). The COVID infodemic phenomenon – an oversupply of COVID information, including false or misleading information, and the quick diffusion of fake news, photos, and videos – is a current example of objectivity issues on social media. It is very contagious and grows exponentially, much like the virus. It also makes the COVID-19 pandemic response activities more difficult.

In addition, a study conducted by Puschmann (2017) shows that if users choose to read radical, bizarre or racist news, search engines will assist them locate it. However, there is no consensus about the effects of YouTube algorithm filtering on radicalization. While some studies suggest an increase on radicalization exposure (e.g. Faddoul et al., 2020; Ribeiro et al., 2020), other research, like Ledwich and Zaitsev's (2020), suggests that the YouTube recommendation algorithm does not increase radicalisation.

The most important social media firms (YouTube, Facebook, Instagram, Tiktok, and Twitter) have all recently launched active initiatives to combat the diffusion of disinformation and conspiracy theories on their platforms. Some social media firms are deleting accounts that share this type of content, as well as deleting posts, articles and images. However, many people think that social media firms are still too slow and hesitant to take action against groups benefitting from conspiracy theories.

A recent example of algorithmic bias is the spread of anti-vaccine videos on YouTube. Some research (e.g. Abul-Fottouh et al., 2020) suggests that pro-vaccine YouTube videos are more likely to promote other pro-vaccine YouTube videos than anti-vaccine YouTube videos, and vice-versa. Anti-vaccine YouTube videos may have been less visible due to YouTube's demonetization policy (also referred as "Adpocalypse") for sensitive topics. This YouTube policy refers to the practice in which YouTube video creators are denied paid adverts in their videos of sensitive topics, resulting in a financial loss.

It is important to highlight that sometimes algorithmic bias is not intentional and actually might be caused by the datasets used to train the algorithms. There are two main data problems: insufficient training data and data bias. Algorithms in machine learning rely on datasets, also called training sets, to improve the learning predictions of algorithms. An algorithm learns a model from the training data that it can apply to other users or items and predict what the correct outputs should be for them. A technique known as supervised learning is used to do this.

Many times, in these AI algorithmic learning contexts, the training data is considered to be representative of the target group or population. But, in case some groups are less represented, the model's predictions for unrepresented or underrepresented groups may be imbalanced and biased. There is also the problem of social media users not representing the general population (Mellon & Prosser, 2017). Finally, the topics and views expressed on social media platforms might vary significantly over time and space (Mellon & Prosser, 2017; Migliaccio et al., 2019). As a result, algorithms must learn with new training sets on a regular basis.

Overall, researchers and social firms that use algorithms need to improve their rigor in terms of testing, executing, and managing the representativeness of training sets. Additionally, some studies (Turner Lee, 2018; Cowgill et al., 2020) suggest that lack of diversity in the algorithm developers creating the training set could lead to underrepresentation of specific groups. Oppositely, the overrepresentation of training sets (i.e. too much data) can skew the decision toward a certain direction.

In conclusion, the algorithms themselves do not hurt the main principle of objectivity. Yet, the way some platforms choose to use these algorithms may cause a problem. These platforms have the power to decide whether a story can be popular or not, depending on the database of each of the users. One solution is to control the term of privacy of these platforms and minimize the harm they cause. Another solution can be to warn users and educate them more about the topic of fake news and how to protect themselves from the harm that causes these algorithms (Edwards & Veale, 2018).

## 3.4 Discussion

With billons of users, social media platforms will continue using algorithm curation techniques. Social media just started using algorithmic curation and it is already posing some challenges that need to be addressed. From a critical approach, algorithmic curation is essentially about power – who controls what we see and how we perceive it. Social media platforms, in this view, are not neutral and often they serve as content curators.

One of the most significant drawbacks of utilizing algorithms in specific social media activities is that the process involves a significant amount of decision-making based on a set of human values. Moreover, these algorithms are designed and programmed by individuals with their own viewpoints, attitudes and even prejudices (Mager, 2012; Kitchin, 2017). This has implications for the dissemination of information (Gillespie, 2014) and how the public sphere uses it (Morozov, 2011; Crawford, 2013; Seaver, 2017). Also, it has implications in the social media user's perception of being well-informed (Weeks et al., 2017; Fletcher & Nielsen, 2018; Thurman et al., 2019; Feezell et al., 2021).

Another important debate is related to algorithmic services accountability (Diakopoulos, 2016; Kemper & Kolkman, 2019), that is, who is responsible for the outcome of a firm's algorithmic decisions (Fink, 2018; Lepri et al., 2018; Buhmann et al., 2020). Some researchers (e.g. Fox, 2007; Kim & Moon, 2021) argue that transparency must be a prerequisite for algorithm accountability.

In terms of objectivity, while algorithm representation can be enhanced, we must keep in mind that most real-world data is skewed by default. This indicates that algorithm designers can reduce data bias, but not completely eliminate it. Automatic procedures are human-made, and therefore do not eradicate, but rather reproduce, human bias. However, some algorithm design choices are better than others. The problem is getting worse with new data protection and privacy regulations being adopted. We need to work on both dataset representation and model design, if we wish to reduce algorithm bias.

There is also an important aspect related to social media education. In that regard, students have historically been taught how to critically assess content rather than how social media platforms might alter that content (D'Ignazio & Bhargava, 2015; Head et al., 2020; Mihailidis, 2018). Algorithm bias can be mitigated through social media education, which should be included in any strategy. Most of the users never check their social media platforms settings, particularly the privacy settings. Furthermore, some social media users struggle with online searching and only know how to conduct basic searches. There is a final aspect related with only checking the top search results. There is sometimes no argumentation for algorithmic bias just because the top result is not what the social media user expected. If the algorithm's filtering process is transparent, it is possible to justify why some results are not at the top of the list.

Finally, legislation plays a critical role in social media algorithm curation (Reviglio & Agosti, 2020; Zuiderveen Borgesius, 2020). Definitively, everyone agrees that regulation is needed to improve the deployment of social media algorithms. While some users advocate for tighter rules on social media algorithm management, others advocate for the abolition of social media censorship. Over the last few years, some people are proposing that social platforms should improve the social algorithms by removing AI to make decisions related to content curation (Morgese, 2020). Some governments have been actively analyzing and developing new legal systems in recent years in order to reduce algorithmic bias and promote transparency and impartiality. Since governments also use algorithms, they have significant market power and control over many key algorithmic use cases. For example, the United States government is introducing legislation to counteract algorithmic bias and establish a new online transparency environment, particularly in sectors such as education, healthcare and the financial sector.

## 3.5 Conclusion

This chapter discusses the challenges of using algorithms in social media. The scholarly literature reviewed backs up the idea that the algorithmic bias challenges posed by these technologies warrant a discussion from a socio-technical and regulatory standpoint. Because of a variety of factors, resolving the algorithmic bias problem is difficult. The first reason is related to the definition of algorithmic bias, misinformation, disinformation and objectivity. The second reason is that it is not always obvious during the algorithm creation that the model may have a bias problem. The third major reason is that the data training set used may be biased. Finally, there is sometimes a lack of social context because algorithms are frequently designed to be used in different contexts, which may result in a lack of testing for specific contexts (Hao, 2019).

The first step in implementing effective algorithmic strategies is to understand the many origins of algorithm bias. It needs thinking beyond how they work, and why and where they are used. This is not only a request that social media firms reveal their internal way of working and reveal their undeclared criteria. It is a societal question that needs to be addressed by society in general (Olhede & Wolfe, 2018).

In terms of research, algorithm bias has been analyzed in the political arena but it needs to expand to other areas like healthcare. In general, there is a consensus about the need to understand algorithms and their impact on the public sphere. This debate needs to think beyond how algorithms work, where they are used and how they are funded. Rather than seeing algorithms as just lines of codes or sophisticated mathematical models, it requires analysing them from a socio-technical perspective (Kitchin, 2017; Shin, 2019; Selbst et al., 2019). A socio-technical approach to social media algorithms adoption should aim to reveal the intricate workings of social media algorithms, including both the process of filtering content and the social process of transforming it into a legitimate solution. These social media algorithms are supposed to function without the need for human participation, and there is some skepticism about the legitimacy of the process. As a result, it appears that algorithms are reproducing certain contemporary human-centric systems, which have some vulnerabilities related to bias issues. Therefore, algorithms can act as an amplifier of bias that exist in humans, and increase inequalities or discriminations (Karimi et al., 2018). Often, human bias is being mirrored by algorithms, and society needs to reflect on this. In some cases, algorithms reflect the skewed nature of our questions and data.

Algorithmic use, like any new technology advance, necessitates a thorough examination of its technical, social, regulatory and business implications. Technology is ushering in a new era in which machines are taking over human functions. We are seeing an increase in human-machine interactions, which will soon become the new normal. Technology is still in its infancy, and it lacks the technological advancements necessary to completely replace people in many decision-making processes. However, it is rapidly evolving, and characteristics such as AI consciousness will be a significant step forward in enhancing algorithm decision-making. Society and other different stakeholders must consider the best approach to use algorithms, rather than viewing them as a threat, but as an opportunity. Algorithmic processes will augment our intelligence by thoroughly examining data and content in ways that humans cannot. Overall, the deployment of algorithms will open up new possibilities and capacities for improving the human experience. Both humans and machines must progress together as part of this future voyage.

# References

Abu Arqoub, O., Elega, A., Özad, B., Dwikat, H. & Oloyede, F. (2020) Mapping the scholarship of fake news research: A systematic review, *Journalism Practice*. DOI: 10.1080/17512786.2020.1805791

Abul-Fottouh, D., Song, M., & Gruzd, A. (2020). Examining algorithmic biases in YouTube's recommendations of vaccine videos. *International Journal of Medical Informatics*, 104175. DOI: 10.1016/j.ijmedinf.2020.104175

Adamopoulou, E., & Moussiades, L. (2020). Chatbots: History, technology, and applications. *Machine Learning with Applications*, 2. DOI:10.1016/j.mlwa.2020.100006

Adiwardana, D., Luong, M.-T., So, D. R., Hall, J., Fiedel, N., Thoppilan, R., Yang, Z., Kulshreshtha, A., Nemade, G., Lu, Y., & Le, Q. V. (2020). Towards a human-like open-domain chatbot, *Google Research*, https://arxiv.org/pdf/2001.09977.pdf

Angwin, J., & Parris Jr., T. (2016). Facebook lets advertisers exclude users by race. Retrieved July 17, 2021, from https://www.propublica.org/article/facebook-lets-advertisers-exclude-users-by-race

Angwin, J., Varner, M., & Tobin, A. (2017). Facebook enabled advertisers to reach 'Jew Haters'. Retrieved July 17, 2021, from https://www.propublica.org/article/facebook-enabled-advertisers-to-reach-jew-haters

Araújo, T., & Casais, B. (2020). Customer acceptance of shopping-assistant chatbots. In A. Rocha, J. Reis, M. Peter, & Z. Bogdanović (eds) *Marketing and smart technologies*, 278–287. Springer: Singapore.

Assenmacher, D., Frischlich, L., Clever, L., Quandt, T., Trautmann, H., & Grimme, C. (2020). Demystifying social bots: On the intelligence of automated social media actors. In: *Social Media & Society*, 6(3), 1–14.

Bakshy, E., Messing, S., & Adamic, L. (2015). Exposure to ideologically diverse news and opinion on Facebook. *Science*, aaa1160. DOI:10.1126/science.aaa1160

Bessi, A., & Ferrara, E. (2016). Social bots distort the 2016 U.S. Presidential election online discussion. *First Monday*, 21(11). DOI:10.5210/fm.v21i11.7090

Boczkowski, P., Mitchelstein, E., & Matassi, M. (2018). News comes across when I'm in a moment of leisure': Understanding the practices of incidental news consumption on social media. *New Media & Society*, 20(10), 3523–3539. https://doi.org/10.1177/1461444817750396

Borgesius, Z., Trilling, D., Möller, J., Bodó, B., De Vreese, C. H., & Helberger, N. (2016). Should we worry about filter bubbles? *Internet Policy Review*, 5(1), 1–16. DOI:10.14763/2016.1.401

Boxell, L., Gentzkow, M., & Shapiro, J. (2020). Cross-country trends in affective polarization. NBER Working Paper No. 26669, https://www.nber.org/system/files/working_papers/w26669/w26669.pdf

Bozdag, E. (2013). Bias in algorithmic filtering and personalization. *Ethics and Information Technology*, 15(3), 209–227. https://doi.org/10.1007/s10676-013-9321-6

Buhmann, A., Paßmann, J., & Fieseler, C. (2020). Managing algorithmic accountability: balancing reputational concerns, engagement strategies, and the potential of rational discourse. *Journal Business Ethics*, 163, 265–280. https://doi.org/10.1007/s10551-019-04226-4

Burrell, J. (2016). How the machine thinks: Understanding opacity in machine learning algorithms. *Big Data & Society*, 3(1), 1–12. https://doi.org/10.1177/2053951715622512

Calvaresi, D., Ibrahim, A., Calbimonte, J.P., Schegg, R., Fragniere, E., Schumacher, M. (2021) The evolution of chatbots in tourism: A systematic literature review. In W. Wörndl, C. Koo, & J. L. Stienmetz (Eds.), *Information and communication technologies in tourism 2021*. Cham: Springer. https://doi.org/10.1007/978-3-030-65785-7_1

Chitra, U., & Musco, C. (2020). Analyzing the impact of filter bubbles on social network polarization. In *13th ACM International Conference on Web Search and Data Mining* (pp. 115–123), Houston, United States.

Chung, M., Ko, E., Joung, H., & Kim, S. J. (2020). Chatbot e-service and customer satisfaction regarding luxury brands. Journal of Business Research, 117, 587–595. https://doi.org/10.1016/j.jbusres.2018.10.004

Ciechanowski, L., Przegalinska, A., Magnuski, M., & Gloor, P. (2019). In the shades of the uncanny valley: An experimental study of human–chatbot interaction. *Future Generation Computer Systems*, 92, 539–548. https://doi.org/10.1016/j.future.2018.01.055

Cinelli, M., Morales, G., Galeazzi, A., Quattrociocchi, W., & Starnini, M. (2021). The echo chamber effect on social media. *Proceedings of the National Academy of Sciences*, 118(9), e2023301118. DOI:10.1073/pnas.2023301118

Cinelli, M., Quattrociocchi, W., Galeazzi, A., Valensise, C., Brugnoli, E., Schmidt, A., Zola, P., Zollo, F., & Scala, A. (2020). The COVID-19 social media infodemic. *Scientific Report*, 10, 16598.

Citron, D. (2014). *Hate crimes in cyberspace*. Cambridge: Harvard University Press.

Coeckelbergh, M. (2020). Artificial intelligence, responsibility attribution, and a relational justification of explainability. *Science and Engineering Ethics*, 26(4), 2051–2068. https://doi.org/10.1007/s11948-019-00146-8

Costa, P. (2018). Conversing with personal digital assistants: On gender and artificial intelligence. *Journal of Science and Technology of the Arts*, 10(3), 59–79. http://dx.doi.org/10.7559/citarj.v10i3.563

Cowgill, B., Dell'Acqua, F., Deng, S., Hsu, D., Verma, N., & Chaintreau, A. (2020). Biased Programmers? Or Biased Data? A Field Experiment in Operationalizing AI Ethics, *Proceedings of the 21st ACM Conference on Economics and Computation*, July 2020, 679–681. https://doi.org/10.1145/3391403.3399545

Cowgill, B. & Tucker, C. E. (2020). Algorithmic Fairness and Economics. Columbia Business School Research Paper, Available at SSRN: https://ssrn.com/abstract=3361280 or http://dx.doi.org/10.2139/ssrn.3361280

Crawford, K. (2013). The Hidden Biases in *Big Data*. Retrieved from Harvard Business Review: https://hbr.org/2013/04/the-hidden-biases-in-big-data

Dahlgren, P. (2021). A critical review of filter bubbles and a comparison with selective exposure. *Nordicom Review*, 42(1), 15–33. https://doi.org/10.2478/nor-2021-0002

de Cosmo, L. M., Piper, L., & Di Vittorio, A. (2021). The role of attitude toward chatbots and privacy concern on the relationship between attitude toward mobile advertising and behavioral intent to use chatbots. *Italian Journal of Marketing*, 2021, 83–102. https://doi.org/10.1007/s43039-021-00020-1

Di Domenico, G., Sit, J., Ishizaka, A., & Nunan, D. (2021). Fake news, social media and marketing: A systematic review. *Journal of Business Research*, 124, 329–341. https://doi.org/10.1016/j.jbusres.2020.11.037

Di Domenico, G., & Visentin, M. (2020). Fake news or true lies? Refections about problematic contents in marketing. *International Journal of Market Research*, 62(2). https://doi.org/10.1177/1470785320934719

Diakopoulos, N. (2013). Algorithmic Accountability Reporting: On the Investigation of Black Boxes. https://doi.org/10.7916/D8ZK5TW2

Diakopoulos, N. (2016). Accountability in algorithmic decision making. *Communications of ACM*, 59(2), 58–62. https://doi.org/10.1145/2844110

Diakopoulos, N., & Koliska, M. (2016). Algorithmic transparency in the news media. *Digital Journalism*, 5(7), 809–828. https://doi.org/10.1080/21670811.2016.1208053

D'Ignazio, C., & Bhargava, R. (2015). Approaches to Building Big Data Literacy [Paper presentation]. Bloomberg Data for Good Exchange Conference, New York. https://bit.ly/33lQ3Eq

Dubois, E., & Blank, G. (2018). The echo chamber is overstated: The moderating effect of political interest and diverse media. *Information, Communication & Society*, 21(5), 729–745. https://doi.org/10.1080/1369118X.2018.1428656

Edwards, L, & Veale, M (2018). Enslaving the algorithm: From a "right to an explanation" to a "right to better decisions"? *IEEE Security & Privacy*, 16(3), 46–54. DOI: 10.1109/MSP.2018.2701152

Ettlinger, N. (2018). Algorithmic affordances for productive resistance. *Big Data & Society*, 5(1), 1–13. https://doi.org/10.1177/2053951718771399

Faddoul, M., Chaslot, G., & Farid, H. (2020). A longitudinal analysis of YouTube's promotion of conspiracy videos. arXiv preprint arXiv:2003.03318

Farkas, E. (2016). Campaigns with branded emojis can supercharge video ads and drive earned media. See how it works. Retrieved July 12, 2021 from https://marketing.twitter.com/en/insights/best-practices-for-supercharging-campaigns-with-branded-emojis

Farzindar, A., & Inkpen, D. (2017). Natural language processing for social media, second edition. *Synthesis Lectures on Human Language Technologies*, 10(2), 1–195. DOI:10.2200/S00809ED2V01Y201710HLT038

Feezell, J., Wagner, J., & Conroy, M. (2021). Exploring the effects of algorithm-driven news sources on political behavior and polarization. *Computers in Kuman Behavior*, 116, 106626. https://doi.org/10.1016/j.chb.2020.106626

Ferreira, S., Antunes, M., & Correia, M. (2021). Exposing manipulated photos and videos in digital forensics analysis. *Journal of Imaging*, 7(7), 102. DOI:10.3390/jimaging7070102

Fink, K. (2018). Opening the government's black boxes: freedom of information and algorithmic accountability, Information, Communication & Society, 21:10, 1453–1471, DOI: 10.1080/1369118X.2017.1330418

Flaxman, S., Goel, S., & Rao, J. (2016). Filter bubbles, echo chambers, and online news consumption. *Public Opinion Quarterly*, 80, 298–320. https://doi.org/10.1093/poq/nfw006

Fletcher, R., & Nielsen, R. (2018). Are people incidentally exposed to news on social media? A comparative analysis. *New Media & Society*, 20(7), 2450–2468. https://doi.org/10.1177/1461444817724170

Følstad, A., & Brandtzæg, P. (2017). Chatbots and the new world of HCI. *Interactions*, 24(4), 38–42. DOI:10.1145/3085558

Fouquaert, T., & Mechant, P. (2021). Making curation algorithms apparent: A case study of 'Instawareness' as a means to heighten awareness and understanding of Instagram's algorithm. *Information, Communication & Society*. DOI:10.1080/1369118x.2021.1883707

Fox, J. (2007). The uncertain relationship between transparency and accountability. *Development in Practice*, 17(4–5), 663–671. https://doi.org/10.1080/09614520701469955

Gardner, E. (2020). YouTube Alleged to Racially Profile Via Artificial Intelligence, Algorithms, Hollywood reporter. Retrieved on July 19, 2021, https://www.hollywood-reporter.com/business/business-news/youtube-alleged-racially-profile-artificial-intelligence-algorithms-1298926/

Gehl, R., & Bakardjieva, M. (2017). *Socialbots and their friends: Digital media and the automation of sociality* (1st ed.). New York: Routledge.

Gillespie, T. (2014). The relevance of algorithms. In T. Gillespie, P. Boczkowski, & K. Foot (Eds.), *Media technologies: Essays on communication, materiality, and society* (pp. 167–194). Cambridge, MA: MIT Press.

Goel, S., Anderson, A., Hofman, J., & Watts, D. (2015). The structural virality of online diffusion. *Management Science*, 62(1), 180–196. https://doi.org/10.1287/mnsc.2015.2158

Grimmelmann, J. (2008). The Google dilemma. *New York Law School Law Review*, 53, 939–950.

Grinberg, N., Joseph, K., Friedland, L., Swire-Thompson, B., Lazer, D. (2019). Fake news on Twitter during the 2016 U.S. presidential election. *Science*, 363, 374–378. DOI:10.1126/science.aau2706

Haim, M., Graefe, A., & Brosius, H. (2017). Burst of the filter bubble? Effects of personalization on the diversity of Google News. *Digital Journalism*. DOI: 10.1080/21670811. 2017.1338145

Hao, K. (2019). This is how AI bias really happens – and why it's so hard to fix. *MIT Technology Review*. Retrieved July 10, 2021, from https://www.technologyreview. com/2019/02/04/137602/this-is-how-ai-bias-really-happensand-why-its-so-hard-to-fix/

Head, A. J., Fister, B., & MacMillan, M. (2020). Information Literacy in the Age of Algorithms: Student Experiences with News and Information, and the Need for Change. Project Information Literacy. Retrieved from https://projectinfolit.org/publications/ news-study/

Hosanagar, K., Fleder, D., Lee, D., & Buja, A. (2014). Will the global village fracture into tribes: Recommender systems and their effects on consumers. *Management Science*, 60(4), 805–823, DOI:10.1287/mnsc.2013.1808

Howard, P., Woolley, S., & Calo, R. (2018) Algorithms, bots, and political communication in the US 2016 election: The challenge of automated political communication for election law and administration, *Journal of Information Technology & Politics*, 15(2), 81–93, DOI: 10.1080/19331681.2018.1448735

Hussein, E., Juneja, P., & Mitra, T. (2020). Measuring Misinformation in Video Search Platforms: An Audit Study on YouTube. *Proceedings of the ACM on Human-Computer Interaction*, 4(CSCW1), 048:1–048:27. https://doi.org/10.1145/3392854

Hwang, S., & Kim, J. (2021). Toward a chatbot for financial sustainability. *Sustainability Journal*, 13, 3173. https://doi.org/10.3390/su13063173

Introna, L. (2016). Algorithms, governance, and governmentality. *Science, Technology, & Human Values*, 41(1), 17–49. https://doi.org/10.1177/0162243915587360

Jang, M., Jung, Y., & Seongcheol, K. (2021). Investigating Managers' understanding of chatbots in the Korean financial industry. *Computers in Human Behavior*, 120(1), 106747, DOI:10.1016/j.chb.2021.106747

Jussupow, E., Benbasat, I., & Heinzl, A., (2020). Why are we averse towards algorithms? A comprehensive literature review on algorithm aversion. In *European Conference on Information Systems (ECIS) 2020 Proceedings* (pp. 1–18).

Kahiga, A. (2019). A model for adoption of chatbots in Kenya: A case study of Zuku Telegram Bot. [Doctoral dissertation, University of Nairobi]. University of Nairobi. http://erepository.uonbi.ac.ke/handle/11295/107169

Kaiser, J., & Rauchfleisch, A. (2020). Birds of a feather get recommended together: Algorithmic homophily in YouTube's channel recommendations in the United States and Germany. *Social Media + Society*, 6(4). https://doi.org/10.1177/2056305120969914

Kang, H. J., & Kim, S. I. (2017). Evaluation on the usability of chatbot intelligent messenger mobile services: focusing on Google (Allo) and Facebook (M messenger). Journal of the Korea Convergence Society, 8(9), 271–276. https://doi.org/10.15207/ JKCS.2017.8.9.271

Kaplan, A., & Haenlein, M. (2010). Users of the world unite! The challenges and opportunities of social media. *Business Horizons*, 53(1), 59–68.

Kaptein, M., Markopoulos, P., Ruyter, B., & Aarts, E. (2015). Personalizing persuasive technologies: Explicit and implicit personalization using persuasion profiles. *International Journal of Human-Computer Studies*, 77, 38–51. https://doi.org/10.1016/j.ijhcs.2015.01.004

Karimi, F., Génois, M., Wagner, C., Singer, P., & Strohmaier, M. (2018). Homophily influences ranking of minorities in social networks. *Scientific Reports*, 8, 1–12.

Kemper, J., & Kolkman, D. (2019). Transparent to whom? No algorithmic accountability without a critical audience. *Information, Communication & Society*, 22(14), 2081–2096. https://doi.org/10.1080/1369118X.2018.1477967

Khan, R., Shrivastava, P., Kapoor, A., Tiwari, A., & Mittal, A. (2020). Social media analysis with AI: Sentiment analysis techniques for the analysis of Twitter Covid-19 data. *Journal of Critical Reviews*, 7(9), 2761–2774. DOI: 10.31838/jcr.07.09.437

Kim, K., & Moon, S. (2021). When Algorithmic transparency failed: Controversies over algorithm-driven content curation in the South Korean digital environment. *American Behavioral Scientist*, 65(1). DOI:10.1177/0002764221989783

Kitchin, R. (2017). Thinking critically about and researching algorithms. *Information Communication & Society*, 20(1), 14–29. https://doi.org/10.1080/1369118X.2016.1154087

Klonick, K. (2018). The new governors: The people, rules, and processes governing online speech. *Harvard Law Review*, 1598–1670. Available at SSRN: https://ssrn.com/abstract=2937985

Ledwich, M., & Zaitsev, A. (2020). Algorithmic extremism: Examining YouTube's rabbit hole of radicalization. First Monday. DOI:10.5210/fm.v25i3.10419

Lee, J., & Xu, W. (2018). The more attacks, the more retweets: Trump's and Clinton's agenda setting on Twitter. *Public Relations Review*, 44(2), 201–213. https://doi.org/10.1016/j.pubrev.2017.10.002

Lee, M. (2018). Understanding perception of algorithmic decisions: Fairness, trust, and emotion in response to algorithmic management. *Big Data & Society*, 5(1), 1–16. https://doi.org/10.1177/2053951718756684

Leetaru, K. (2018). Without transparency, democracy dies in the darkness of social media. *Forbes*, 25 January 2020. Retrieved July 7, 2021, from https://www.forbes.com/sites/kalevleetaru/2018/01/25/without-transparency-democracy-dies-in-the-darkness-of-social-media/

Lepri, B., Oliver, N., Letouzé, E., Pentland, A., & Vinck, P. (2018). Fair, transparent, and accountable algorithmic decision-making processes. *Philosophy & Technology*, 31(4), 611–627. https://doi.org/10.1007/s13347-017-0279-x

Levordashka, A., & Utz, S. (2016). Ambient awareness: From random noise to digital closeness in online social networks. *Computers in Human Behavior*, 60, 147–154. https://doi.org/10.1016/j.chb.2016.02.037

Levy, R. (2021). Social media, news consumption, and polarization: Evidence from a field experiment. *American Economic Review*, 111(3), 831–870. http://dx.doi.org/10.2139/ssrn.3653388

Li, L., Lee, K., Emokpae, E., & Yang, S. (2021). What makes you continuously use chatbot services? Evidence from Chinese online travel agencies. *Electronic Markets*, 1–25. DOI:10.1007/s12525-020-00454-z

Long, J., Yuan, J., & Lee, H. M. (2019). How to program a chatbot: An introductory project and student perceptions. *Issues in Informing Science and Information Technology*, 16, 1–31. https://doi.org/10.28945/4282

Luo X., Tong S., Fang Z., Qu Z. (2019). Frontiers: Machines vs. Humans: The impact of artificial intelligence chatbot disclosure on customer purchases. *Marketing Science*, 38 (6), 937–947, https://doi.org/10.1287/mksc.2019.1192

Mager, A. (2012). Algorithmic ideology: How capitalist society shapes search engines. *Information, Communication & Society*, 15(5), 769–787. https://doi.org/10.1080/1369118X.2012.676056

Marx, J., Brünker, F., Mirbabaie, M., & Hochstrate, E. (2020). 'Conspiracy machines' – The role of social bots during the COVID-19 'Infodemic'. In *Australasian Conference on Information Systems (ACIS) 2020 Proceedings* (p. 82), Wellington (NZ).

Masche, J., & Le, N.-T. (2018). A review of technologies for conversational systems. *Advances in Intelligent Systems and Computing*, 212–225. http://dx.doi.org/10.1007/978-3-319-61911-8_19

Melián-González, S., Gutierrez-Taño, D., & Bulchand-Gidumal, J. (2019). Predicting the intentions to use chatbots for travel and tourism. *Current Issues in Tourism*, 24(1), 1–19 http://dx.doi.org/10.1080/13683500.2019.1706457

Mellon, J., & Prosser, C. (2017). Twitter and Facebook are not representative of the general population: Political attitudes and demographics of British social media users. *Research & Politics*, 4(3). http://dx.doi.org/10.1177/205316801772000

Meng, J., & Dai, Y. (2021). Emotional support from AI chatbots: Should a supportive partner self-disclose or not?, *Journal of Computer-Mediated, Communication*, zmab005, https://doi.org/10.1093/jcmc/zmab005

Messing, S., & Westwood, S. (2014). Selective exposure in the age of social media: Endorsements trump partisan source affiliation when selecting news online. *Communication Research*, 41(8), 1042–1063. http://dx.doi.org/10.1177/0093650212466406

Migliaccio, F., Carrion, D., & Ferrario, F. (2019). Semantic validation of social media geographic information: A case study on Instagram data for expo Milano 2015. *4th International Society for Photogrammetry and Remote Sensing (ISPR) Geospatial Week*, 42(2), 1321–1326.

Mihailidis, P. (2018). Civic media literacies: Re-imagining engagement for civic intentionality. *Learning, Media and Technology*, 43 (2), 152–164. https://doi.org/10.1080/17439884.2018.1428623

Mittelstadt, B., Allo, P., Tadeo, M., Yachter, S., & Floridi, L. (2016). The ethics of algorithms: Mapping the debate. *Big Data and Society*, 3(2), 1–21. https://doi.org/10.1177/2053951716679679

Morgese, J. 2020. 3 reforms social media platforms should make in light of 'The Social Dilemma'. TechCrunch. Retrieved from https://techcrunch.com/2020/10/22/3-reforms-social-media-platforms-should-make-in-light-of-the-social-dilemma/

Morozov, E. (2011). *The net delusion: The dark side of internet freedom*. New York: Public Affairs.

Mothes, C., & Ohme, J. (2019). Partisan selective exposure in times of political and technological upheaval: A social media field experiment. *Media and Communication*, 7(3), 42. DOI:10.17645/mac.v7i3.2183

Narayanan, A. (2018). Translation tutorial: 21 fairness definitions and their politics. In *Proceedings of Association Computing Machinery Conference on. Fairness, Accountability, and Transparency*, New York, 2018.

Olhede, S., & Wolfe, P. (2018). The growing ubiquity of algorithms in society: Implications, impacts and innovations. *Philosophical Transactions, Series A, Mathematical, Physical, and Engineering Sciences*, 376(2128), 20170364. https://doi.org/10.1098/rsta.2017.0364

Pancer, E., & Poole, M. (2016). The popularity and virality of political social media: Hashtags, mentions, and links predict likes and retweets of 2016 US presidential nominees' tweets. *Social Influence*, 11(4), 259–270. https://doi.org/10.1080/15534510.2016.1265582

Pariser, E. 2011. *The filter bubble: What the Internet is hiding from you*. New York: The Penguin Group.

Pasquale, F. (2015). *The black box society: The secret algorithms that control money and information.* Cambridge, MA: Harvard University Press.

Pastor-Galindo, J., Zago, M., Nespoli, P., Lopez, S., Huertas, A., Gil, M., Ruiperez-Valiente, J., Martinez Perez, G., & Gomez, F. (2020). Spotting political social bots in Twitter: A use case of the 2019 Spanish general election. *IEEE Transactions on Network and Service Management,* 17(4), 2156–2170. DOI:10.1109/TNSM.2020.3031573

Prasetya, S., Erwin, A., & Galinium, M. (2018). Implementing Indonesian language chatbot for ecommerce site using artificial intelligence markup language (AIML). In *Prosiding Seminar Nasional Pakar* (pp. 313–322).

Preston, S., Anderson, A., Robertson, D., Shephard M., & Huhe, N. (2021). Detecting fake news on Facebook: The role of emotional intelligence. *PLoS One,* 16(3), e0246757. https://doi.org/10.1371/journal.pone.0246757

Puschmann, C. (2017). How significant is algorithmic personalization in searches for political parties and candidates? Part II [Web log post]. Retrieved from https://www.hiig.de/en/how-significant-is-algorithmic-personalization-in-searches-for-political-parties-and-candidates-part-ii/

Rader, E., & Gray, R. (2015). Understanding user beliefs about algorithmic curation in the Facebook news feed. *Proceedings of the 33rd Annual ACM Conference on Human Factors in Computing Systems - CHI'15* (pp. 173–182).

Rainie, L., & Anderson, J. (2017). *Code-dependent: Pros and cons of the algorithm age.* Washington, DC: Pew Internet & American Life Project. Retrieved from https://www.pewresearch.org/internet/2017/02/08/code-dependent-pros-and-cons-of-the-algorithm-age/

Reviglio, U., & Agosti, C. (2020). Thinking outside the black-box: The case for "algorithmic sovereignty" in social media. *Social Media +Society,* 1–12. https://doi.org/10.1177/2056305120915613

Ribeiro, M., Ottoni, R., West, R., Almeida, V., & Meira Jr, W. (2020). Auditing radicalization pathways on Youtube. In *Proceedings of the 2020 Conference on Fairness, Accountability, and Transparency* (pp. 131–141).

Ricci, F., Rokach, L., & Shapira, B. (2015). *Recommender systems handbook* (1–34). Boston: Springer. 10.1007/978-1-4899-7637-6_1

Roth, P. L., Thatcher, J. B., Bobko, P., Matthews, K. D., Ellingson, J. E., & Goldberg, C. B. (2020). Political affiliation and employment screening decisions: The role of similarity and identification processes. Journal of Applied Psychology, 105(5), 472–486. https://doi.org/10.1037/apl0000422

Ryngksai, I., & Chameikho, L. (2014). Recommender systems: Types of filtering techniques. *International Journal of Engineering Research & Technology (IJERT),* 3(11), 251–254.

Safi, Z., Abd-Alrazaq, A., Khalifa, M., & Househ, M. (2020). Technical aspects of developing chatbots for medical applications: Scoping review. *Journal of Medical Internet Research,* 22(12), e19127. DOI: 10.2196/19127

Schirch, L. (Ed.). (2021). *social media impacts on conflict and democracy: The techtonic shift* (1st ed.). London: Routledge. https://doi.org/10.4324/9781003087649

Schuchard, R., & Crooks, A. (2021). Insights into elections: An ensemble bot detection coverage framework applied to the 2018 U.S. midterm elections. *PLoS One,* 16(1), e0244309. https://doi.org/10.1371/journal.pone.0244309

Seaver, N. (2017). Algorithms as culture: Some tactics for the ethnography of algorithmic systems. *Big Data & Society,* 4(2). https://doi.org/10.1177/2053951717738104

Selbst, A., Boyd, D., Friedler, S.; Venkatasubramanian, S., & Vertesi, J. (2019). Fairness and abstraction in sociotechnical systems. In *Proceedings of the ACM Conference on Fairness, Accountability, and Transparency (FAT\*)* (pp. 59–68), Atlanta, GA, USA, 29–31, January 2019. https://ssrn.com/abstract=3265913

Shevat, A. (2017). *Designing bots: Creating conversational experiences.* Massachusetts: O'Reilly Media, Inc.

Shin, D. (2019). Toward fair, accountable, and transparent algorithms: Case studies on algorithm initiatives in Korea and China. *Javnost: The Public, Journal of the European Institute for Communication and Culture,* 26(3), 1–17. https://doi.org/10.1080/13183222.2019.1589249

Shin, D. (2021). How do people judge the credibility of algorithmic sources?. *AI & Society, Journal of Knowledge, Culture and Communication,* 1–16. https://doi.org/10.1007/s00146-021-01158-4

Speicher, T., Ali, M., Venkatadri, G., Ribeiro, F., Arvanitakis, G., Benevenuto, F., Gummadi, K. P., Loiseau, P., & Mislove, A. (2018). Potential for discrimination in online targeted advertising. In *FAT 2018 – Conference on Fairness, Accountability, and Transparency* (p. 81), New-York (USA), 1–15. https://hal.archives-ouvertes.fr/hal-01955343

Sterrett, D., Malato, D., Benz, J., Kantor, L., Tompson, T., Rosenstiel, T., Sonderman, J., & Loker, K. (2019). Who shared it?: Deciding what news to trust on social media. *Digital Journalism,* 7(6), 783–801. https://doi.org/10.1080/21670811.2019.1623702

Stieglitz, S., Brachten, F., Ross, B., & Jung, A. (2017). Do social bots dream of electric sheep? A categorisation of social media bot accounts. In *Proceedings of the Australasian Conference on Information Systems 2017,* Hobart, Australia, 4–6 December 2017.

Sunstein, C. (2009). *Republic.com 2.0.* Princeton: Princeton University Press.

Tang, L., Fujimoto, K., Amith M., Cunningham, R., Costantini, R., York, F., Xiong, G., Boom, J., & Tao, C. (2021). "Down the rabbit hole" of vaccine misinformation on YouTube: Network exposure study. *Journal of Medical Internet Research,* 23(1), e23262. DOI: 10.2196/23262

Thorat, P. (2015). Survey on collaborative filtering, content-based filtering and hybrid recommendation system. *International Journal of Computer Applications,* 110(4), 31–36. DOI:10.5120/19308-0760

Thurman, N., Moeller, J., Helberger, N., & Trilling, D. (2019). My friends, editors, algorithms, and I: Examining audience attitudes to news selection. *Digital Journalism,* 7(4), 447–469. DOI:10.1080/21670811.2018.1493936

Thurman, N., & Schifferes, S. (2012). The future of personalization at news websites. *Journalism Studies,* 13(5–6), 775–790. https://doi.org/10.1080/1461670X.2012.664341

Tsamados, A., Aggarwal, N., Cowls, J., Morley, J., Roberts, H., Taddeo, M., & Floridi, L. (2021). The ethics of algorithms: Key problems and solutions. *AI & Society* DOI:10.1007/s00146-021-01154-8

Turner Lee, N. (2018). Detecting racial bias in algorithms and machine learning. Journal of *Information, Communication and Ethics in Society,* 16(39), 252–260. https://doi.org/10.1108/JICES-06-2018-0056

Vicario, M., Quattrociocchi, W., Scala, A., & Zollo, F. (2019). Polarization and fake news: Early warning of potential misinformation targets. *ACM Transactions on the Web (TWEB),* 13, 1–22. DOI:10.1145/3316809

Vosoughi, S., Roy, D., & Aral, S. (2018). The spread of true and false news online. *Science,* 359(6380), 1146–1151. DOI: 10.1126/science.aap9559

Ward, J. (2009). Truth and Objectivity. In L. Wilkins, & C. G. Christians (Eds.), *Handbook of mass media ethics.* New York: Routledge.

Weeks, B., Lane, D., Kim, D., Lee, S., & Kwak, N. (2017). Incidental exposure, selective exposure, and political information sharing: Integrating online exposure patterns and expression on social media. *Journal of Computer-Mediated Communication,* 22 (6), 363–379. https://doi.org/10.1111/jcc4.12199

Westerlund, M. (2019). The emergence of deepfake technology: A review. *Technology Innovation Management Review,* 9, 39–52. DOI: 10.22215/timreview/1282

Willson, M. (2017). Algorithms (and the) everyday. *Information, Communication & Society*, 20(1), 137–150. https://doi.org/10.1080/1369118X.2016.1200645

Xu, A., Liu, Z., Guo, Y., Sinha, V., & Akkiraju, R. (2017). A new chatbot for customer service on social media. In *Proceedings of the 2017 CHI conference on human factors in computing systems* (pp. 3506–3510). New York, NY, USA: ACM, http://dx.doi.org/10.1145/3025453.3025496

Yang, K., Varol, O., Davis, C., Ferrara, E., Flammini, A., & Menczer, F. (2019). Arming the public with artificial intelligence to counter social bots. *Human Behavior and Emerging Technologies*, 1(1), 48–61. http://dx.doi.org/10.1002/hbe2.115

Yeung, K. (2018). Five fears about mass predictive personalisation in an age of surveillance capitalism. *International Data Privacy Law*, 8, 258–269. http://dx.doi.org/10.1093/idpl/ipy020

Zarouali, B., Boerman, S., & Vreese, C. (2021). Is this recommended by an algorithm? The development and validation of the algorithmic media content awareness scale (AMCA-scale). *Telematics and Informatics*, 62(2), 101607, http://dx.doi.org/10.1016/j.tele.2021.101607

Zerilli, J., Knott, A., & Maclaurin, J. (2018). Transparency in algorithmic and human decision-making: Is there a double standard? *Philosophy & Technology*, 32, 661–683, https://doi.org/10.1007/s13347-018-0330-6

Zhou, H., Huang, M., Zhang, T., Zhu, X., & Bing, L. (2018). Emotional chatting machine: emotional conversation generation with internal and external memory. In *Proceedings of the 32nd AAAI Conference on Artificial Intelligence* (pp. 730–739), Louisiana, LA, USA.

Zimmer, F., Scheibe, K., Stock, M., & Stock, W. (2019). Echo chambers and filter bubbles of fake news in social media. Man-made or produced by algorithms? In *8th Annual Arts, Humanities, Social Sciences & Education Conference* (pp. 1–22). Honolulu, Hawaii University.

Zuiderveen Borgesius, F. (2020). Strengthening legal protection against discrimination by algorithms and artificial intelligence. *The International Journal of Human Rights*, 24(10), 1572–1593. https://doi.org/10.1080/13642987.2020.1743976

# 4 Reviewing the Commercial and Social Impact of Social Media Influencers

*Chen Lou, Tiffany Chee and Xuan Zhou*

## 4.1 Introduction

The proliferation of mobile technology and social media has rendered individuals easy access to crafting content and sharing personal lives online, and this climate lays a foundation for the boom of social media influencers – a group of social media users who have achieved a quasi-celebrity status in the digital world (Bailis, 2021; Lou, 2021). Over the past few years, an increasing number of practitioners recognize the value of social media influencers in boosting brand awareness and facilitating consumer conversations, especially in view of the lessened effectiveness of traditional advertising tactics (Baker, 2021). First, influencer marketing can be a potent tool for brands to advertise products and increase conversion rate, because consumers exhibit much higher levels of trust in social media influencers than other types of endorsers (Fertik, 2020). Second, non-profit organizations can also establish partnerships with influencers to strengthen credibility, cultivate images and gear up message diffusion (Yu, 2020). In other words, influencer marketing can be integrated to various campaigns appealing to a wide range of enterprises and initiatives.

In terms of social media platforms affording the presence of influencers and influencer marketing, a majority of marketers consider Instagram (89%) the most impactful channel, followed by YouTube (70%), Facebook (45%), Twitter (33%), LinkedIn (19%) and Pinterest (15%), among others (Bailis, 2021). On these digital platforms, social media influencers can create content in a variety of modalities, such as photos, short videos, and vlogs, discuss topics ranging from everyday lives to professional tips, and naturally weave promotional information into their posts. Notably, the market value of influencer marketing has grown from US$1.7 billion in 2016 to US$9.7 billion in 2020, and is forecasted to continually jump to US$13.8 billion by the end of 2021 (Influencer Marketing Hub, 2021). The outbreak of COVID-19 pandemic did not refrain this industry's growth. Instead, the pandemic accelerated the boom of influencer marketing, since more businesses, brands and organizations have been moving to online spaces and contemplating building a strong online presence to reap and engage with their target audiences. In light of the uptrend of influencer marketing, a growing body of literature has documented how marketers can capitalize on social media influencers to support strategic communication efforts. Prior researchers have mostly focused on three

DOI: 10.4324/9781003134176-5

main pillars – the influencer's perspective, the brand's perspective and consumer receptivity – to understand how different stakeholders can work together to meet strategic objectives (Sundermann & Raabe, 2019). Past literature also often focuses on three factors involved in the process – source, message and audience – to investigate the commercialization of social media influencers and their roles in advertising effectiveness and branding strategies (Hudders et al., 2021). However, considering the tremendous social capital of social media influencers, we believe that there is a sizable amount of untapped potential beyond the commercial sphere. Therefore, this book chapter presents a systematic literature review to uncover the broader impact of social media influencers – both commercially and socially.

In the following, we first define social media influencers, hereafter referred to as influencers, and review the relationship between influencers and their followers – parasocial relation. Then, we discuss at length the methodology and framework that guide the development of this review. Last, we synthesize the gathered findings and sort them into four streams – commercial effects, cultural effects, prosocial potential and effectiveness – to offer multi-faceted insights on the effects of influencer marketing. This chapter concludes with a suggested agenda for future research.

## 4.2 Social Media Influencers

Social media has led to the rise of micro-celebrities, known as influencers, who curate their image on social media platforms, mediatizing their everyday life to garner an online following comparable to that of celebrities (Raun, 2018). In this review, we define influencers as individuals who earned their fame solely through their social presence on social media platforms such as Instagram, Facebook, YouTube and Twitter (Lou & Yuan, 2019; Sundermann & Raabe, 2019). As independent content creators, influencers monetize their social following and online identity on these platforms to establish their social presence (Abidin, 2016; Campbell & Farrell, 2020; Khamis et al., 2016). Yet contrary to celebrities, influencers are perceived as more accessible, authentic and relatable, and can develop high-quality relationships with their audiences (De Veirman et al., 2017; Enke & Borchers, 2019; Lou, 2021).

These high-quality relationships are known as parasocial relationships. A parasocial relationship (PSR) is an illusory, non-reciprocal relationship that audiences perceive to have with a particular media personality (Horton & Wohl, 1956). More recently, Lou (2021) defines this relation as a more enhanced version of parasocial relation – or the so-called trans-parasocial relation – and describes it as collectively reciprocal, (a)synchronously interactive and co-created. Indeed, the interactive nature of social media platforms allows influencers to address their followers directly through their posts, thus overcoming the fourth wall and intensifying PSRs (Kyewski et al., 2018). According to Berryman and Kavka (2017), such posts are an "expressive performance of vulnerability" (p. 313) that appears to invite the audience into the influencer's personal life.

Influencers connect with their audiences through strategic self-presentation to portray an authentic, intimate and relatable image (Djafarova & Trofimenko, 2019;

Marôpo et al., 2020). Since influencers can connect effectively with their audiences, they are choice endorsers who help humanize brands, allowing brands to connect with their audiences in a more relatable and authentic manner.

## 4.3 Methodology

To identify relevant articles for this review, the following keywords were selected: influencer marketing, social media influencer, blogger, vlogger, microcelebrity, microinfluencer, social media celebrity, key opinion leader. We chose the Scopus database due to its extensive multidisciplinary database of peer-reviewed social science research articles (Ye et al., 2021). A keyword search yielded 3,573 peer-reviewed articles in English. We then conducted backward and forward searches to identify related articles that may have been omitted. The extensive list was then further refined to only include articles about the commercial or social impact of influencers, resulting in a list of 142 articles.

## 4.4 Proposed Framework

To obtain a holistic understanding of the impact of influencers, we organized the articles into four main pillars for analysis – commercial effects, cultural effects, prosocial potential and effectiveness (see Table 4.1).

The first pillar, commercial effects, explores how influencer marketing affects consumer behavior, specifically in terms of purchase intentions and brand awareness. These effects are often moderated by (1) perceived credibility, (2) an influencer's number of followers, (3) the extent of parasocial interaction (PSI) and (4) the presence of ad disclosures. In addition, with social media platforms becoming increasingly accessible to children and teenagers, it is also worth investigating the impact of influencers on youth consumer behavior.

The second pillar of cultural effects investigates how the definition of celebrity has transformed with time and how influencers are the leading trendsetters in

*Table 4.1* Theoretical framework for organizing research on the impact of influencers.

| Chemical Effects | Influencer Characteristics and Effects on Consumer Behavior | Credibility No. of Followers Extent of PSI Ad Disclosure |
| --- | --- | --- |
| | Youth Consumer Effects | |
| Cultural Effects | Transforming the Meaning of Celebrity | |
| | Navigating Identities | |
| | Trends | |
| Prosocial Potential | Health Communication | |
| | Breaking Stereotypes, Changing Perceptions | |
| | Creating Safe Spaces | |
| | Digital Activism | |
| | Potential for Misinformation | |
| Effectiveness | Audience Perception | |
| | Comparison to Celebrities and Traditional Advertising | |

today's landscape. We will then dive deeper to explore how influencers can potentially be role models for individuals struggling to navigate their own religious, sexual, gender or cultural identities.

The third pillar of prosocial potential analyzes the strategic use of influencers in health communication and digital activism. While we explore how influencers can take the lead in breaking stereotypes and changing perceptions, we will also look further into the risk of misinformation and fake news.

Finally, this review investigates how influencers are perceived by their audiences. In particular, does this perception correlate with the image they are trying to portray? In addition, we will also compare the effectiveness of influencers against that of celebrities and traditional advertising.

## 4.5 Findings

### 4.5.1 Commercial Effects

#### 4.5.1.1 Characteristics of Influencers and their Effects on Consumer Behavior

While this review aims to uncover the potential of influencers beyond the commercial sphere, strategic influencer marketing research is vital to preface the discussion in the subsequent sections.

Brands leverage on the large following and established credibility of these influencers to drive brand engagement, build brand loyalty and increase purchase intentions (Campbell & Farrell, 2020; Chetioui et al., 2020; Ki & Kim, 2019; Lou & Kim, 2019). Researchers have identified that credibility, attractiveness, similarity and authenticity affect an influencer's success in achieving strategic outcomes (Baker & Rojek, 2019; Daniel et al., 2018; Djafarova & Trofimenko, 2019; Marôpo et al., 2020). Figure 4.1 provides an overview of how these factors interact with each other.

4.5.1.1.1 SOURCE CREDIBILITY THEORY

The Source Credibility Theory pioneered by Ohanian (1991) has been reiterated in numerous studies (Abdullah et al., 2020; Balaban & Mustătea, 2019; Pick, 2020). The theory posits that credibility is measured in three dimensions – expertise, attractiveness and trustworthiness.

*Expertise* is measured by how knowledgeable or experienced an influencer is with regards to their respective niche. It can also be determined by the degree of congruence between influencers and their promoted products/services – also known as endorser-product fit (Alotaibi et al., 2019). If there is a poor endorser-product fit, audiences will become more cognizant of the message's commercial intent and regard the influencers as less credible (Breves et al., 2019; Martínez-López et al., 2020).

*Attractiveness* encompasses physical attractiveness (i.e., perceived beauty of the influencer) and social attractiveness (i.e., likability and familiarity of the influencer) (Choi & Lee, 2019; Sokolova & Kefi, 2020). Both are positively associated with credibility and even purchase intentions, particularly for microinfluencers[1] (Lou &

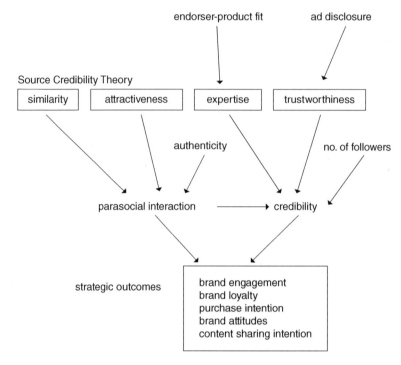

*Figure 4.1* Model describing the relationship between different factors in influencer marketing.

Kim, 2019). In one study, audiences were more attracted to images featuring both the influencer and the product than images of the product alone (Jin & Muqaddam, 2019). However, some researchers suggest that these effects are also affected by the size of an influencer's following. This will be explained in greater detail in subsequent sections.

*Trustworthiness* refers to an influencer's integrity and is determined by whether s/he is biased or has ulterior motives in promoting certain products (Abdullah et al., 2020). Audiences often assess an influencer's trustworthiness by their authority, objectivity and perceived expertise (Martínez-López et al., 2020). Furthermore, audiences consider ad disclosures to determine whether influencers have a conflict of interest. This will be explored later in the review.

While similarity was not identified in Ohanian's original theory, some researchers have found it to be another crucial factor that affects perceived credibility. *Similarity* refers to the degree of likeness between influencers and their followers' background, interests, attitudes, social status and lifestyle (Abdullah et al., 2020; Taillon et al., 2020). Some researchers suggest that similarity forms the basis for how trends begin – audiences are more inclined to think that they also need the product/service used by influencers (Abdullah et al., 2020). This phenomenon could also be attributed to consumers' perception of the influencer as their ideal self-image (Liu et al., 2020).

4.5.1.1.2 NUMBER OF FOLLOWERS

Fame has become more quantifiable in today's social media environment – individuals associate the popularity of influencers with the number of their followers (Martínez & Olsson, 2019). Generally, researchers have found that an influencer's popularity relates directly to their perceived credibility and ability to influence purchase intentions (Hill et al., 2020). In addition, as audiences use popularity as a measure of an influencer's impact, audiences are more likely to be persuaded by an influencer when they consider him/her to have greater influential power (De Veirman et al., 2017; Jiménez-Castillo & Sánchez-Fernández, 2019).

However, some researchers suggest that the number of followers an influencer has should be considered relative to the number of accounts an influencer follows. If the disparity between the two is too great, audiences may regard the influencer as less trustworthy, credible, and authentic (De Veirman et al., 2017). On the other hand, if the difference is too minute, the influencer may be perceived as less of an opinion leader (Valsesia et al., 2020).

Research also found that for influencers with more followers and a more established presence, attractiveness and style may play against their interests. Some researchers argue that this is because followers "suspect a lack of authenticity behind the influencer's pleasantness, appearance, and even integrity, or that they see a forced attempt at sympathy and credibility" (Berne-Manero & Marzo-Navarro, 2020, p.12).

4.5.1.1.3 EXTENT OF PARASOCIAL INTERACTION

As mentioned earlier, the interactive nature of social media facilitates the development of PSRs between influencers and their audiences. PSI is driven by the attractiveness and similarity of influencers (Handriana et al., 2019; Sokolova & Kefi, 2020; Yuan & Lou, 2020) and is further strengthened by the perceived authenticity and entertainment value of influencer-generated content (Lou & Kim, 2019; Reinikainen et al., 2020). Authenticity is key to developing a strong emotional attachment with the audience, turning them into a sustainable fan base with whom influencers can build a community (Ezzat, 2020; Jun & Yi, 2020).

Researchers found that PSI is a secondary dimension that positively influences purchases and content sharing intentions (i.e., electronic word-of-mouth) (Lee & Watkins, 2016; Lou & Kim, 2019; Ki et al., 2020). This is attributed to the perception that influencers are authentic and credible, just as one would perceive their friends (Hwang & Zhang, 2018). The effect of PSI is particularly pronounced among Generation Z consumers, as researchers found that PSI is a much stronger predictor of purchase intentions than credibility (Sokolova & Kefi, 2020).

4.5.1.1.4 AD DISCLOSURE

While most researchers agree that ad disclosures increase ad recognition and brand/product recall (Boerman, 2020; De Jans & Hudders, 2020; Evans et al., 2017), it remains highly contested whether ad disclosures significantly affect brand attitudes or purchase intentions. Evans et al. (2017) found that ad disclosures led to negative brand attitudes, yet other studies found that they have no significant impact on brand attitudes or purchase intentions (Coco & Eckert, 2020; Stubb & Colliander, 2019).

With increased advertising literacy and awareness of commercial intent, some researchers argue that advertising disclosures may no longer be necessary (Balaban & Mustătea, 2019; Boerman, 2020). Coco and Eckert (2020) also found that regardless of ad disclosures, purchase intentions were primarily influenced by prior interest and perceived authenticity of product reviews. Additionally, endorser-product fit and product relevance were more crucial (Balaban & Mustătea, 2019; Benito et al., 2020).

Another study by Lou et al. (2020) found that ad disclosures have little impact among individuals with poor advertising literacy toward influencer marketing (i.e., advertising literacy interventions have to be accompanied by these disclosures for maximum benefit). This observation remains the case for children who are likely to face difficulty recognizing advertisements and sponsorships (Boerman & van Reijmersdal, 2020). The topic of influencer marketing to children will be detailed further in the next section.

Nonetheless, ad disclosures may still be an essential tool of transparency. Influencers are perceived to be, first, content creators, and, second, endorsers. The lack of ad disclosures in content featuring sponsored products may reduce trust in influencers, leading to the perception of staged authenticity that may be detrimental to influencers' reputation in the long run (de Carvalho & Marôpo, 2020). However, some researchers suggest that such disclosures trigger skepticism among the audience (De Jans & Hudders, 2020).

### 4.5.1.2 Youth Consumer Effects

Within the area of strategic communication, there are constant debates on the effects of ad disclosures on children and youths. On one hand, most research suggests that children require cues to recognize advertising (De Jans & Hudders, 2020) and face more difficulty in identifying advertising embedded in social media content (Coates et al., 2019b). On the other hand, some suggest that children can now recognize advertising but still lack the cognition to be critical about it (Coates et al., 2020; Martínez & Olsson, 2019). However, van Reijmersdal et al. (2020) found that children who accurately recognize advertisements are capable of developing a critical attitude toward sponsored content.

Yet, it remains unclear whether ad disclosures affect children's consumption behavior. Some found that ad disclosures have no significant effects (Coates et al., 2019a; Smit et al., 2020), some found that ad disclosures led to increased product interest (Coates et al., 2019b), while others found that ad disclosures led to negative brand attitudes (Hoek et al., 2020). Meanwhile, in addition to governmental regulations, Lin et al. (2019) found that parents' social media habits also affect children's perceptions of influencers. Given the conflicting results in this area, further research is needed to develop effective policies to mitigate the effects of advertising on children.

### 4.5.2 Cultural Effects

#### 4.5.2.1 Transforming the Meaning of Celebrity

As youths have grown up with the prevalence of social media platforms, such as Facebook, Instagram and Snapchat, in their lives, their worldviews are very much affected by their interactions and observations on these platforms (Bond, 2016; Garwol, 2020; Martínez & Olsson, 2019; van Eldik et al., 2019). Influencers have overtaken celebrities as their favorite social media personalities (Argyris et al., 2021; O'Neil-Hart & Blumenstein, 2016; Sugihartati & Egalita, 2019), and they find themselves relating more to influencers than traditional celebrities (Marôpo et al., 2020).

There seems to be a lowered "barrier to entry" to celebrityhood, as grassroots have direct access to the public through digital networks and can garner visibility using various strategies (Deller & Murphy, 2020; Velasco, 2021). Previously, celebrities comprised public figures with "an acknowledged talent, accomplishment or skill" (Baker & Rojek, 2019, p. 393), such as politicians, sportsmen or entertainers. However, today influencers enjoy a pseudo-celebrity status by sharing niche topics with their followers (Baker & Rojek, 2019).

This lowered barrier to entry also comes with a quicker fall. Today, we witness a "cancel culture" where individuals who make posts breaching the rules of social acceptability are boycotted through "public shaming, deplatforming, or demanding that they be fired" (Velasco, 2021, p.3). In one example, influencer Cat Arambulo-Antonio was "canceled" for making harsh and insensitive remarks about individuals working during the COVID-19 pandemic, resulting in brands ending their partnership with her following public outcry (Velasco, 2021). The ease of collective action to "cancel" such public figures suggests that celebrityhood has less permanence than before.

#### 4.5.2.2 Navigating Identities

A secondary social function of influencers arises in their position as opinion or community leaders on social media. They also function as role models – a particularly salient role among minority communities – who serve to fill the gap in media representation while setting the narrative straight with their personal experiences (Andrews, 2021). For example, some influencers have been lauded for their authentic and inclusive performance of masculinity that challenges heteronormative gender behaviors (Morris & Anderson, 2015).

Most studies identified in this review focused on queer influencers and their interactions with their respective communities. With their influence and social presence, queer influencers are well-positioned to fight for social justice, "using their lifestyle narratives and platforms to personalize and promote causes pertaining to politics and LGBT advocacy" (Abidin, 2019, p. 614). They also act as central nodes on social media platforms that have become safe spaces for queer youths who are still figuring out their identities.

However, some researchers are looking at the work of queer influencers from a different perspective. They suggest that their style of content creation can be equated to queerbaiting – a technique that has been criticized as manipulative, as it exploits the trust of followers and the excitement of being represented for commercial gains (Abidin, 2019; Lovelock, 2017). Some examples include collaborating with other influencers to create a spectacle or dropping hints on social media to get viewers to speculate about an influencer's sexuality or relationship status. In addition, there is a trove of "coming-out" videos on YouTube that demonstrate how influencers mediatize and commercialize the acceptance of their identities, projecting a vulnerable image in a public space (Lovelock, 2017).

### 4.5.2.3 Trends

While fashion trends used to be dictated by fashion magazines or celebrities' looks on the red carpet, the rise of influencers has led to an entirely new group of opinion leaders in the fashion industry. This can be attributed to the rapid diffusion of content on social media and the bandwagon effect of seeing multiple influencers dressing a certain way on different platforms (Triani & Vusparatih, 2019).

Influencers also utilize affiliate links and promotional codes to entice their followers to take immediate action. Research indicates that this has a significant impact on impulsive purchase decisions especially among Generation Z females (Djafarova & Bowes, 2021).

### 4.5.3 Prosocial Potential

#### 4.5.3.1 Health Communication

With influencer marketing, authorities can engage with harder-to-reach communities, such as youths or community minorities, through key opinion leaders in their social media networks (Kostygina et al., 2020; Ling et al., 2020; McCosker, 2018). However, while most researchers agree that influencer marketing yields greater reach and visibility, it remains unclear whether such campaigns lead to significant attitudinal and behavioral changes.

In one example, non-profit organization engaged influencers to address misconceptions about flu vaccines and encourage vaccine uptake on social media, resulting in improved attitudes toward the vaccines (Bonnevie et al., 2020). Kostygina et al. (2020) suggest that content type may also be a factor, as individuals can rapidly reproduce and share memes through social media networks.

A few studies focused on how organizations can rely on influencer marketing to promote healthier lifestyles. Sokolova and Perez (2021) found that PSR drives non-exercising viewers to continue viewing exercise videos of the influencers as they look forward to seeing the influencer. However, stronger PSR does not necessarily correlate to a stronger intention to exercise (Sokolova & Perez, 2021). Yet, there is still strong evidence suggesting that influencers and their viewer community can be considered a form of mutual social support to maintain exercising behavior (Sokolova & Perez, 2021).

Engagement with fitness influencer content has also been associated with "favorable health behaviors, at least in relation to physical activity, nutrition, and preventive activities" (Duplaga, 2020, p. 13). However, just as influencers are capable of encouraging positive health behaviors, the opposite is also true. Some studies suggest that viewing fitness influencer content is also associated with increased use of e-cigarettes and alcohol (Duplaga, 2020). This sheds light on a possible risk of health-based influencer marketing – influencers may give advice that is not evidence-based, potentially promoting health-damaging behavior (Duplaga, 2020; Hendriks et al., 2020). Hence, there is a need to explore partnerships between governmental authorities and social media platform developers to implement robust content regulation to reduce the risk of misinformation.

### 4.5.3.2 Breaking Stereotypes, Changing Perceptions

The presence of influencers on social media also results in the redefinition of beauty in the social context. According to Hund (2017), most popular influencers share key commonalities; they have a global identity, are business savvy and exemplify Eurocentric beauty standards. Fitness influencers, in particular, successfully promote exercise regimes by reinforcing the narrative that individuals can only be happy if they have the "ideal" body (Pilgrim & Bohnet-Joschko, 2019). Such a narrative comes with a price – individuals who view images featuring the "ideal" body type report lower body satisfaction and moods (Lowe-Calverley & Grieve, 2021; Tiggemann & Anderberg, 2020).

From a macroscopic perspective, the pervasiveness of social media exacerbated the situation of body dissatisfaction, since digital platforms allow for high exposure to real-time information of what other people are doing, causing audiences to compare their own lives to influencers' posts on "my ordinary day" (Chae, 2018). Unfortunately, most individuals fail to rationalize that influencer posts are carefully curated and strategically shared with the rest of the world, leading to envy of an unattainable lifestyle (Chae, 2018). While this can be particularly damaging, some researchers posit that such social comparison could potentially motivate individuals to engage in self-improvement, as they view the positive results shared by influencers as achievable (Pilgrim & Bohnet-Joschko, 2019; Sokolova & Perez, 2021).

### 4.5.3.3 Creating Safe Spaces

Influencers can create communities with their followers both online and offline. Unlike celebrity fandoms, there is a higher level of interaction between influencers and their followers, with influencers holding their position as a central node in the community network. Within this community, influencers have the power to kickstart conversations and set the tone for the type of interactions that take place in virtual spaces.

A recent study conducted by De Wit et al. (2020) examined how Twitch communities navigate vocalizing issues on mental health. They found that the Twitch streamers (i.e., influencers) shared their life struggles and talked about personal experiences openly with their community, creating an environment that normalizes the vocalizing of one's feelings and thoughts when experiencing a difficult time. The authors found that viewers not only participated in open conversations with the community (whether or not led by the influencer) but were also able to translate their online behaviors into real-life interactions. This can also be perceived as a simple manifestation of digital activism in an influencer's daily life. While they are not kickstarting a social movement or mobilizing their community to make social change, they are still using a social media platform for the greater good of society, even if they never had conscious intentions to do so.

#### 4.5.3.4 Risk: Potential for Misinformation

As influencers develop strong PSRs with their audiences and cultivate trust in their community, there also lies the risk of misinformation and harmful influence. In the first scenario, loyal followers could have "blind confidence" in the influencer, where they believe that the influencer has a good record and will maintain this standard forever (de Carvalho & Marôpo, 2020, p. 101). In the second scenario, followers cast a "positive halo" on influencers, dismissing influencers' negative qualities and believing that they could do nothing wrong (Djafarova & Rushworth, 2017). A similar halo effect also materializes when credibility is automatically transferred from endorsers to brands (Hu et al., 2019).

While most influencers do not actively promote detrimental behaviors, there is always a possibility that the content they produce contains inaccuracies or prejudices. For example, influencers who posted content perpetuating stereotypes relating to mental health led followers to create similar response posts that stigmatized individuals with mental health issues, revealing that audiences are influenced by opinion leaders (Wang & Liu, 2016). As social media platforms increasingly witness the occurrence of mental health issues conversations, influencers have a greater responsibility to present factually accurate information and not perpetuate falsehoods (Wang & Liu, 2016).

### 4.5.4 Effectiveness

#### 4.5.4.1 Audience Perception

Influencers are largely looked up to as role models, whose followers seek to mimic, as well as sparkles of inspiration (Balaban & Mustătea, 2019). They are also perceived to be sources of information and are lauded for their willingness to share their own experiences (Freberg et al., 2011). Macroinfluencers are considered more credible and knowledgeable in their respective niches, while microinfluencers are associated with intimacy and friendliness (Berne-Manero & Marzo-Navarro, 2020).

An interesting study found that followers are occasionally embarrassed about their interactions with influencers; therefore, they choose to engage less overtly or conceal their engagement with influencer content by creating secondary social media accounts which are hidden away from their peers (Abidin, 2016).

#### 4.5.4.2 Comparison to Celebrity Endorsers and Traditional Advertising

Compared to typical brand commercials, influencers are perceived to be more credible and generate more positive brand attitudes (Alotaibi et al., 2019).

Researchers suggest two primary reasons for this. First, as a form of native advertising, branded content posted by influencers fit naturally in their media environment (i.e., social media platforms) and can look like organically created user-generated content (UGC) which lends greater credibility. It also helps that the audience is already relatively engaged on these social media platforms (Johnson et al., 2019). Second, influencers are ambassadors who serve to humanize a brand, reducing the social distance between a brand and its target audience. However, some researchers argue that while influencers are more admired, audiences find them less credible than brands (De Jans et al., 2020). For these reasons, although both influencers and celebrity endorsers can yield significant positive results for brands (Agnihotri & Bhattacharya, 2021; Almaida et al., 2020), influencer marketing is overall more effective than traditional marketing. Researchers find that influencers can build stronger PSRs with their audiences and are hence perceived to be more relatable and credible than their celebrity counterparts (Alotaibi et al., 2019; Jin et al., 2019). However, there are two boundaries when it comes to which endorser yields better results. First, celebrity endorsers can build a stronger endorser-brand association if they work exclusively with a specific brand, while influencers endorse multiple products at once (Almaida et al., 2020). Second, endorser effectiveness may vary for different countries, as one research by Agnihotri & Bhattacharya (2021) showed that celebrity endorsements yield better results in India, where wealth and social status trumps relatability.

## 4.6 Conclusion

This chapter presents the current state of research in the field of influencer marketing from a multi-dimensional perspective, exploring the commercial, cultural and prosocial potential of influencers beyond a merely business-related standpoint. This systematic literature review of 142 articles synthesizes key findings in extant studies on influencer effects and contributes to a deeper understanding of influencers' roles in commerce and broader societal and influencer marketing effectiveness. Not only do most researchers recognize the strategic commercial value of influencers, there is also a consensus that influencers are capable of producing positive results in non-commercial partnerships. This suggests that both governmental authorities and non-governmental organizations can consider using influencer marketing to disseminate important messages effectively in this digital climate.

First, influencers pay an indispensable part in facilitating consumer decision-making and shaping purchase behavior. In general, consumers can evaluate influencers' product recommendation based on (1) influencers' credibility cues, including expertise, attractiveness, trustworthiness and similarity, (2) influencers' follower size, (3) the extent of parasocial interaction between influencers and followers and (4) sponsorship disclosure. However, a special consumer group – youth consumers – deserves particular attention and care from researchers, marketers and policy makers, considering the unclear effects of sponsorship disclosures on youth consumers' recognition and attitudinal development. Regulations and parental mediation can be effective avenues to protect youth consumers and guide their consumption during daily exposure to social media and influencers' posts.

Second, the emergence of influencers helps cultivate a cultural environment with more equality, inclusivity and diversity. The ease of creating content and disseminating it to a wide public tremendously lowered the barrier to entry to celebrityhood. Yet, this flat online communication structure engenders a risk of being "canceled" or boycotted by audiences. In addition, minorities, especially LGBTQ+ individuals, can find social support from queer influencers and other in-group social media users, which helps them navigate their identities.

Third, there is a huge potential for influencers to effectively promote prosocial causes for societal good. For instance, health professionals can leverage influencers to launch health campaigns, broadcast healthy lifestyles, and encourage sustainable behaviors. Meanwhile, as more influencers join in the movement to advocate body positivity, they are indeed challenging stereotypes and re-defining the societal beauty norms in a larger sense. Moreover, by virtue of increased parasocial inter-action between influencer and followers, social media become a relatively safe space for communal discussion and information exchange. Nevertheless, misinfor-mation and fake news can also spread across the online community, which under-lines the importance of both governmental regulations and platforms' efforts.

Overall, this review highlights that the current state of influencer marketing research is highly skewed toward investigating its role in the commercial and branding domain. Thus, future research is expected to delineate the cultural and societal effects of influencers and audience receptivity to prosocial influencer mar-keting. This review can then inform effective policies to regulate prosocial influ-encer marketing given the risks. Furthermore, researchers can observe a vast repository of research to investigate how different characteristics of influencers and the content they produce may impact strategic outcomes. Just as these researchers have generated insightful findings for the industry of strategic communications, it is necessary to replicate these studies in a social marketing context so that different stakeholders can best capitalize on influencers to benefit the society.

## Note

1  Microinfluencers are individuals with between 10k and 100k followers. Macroinfluencers have between 100k to 1 million followers while megainfluencers have more than a million followers.

## References

Abdullah, T., Deraman, S. N. S., Zainuddin, S. A., Azmi, N. F., Abdullah, S. S., Anuar, N. I. M., Mohamad, S. R., Zulkiffli, W. F. W., Hashim, N. A. A. N., Abdullah, A. R., Rasdi, A. L. M. & Hasan, H. (2020). Impact of social media influencer on Instagram user purchase intention towards the fashion products: The perspectives of students. *European Journal of Molecular and Clinical Medicine*, 7(8), 2589–2598.

Abidin, C. (2016). Visibility labour: Engaging with Influencers' fashion brands and #OOTD advertorial campaigns on Instagram. *Media International Australia*, *161*(1), 86–100. https://doi.org/10.1177/1329878X16665177

Abidin, C. (2019). Yes Homo: Gay influencers, homonormativity, and queerbaiting on YouTube. *Continuum*, *33*(5), 614–629. https://doi.org/10.1080/10304312.2019.1644806

Agnihotri, A. & Bhattacharya, S. (2021). Endorsement effectiveness of celebrities versus social media influencers in the materialistic cultural environment of India. *Journal of International Consumer Marketing*, *33*(3), 280–302. https://doi.org/10.1080/08961530.20 20.1786875

Almaida, A., Baumassepe, A. N. & Azzahra, W. F. (2020). Social media influencers vs. brand ambassadors for brand image. *Opción*, *35*(20), 2899–2921.

Alotaibi, T. S., Alkhathlan, A. A. & Alzeer, S. S. (2019). Instagram shopping in Saudi Arabia: What influences consumer trust and purchase decisions? *International Journal of Advanced Computer Science and Applications*, *10*(11), 605–613. https://doi.org/10.14569/IJACSA.2019.0101181

Andrews, G. (2021). YouTube queer communities as heterotopias: Space, identity and "realness" in queer South African vlogs. *Journal of African Cultural Studies*, *33*(1), 84–100. https://doi.org/10.1080/13696815.2020.1792275

Argyris, Y. A., Muqaddam, A. & Miller, S. (2021). The effects of the visual presentation of an influencer's extroversion on perceived credibility and purchase intentions – moderated by personality matching with the audience. *Journal of Retailing and Consumer Services*, *59*, 1–14. https://doi.org/10.1016/j.jretconser.2020.102347

Bailis, R. (2021). The state of influencer marketing: 10 Influencer marketing statistics to inform where you invest. *Big Commerce*. https://www.bigcommerce.com/blog/influencer-marketing-statistics/#what-makes-a-quality-influencer

Baker, K. (2021). What will influencer marketing look like in 2021? *HubSpot*. https://blog.hubspot.com/marketing/how-to-work-with-influencers?toc-variant-b=

Baker, S. A. & Rojek, C. (2019). The Belle Gibson scandal: The rise of lifestyle gurus as micro-celebrities in low-trust societies. *Journal of Sociology*, *56*(3), 388–404. https://doi.org/10.1177/1440783319846188

Balaban, D. & Mustătea, M. (2019). Users' perspective on the credibility of social media influencers in Romania and Germany. *Romanian Journal of Communication and Public Relations*, *21*(1), 31–46. https://doi.org/10.21018/rjcpr.2019.1.269

Benito, S. M., Illera, A. E. & Fernández, E. O. (2020). YouTube celebrity endorsement: Audience evaluation of source attributes and response to sponsored content. A case study of influencer Verdeliss. *Communication and Society*, *33*(3), 149–166. https://doi.org/10.15581/003.33.3.6

Berne-Manero, C. & Marzo-Navarro, M. (2020). Exploring how influencer and relationship marketing serve corporate sustainability. *Sustainability*, *12*(11), 1–19. https://doi.org/10.3390/su12114392

Berryman, R. & Kavka, M. (2017). 'I guess a lot of people see me as a big sister or a friend': The role of intimacy in the celebrification of beauty vloggers. *Journal of Gender Studies*, *26*(3), 307–320. https://doi.org/10.1080/09589236.2017.1288611

Boerman, S. C. (2020). The effects of the standardized Instagram disclosure for micro- and meso-influencers. *Computers in Human Behavior*, *103*, 199–207. https://doi.org/10.1016/j.chb.2019.09.015

Boerman, S. C. & van Reijmersdal, E. A. (2020). Disclosing influencer marketing on YouTube to children: The moderating role of para-social relationship. *Frontiers in Psychology*, *10*, 1–15. https://doi.org/10.3389/fpsyg.2019.03042

Bond, B. J. (2016). Following your "friend": Social media and the strength of adolescents' parasocial relationships with media personae. *Cyberpsychology, Behavior, and Social Networking*, *19*(11), 656–660. https://doi.org/10.1089/cyber.2016.0355

Bonnevie, E., Rosenberg, S. D., Kummeth, C., Goldbarg, J., Wartella, E. & Smyser, J. (2020). Using social media influencers to increase knowledge and positive attitudes toward the flu vaccine. *PLoS One*, *15*(10), 1–14. https://doi.org/10.1371/journal.pone.0240828

Breves, P. L., Liebers, N., Abt, M. & Kunze, A. (2019). The perceived fit between Instagram influencers and the endorsed brand: How influencer-brand fit affects source credibility and persuasive effectiveness. *Journal of Advertising Research, 59*(4), 440–454. https://doi.org/10.2501/JAR-2019-030

Campbell, C. & Farrell, J. R. (2020). More than meets the eye: The functional components underlying influencer marketing. *Business Horizons, 63*(4), 469–479. https://doi.org/10.1016/j.bushor.2020.03.003

Chae, J. (2018). Explaining females' envy toward social media influencers. *Media Psychology, 21*(2), 246–262. https://doi.org/10.1080/15213269.2017.1328312

Chetioui, Y., Benlafqih, H. & Lebdaoui, H. (2020). How fashion influencers contribute to consumers' purchase intention. *Journal of Fashion Marketing and Management, 24*(3), 361–380. https://doi.org/10.1108/JFMM-08-2019-0157

Choi, W. & Lee, Y. (2019). Effects of fashion vlogger attributes on product attitude and content sharing. *Fashion and Textiles, 6*(1), 1–18. https://doi.org/10.1186/s40691-018-0161-1

Coates, A. E., Hardman, C. A., Halford, J. C. G., Christiansen, P. & Boyland, E. J. (2019a). Social media influencer marketing and children's food intake: A randomized trial. *Pediatrics, 143*(4), 1–9. https://doi.org/10.1542/peds.2018-2554

Coates, A. E., Hardman, C. A., Halford, J. C. G., Christiansen, P. & Boyland, E. J. (2019b). The effect of influencer marketing of food and a "protective" advertising disclosure on children's food intake. *Pediatric Obesity, 14*(10), 1–9. https://doi.org/10.1111/ijpo.12540

Coates, A. E., Hardman, C. A., Halford, J. C. G., Christiansen, P. & Boyland, E. J. (2020). "It's just addictive people that make addictive videos": Children's understanding of and attitudes towards influencer marketing of food and beverages by YouTube video bloggers. *International Journal of Environmental Research and Public Health, 17*(2), 1–18. https://doi.org/10.3390/ijerph17020449

Coco, S. L. & Eckert, S. (2020). #Sponsored: Consumer insights on social media influencer marketing. *Public Relations Inquiry, 9*(2), 177–194. https://doi.org/10.1177/2046147X20920816

Daniel, E. S., Crawford Jackson, E. C. & Westerman, D. K. (2018). The influence of social media influencers: Understanding online vaping communities and parasocial interaction through the lens of Taylor's Six-Segment Strategy Wheel. *Journal of Interactive Advertising, 18*(2), 96–109. https://doi.org/10.1080/15252019.2018.1488637

De Carvalho, B. J. & Marôpo, L. (2020). "I'm sorry you don't flag it when you advertise": Audience and commercial content on the Sofia Barbosa YouTube channel. *Comunicação E Sociedade, 37*, 93–107. https://doi.org/10.17231/comsoc.37(2020).2394

De Jans, S. & Hudders, L. (2020). Disclosure of vlog advertising targeted to children. *Journal of Interactive Marketing, 52*, 1–19. https://doi.org/10.1016/j.intmar.2020.03.003

De Jans, S., Van de Sompel, D., De Veirman, M. & Hudders, L. (2020). #Sponsored! How the recognition of sponsoring on Instagram posts affects adolescents' brand evaluations through source evaluations. *Computers in Human Behavior, 109*, 1–15. https://doi.org/10.1016/j.chb.2020.106342

De Veirman, M., Cauberghe, V. & Hudders, L. (2017). Marketing through Instagram influencers: The impact of number of followers and product divergence on brand attitude. *International Journal of Advertising, 36*(5), 798–828. https://doi.org/10.1080/02650487.2017.1348035

De Wit, J., Van Der Kraan, A. & Theeuwes, J. (2020). Live streams on Twitch help viewers cope with difficult periods in life. *Frontiers in Psychology, 11*, 1–16. https://doi.org/10.3389/fpsyg.2020.586975

Deller, R. A. & Murphy, K. (2020). 'Zoella hasn't really written a book, she's written a cheque': Mainstream media representations of YouTube celebrities. *European Journal of Cultural Studies*, 23(1), 112–132. https://doi.org/10.1177/1367549419861638

Djafarova, E. & Bowes, T. (2021). 'Instagram made me buy it': Generation Z impulse purchases in fashion industry. *Journal of Retailing and Consumer Services*, 59, 1–9. https://doi.org/10.1016/j.jretconser.2020.102345

Djafarova, E. & Rushworth, C. (2017). Exploring the credibility of online celebrities' Instagram profiles in influencing the purchase decisions of young female users. *Computers in Human Behavior*, 68, 1–7. https://doi.org/10.1016/j.chb.2016.11.009

Djafarova, E. & Trofimenko, O. (2019). 'Instafamous' – credibility and self-presentation of micro-celebrities on social media. *Information Communication and Society*, 22(10), 1432–1446. https://doi.org/10.1080/1369118X.2018.1438491

Duplaga, M. (2020). The use of fitness influencers' websites by young adult women: A cross-sectional study. *International Journal of Environmental Research and Public Health*, 17(17), 1–19. https://doi.org/10.3390/ijerph17176360

Enke, N. & Borchers, N. S. (2019). Social media influencers in strategic communication: A conceptual framework for strategic social media influencer communication. *International Journal of Strategic Communication*, 13(4), 261–277. https://doi.org/10.1080/15531 18X.2019.1620234

Evans, N. J., Phua, J., Lim, J. & Jun, H. (2017). Disclosing Instagram influencer advertising: The effects of disclosure language on advertising recognition, attitudes, and behavioral intent. *Journal of Interactive Advertising*, 17(2), 138–149. https://doi.org/10.1080/152520 19.2017.1366885

Ezzat, H. (2020). Social media influencers and the online identity of Egyptian youth. *Catalan Journal of Communication and Cultural Studies*, 12(1), 119–133. https://doi.org/10.1386/cjcs_00017_1

Fertik, M. (2020). Why is influencer marketing such a big deal right now? *Forbes*. https://www.forbes.com/sites/michaelfertik/2020/07/02/why-is-influencer-marketing-such-a-big-deal-right-now/?sh=3a6ca4b275f3

Freberg, K., Graham, K., McGaughey, K. & Freberg, L. A. (2011). Who are the social media influencers? A study of public perceptions of personality. *Public Relations Review*, 37(1), 90–92. https://doi.org/10.1016/j.pubrev.2010.11.001

Garwol, K. (2020). Influencers–contemporary authorities of the young generation? *European Journal of Sustainable Development*, 9(4), 273–280. https://doi.org/10.14207/ejsd.2020.v9n4p273

Handriana, T., Dananjaya, D. I. T., Lestari, Y. D. & Aisyah, R. A. (2019). Parasocial interaction between YouTube beauty vlogger and millennial consumers in Indonesia. *International Journal of Innovation, Creativity and Change*, 9(8), 181–196.

Hendriks, H., Wilmsen, D., van Dalen, W. & Gebhardt, W. A. (2020). Picture me drinking: Alcohol-related posts by Instagram influencers popular among adolescents and young adults. *Frontiers in Psychology*, 10, 1–9. https://doi.org/10.3389/fpsyg.2019.02991

Hill, S. R., Troshani, I. & Chandrasekar, D. (2020). Signalling effects of vlogger popularity on online consumers. *Journal of Computer Information Systems*, 60(1), 76–84. https://doi.org/10.1080/08874417.2017.1400929

Hoek, R. W., Rozendaal, E., van Schie, H. T., van Reijmersdal, E. A. & Buijzen, M. (2020). Testing the effectiveness of a disclosure in activating children's advertising literacy in the context of embedded advertising in vlogs. *Frontiers in Psychology*, 11, 1–16. https://doi.org/10.3389/fpsyg.2020.00451

Horton, D. & Wohl, R. R. (1956). Mass communication and para-social interaction: Observations on intimacy at a distance. *Psychiatry*, *19*(3), 215–229. https://doi.org/10.1080/00332747.1956.11023049

Hu, H., Zhang, D. & Wang, C. (2019). Impact of social media influencers' endorsement on application adoption: A trust transfer perspective. *Social Behavior and Personality*, *47*(11), 1–12. https://doi.org/10.2224/sbp.8518

Influencer Marketing Hub. (2021). Influencer Marketing Benchmark Report 2021. https://influencermarketinghub.com/influencer_marketing_benchmark_report_2021.pdf

Hudders, L., De Jans, S. & De Veirman, M. (2021). The commercialization of social media stars: A literature review and conceptual framework on the strategic use of social media influencers. *International Journal of Advertising*, *40*(3), 327–375. https://doi.org/10.1080/02650487.2020.1836925

Hund, E. (2017). Measured Beauty: Exploring the aesthetics of Instagram's fashion influencers. *Proceedings of the 8th International Conference on Social Media & Society*, 1–5. https://doi.org/10.1145/3097286.3097330

Hwang, K. & Zhang, Q. (2018). Influence of parasocial relationship between digital celebrities and their followers on followers' purchase and electronic word-of-mouth intentions, and persuasion knowledge. *Computers in Human Behavior*, *87*, 155–173. https://doi.org/10.1016/j.chb.2018.05.029

Jiménez-Castillo, D. & Sánchez-Fernández, R. (2019). The role of digital influencers in brand recommendation: Examining their impact on engagement, expected value and purchase intention. *International Journal of Information Management*, *49*, 366–376. https://doi.org/10.1016/j.ijinfomgt.2019.07.009

Jin, S. V. & Muqaddam, A. (2019). Product placement 2.0: "Do brands need influencers, or do influencers need brands?" *Journal of Brand Management*, *26*(5), 522–537. https://doi.org/10.1057/s41262-019-00151-z

Jin, S. V., Muqaddam, A. & Ryu, E. (2019). Instafamous and social media influencer marketing. *Marketing Intelligence & Planning*, *37*(5), 567–579. https://doi.org/10.1108/MIP-09-2018-0375

Johnson, B. K., Potocki, B. & Veldhuis, J. (2019). Is that my friend or an advert? The effectiveness of Instagram native advertisements posing as social posts. *Journal of Computer-Mediated Communication*, *24*(3), 108–125. https://doi.org/10.1093/jcmc/zmz003

Jun, S. & Yi, J. (2020). What makes followers loyal? The role of influencer interactivity in building influencer brand equity. *Journal of Product and Brand Management*, *29*(6), 803–814. https://doi.org/10.1108/JPBM-02-2019-2280

Khamis, S., Ang, L. & Welling, R. (2016). Self-branding, 'micro-celebrity' and the rise of social media influencers. *Celebrity Studies*, *8*(2), 191–208. https://doi.org/10.1080/19392397.2016.1218292

Ki, C. W. C., Cuevas, L. M., Chong, S. M. & Lim, H. (2020). Influencer marketing: Social media influencers as human brands attaching to followers and yielding positive marketing results by fulfilling needs. *Journal of Retailing and Consumer Services*, *55*, 1–11. https://doi.org/10.1016/j.jretconser.2020.102133

Ki, C. W. C. & Kim, Y. K. (2019). The mechanism by which social media influencers persuade consumers: The role of consumers' desire to mimic. *Psychology and Marketing*, *36*(10), 905–922. https://doi.org/10.1002/mar.21244

Kostygina, G., Tran, H., Binns, S., Szczypka, G., Emery, S., Vallone, D. & Hair, E. (2020). Boosting health campaign reach and engagement through use of social media influencers and memes. *Social Media + Society, April-June 2020*, 1–12. https://doi.org/10.1177/2056305120912475

Kyewski, E., Szczuka, J. M. & Krämer, N. C. (2018). The protagonist, my Facebook friend: How cross-media extensions are changing the concept of parasocial interaction. *Psychology of Popular Media Culture*, 7(1), 2–17. https://doi.org/10.1037/ppm0000109

Lee, J. E. & Watkins, B. (2016). YouTube vloggers' influence on consumer luxury brand perceptions and intentions. *Journal of Business Research*, 69(12), 5753–5760. https://doi.org/10.1016/j.jbusres.2016.04.171

Lin, M. H., Vijayalakshmi, A. & Laczniak, R. (2019). Toward an understanding of parental views and actions on social media influencers targeted at adolescents: The roles of parents' social media use and empowerment. *Frontiers in Psychology*, 10, 1–16. https://doi.org/10.3389/fpsyg.2019.02664

Ling, P. M., Lisha, N. E., Neilands, T. B. & Jordan, J. W. (2020). Join the commune: A controlled study of social branding influencers to decrease smoking among young adult hipsters. *American Journal of Health Promotion*, 34(7), 754–761. https://doi.org/10.1177/0890117120904917

Liu, C., Zhang, Y. & Zhang, J. (2020). The impact of self-congruity and virtual interactivity on online celebrity brand equity and fans' purchase intention. *Journal of Product and Brand Management*, 29(6), 783–801. https://doi.org/10.1108/JPBM-11-2018-2106

Lou, C. (2021). Social media influencers and followers: Theorization of a trans-parasocial relation and explication of its implications for influencer advertising. *Journal of Advertising*, 1–18.

Lou, C. & Kim, H. K. (2019). Fancying the new rich and famous? Explicating the roles of influencer content, credibility, and parental mediation in adolescents' parasocial relationship, materialism, and purchase intentions. *Frontiers in Psychology*, 10, 1–17. https://doi.org/10.3389/fpsyg.2019.02567

Lou, C., & Yuan, S. (2019). Influencer marketing: how message value and credibility affect consumer trust of branded content on social media. *Journal of Interactive Advertising*, 19(1), 58–73.

Lou, C., Ma, W. & Feng, Y. (2020). A sponsorship disclosure is not enough? How advertising literacy intervention affects consumer reactions to sponsored influencer posts. *Journal of Promotion Management*, 27(2), 278–305. https://doi.org/10.1080/10496491.2020.1829771

Lovelock, M. (2017). 'Is every YouTuber going to make a coming out video eventually?' YouTube celebrity video bloggers and lesbian and gay identity. *Celebrity Studies*, 8(1), 87–103. https://doi.org/10.1080/19392397.2016.1214608

Lowe-Calverley, E. & Grieve, R. (2021). Do the metrics matter? An experimental investigation of Instagram influencer effects on mood and body dissatisfaction. *Body Image*, 36, 1–4. https://doi.org/10.1016/j.bodyim.2020.10.003

Marôpo, L., Jorge, A. & Tomaz, R. (2020). "I felt like I was really talking to you!": Intimacy and trust among teen vloggers and followers in Portugal and Brazil. *Journal of Children and Media*, 14(1), 22–37. https://doi.org/10.1080/17482798.2019.1699589

Martínez, C. & Olsson, T. (2019). Making sense of youtubers: How Swedish children construct and negotiate the youtuber Misslisibell as a girl celebrity. *Journal of Children and Media*, 13(1), 36–52. https://doi.org/10.1080/17482798.2018.1517656

Martínez-López, F. J., Anaya-Sánchez, R., Fernández Giordano, M. & Lopez-Lopez, D. (2020). Behind influencer marketing: Key marketing decisions and their effects on followers' responses. *Journal of Marketing Management*, 36(7–8), 579–607. https://doi.org/10.1080/0267257X.2020.1738525

McCosker, A. (2018). Engaging mental health online: Insights from Beyondblue's forum influencers. *New Media & Society*, 20(12), 4748–4764. https://doi.org/10.1177/1461444818784303

Morris, M. & Anderson, E. (2015). 'Charlie is so cool like': Authenticity, popularity and inclusive masculinity on YouTube. *Sociology*, *49*(6), 1200–1217. https://doi.org/10.1177/0038038514562852

O'Neil-Hart, C. & Blumenstein, H. (2016). Why YouTube stars are more influential than traditional celebrities. *Think with Google*. https://www.thinkwithgoogle.com/marketing-strategies/video/youtube-stars-influence/

Ohanian, R. (1991). The impact of celebrity spokespersons' perceived image on consumers' intention to purchase. *Journal of Advertising Research*, *31*(1), 46–54.

Pick, M. (2020). Psychological ownership in social media influencer marketing. *European Business Review*, *33*(1), 1–21. https://doi.org/10.1108/EBR-08-2019-0165

Pilgrim, K. & Bohnet-Joschko, S. (2019). Selling health and happiness how influencers communicate on Instagram about dieting and exercise: Mixed methods research. *BMC Public Health*, *19*(1), 1–9. https://doi.org/10.1186/s12889-019-7387-8

Raun, T. (2018). Capitalizing intimacy: New subcultural forms of micro-celebrity strategies and affective labour on YouTube. *Convergence: The International Journal of Research into New Media Technologies*, *24*(1), 99–113. https://doi.org/10.1177/1354856517736983

Reinikainen, H., Munnukka, J., Maity, D. & Luoma-Aho, V. (2020). 'You really are a great big sister'-parasocial relationships, credibility, and the moderating role of audience comments in influencer marketing. *Journal of Marketing Management*, *36*(3–4), 279–298. https://doi.org/10.1080/0267257X.2019.1708781

Smit, C. R., Buijs, L., van Woudenberg, T. J., Bevelander, K. E. & Buijzen, M. (2020). The impact of social media influencers on children's dietary behaviors. *Frontiers in Psychology*, *10*, 1–6. https://doi.org/10.3389/fpsyg.2019.02975

Sokolova, K. & Kefi, H. (2020). Instagram and YouTube bloggers promote it, why should I buy? How credibility and parasocial interaction influence purchase intentions. *Journal of Retailing and Consumer Services*, *53*, 1–9. https://doi.org/10.1016/j.jretconser.2019.01.011

Sokolova, K. & Perez, C. (2021). You follow fitness influencers on YouTube. But do you actually exercise? How parasocial relationships, and watching fitness influencers, relate to intentions to exercise. *Journal of Retailing and Consumer Services*, *58*, 1–11. https://doi.org/10.1016/j.jretconser.2020.102276

Stubb, C. & Colliander, J. (2019). "This is not sponsored content" – The effects of impartiality disclosure and e-commerce landing pages on consumer responses to social media influencer posts. *Computers in Human Behavior*, *98*, 210–222. https://doi.org/10.1016/j.chb.2019.04.024

Sugihartati, R. & Egalita, N. (2019). Youtubers as micro-celebrities and new idols among the igeneration. *Opción*, *35*(21), 2899–2921.

Sundermann, G. & Raabe, T. (2019). Strategic communication through social media influencers: Current state of research and desiderata. *International Journal of Strategic Communication*, *13*(4), 278–300. https://doi.org/10.1080/1553118X.2019.1618306

Taillon, B. J., Mueller, S. M., Kowalczyk, C. M. & Jones, D. N. (2020). Understanding the relationships between social media influencers and their followers: The moderating role of closeness. *Journal of Product and Brand Management*, *29*(6), 767–782. https://doi.org/10.1108/JPBM-03-2019-2292

Tiggemann, M. & Anderberg, I. (2020). Muscles and bare chests on Instagram: The effect of Influencers' fashion and fitspiration images on men's body image. *Body Image*, *35*, 237–244. https://doi.org/10.1016/j.bodyim.2020.10.001

Triani, D. & Vusparatih, D. S. (2019). "The role of social media instagram in creating youth trend fashion (19–22 Years Old)" (Case Study Of Fashion Influencer On Instagram Towards Binus University Faculty Of Economics And Communication Departement Students Year 2014–2017). *International Journal of Scientific and Technology Research*, *8*(7), 248–250.

Valsesia, F., Proserpio, D. & Nunes, J. C. (2020). The positive effect of not following others on social media. *Journal of Marketing Research*, *57*(6), 1152–1168. https://doi.org/10. 1177/0022243720915467

Van Eldik, A. K., Kneer, J., Lutkenhaus, R. O. & Jansz, J. (2019). Urban influencers: An analysis of urban identity in YouTube content of local social media influencers in a super-diverse city. *Frontiers in Psychology*, *10*, 1–17. https://doi.org/10.3389/fpsyg. 2019.02876

Van Reijmersdal, E. A., Rozendaal, E., Hudders, L., Vanwesenbeeck, I., Cauberghe, V. & van Berlo, Z. M. C. (2020). Effects of disclosing influencer narketing in videos: An eye tracking study among children in early adolescence. *Journal of Interactive Marketing*, *49*, 94–106. https://doi.org/10.1016/j.intmar.2019.09.001

Velasco, J. C. (2021). You are cancelled: Virtual collective consciousness and the emergence of cancel culture as ideological purging. *Rupkatha Journal on Interdisciplinary Studies in Humanities*, *12*(5), 1–7. https://doi.org/10.21659/rupkatha.v12n5.rioc1s21n2

Wang, W. & Liu, Y. (2016). Discussing mental illness in Chinese social media: The impact of influential sources on stigmatization and support among their followers. *Health Communication*, *31*(3), 355–363. https://doi.org/10.1080/10410236.2014.957376

Ye, G., Hudders, L., De Jans, S. & De Veirman, M. (2021). The value of influencer marketing for business: A bibliometric analysis and managerial implications. *Journal of Advertising*, *50*(2), 160–178. https://doi.org/10.1080/00913367.2020.1857888

Yu, H. (2020). How to use influencer marketing for non-profit organization. *Medium*. https://medium.com/swlh/how-to-use-influencer-marketing-for-non-profit-organization-2cfa34cbd841

Yuan, S. & Lou, C. (2020). How social media influencers foster relationships with followers: The roles of source credibility and fairness in parasocial relationship and product interest. *Journal of Interactive Advertising*, *20*(2), 133–147. https://doi.org/10.1080/15252019.2020. 1769514

# 5    The evolution of the influence business

*Antonio Baraybar Fernández*

## 5.1 Power and influence

The Aristotelian consideration of the human being as a social being by nature, brings with it, to a greater or lesser extent, the necessary idea of a power to organize those communities which are built. The outstanding professor and political analyst, Robert Alan Dahl, began his famous essay "The concept of power" asking the question: "What is 'power'?" He went on to say:

> Most people have an intuitive notion of what it means. But scientists have not yet formulated a statement of the concept of power that is rigorous enough to be of use in the systematic study of this important social phenomenon.
>
> (Dahl, 1957: 201)

In the course of his work, he makes reference to how the term and its synonyms are engraved in the language of civilized peoples, with subtly different expressions: power, influence, control, pouvoir, puissance, Match, Herrschaft, imperium, potestas, auctoritas, potentia, etc.

In order to understand the power of influence in our current environment, the definition of power set out by Moisés Naím has been used: "power is the ability to direct or impede the current or future actions of groups and individuals" (Naím, 2013:38). The choice is due to the fact that it is a practical definition with numerous antecedents and parallelisms with others which focus on the social function of power. Therefore, it makes it possible to obtain more in-depth knowledge of the organization of communities, societies and markets; it is fundamental in order to assimilate the trends which are transforming the current, hyper-connected environment in which previously established types of power seem to be dissolving. New technologies are modifying the influence business, however they are mere tools and require other users whose behaviour modifies the dynamic of the generation of information flow and opinion. Irrespective of the area in which it takes place, any conflict dynamic is made up of a combination of four elements between the rival factions: force or coercion, code or obligation, message or persuasion and reward or incentive (MacMillan, 1978). This conceptual framework eliminates possible terminological confusion regarding concepts which are used as synonyms

DOI: 10.4324/9781003134176-6

in everyday situations. Both power and influence seek to affirm or change the behaviour of others but only coercion and reward can really alter the situation; persuasion or influence only seek to act on how conflict is perceived rather than the conflict itself. Consequently, "it is a sub-category of power, in the sense that power does not include only actions which change the situation but also actions which change how the situation is perceived" (Naím, 2013: 52).

Whether it be relationships among people, between people and groups, or between groups which are quite numerous, links of mutual dependence appear among members. Relationships of power will be fixed between the one who hopes to obtain benefits or rewards and the one who can influence or control the behaviour of another depending on the degree of mutual dependence which exists. Therefore the power to influence another consists of the control over the things that they value. In the relationships between social groups and their hierarchies, the motivational component becomes transcendental when it comes to the granting of rewards, be they monetary or prestige (ego), the latter being very highly valued by the receiver (Emerson, 1962:32–41). These approaches make it possible to understand all those individuals who share, create and spread content thanks to new technologies in a low-cost, almost instantaneous, exchange of information. This user-generated content (UGC) constitutes a new power which has destabilized and questioned the previous business structures of the sector of influence. The monetization of creative work is not always the main argument – belonging to communities according to personal interests or the search for social recognition become the reward for the effort which any creation requires.

Above and beyond the significant changes which businesses associated with influence have undergone and the volume of advertising turnover of large companies such as Google or Facebook, the true power of networks is found in their ability to generate or modify the behaviour and opinions of the general public. This aspect becomes essential inasmuch as it is at the heart of western societies and becomes apparent when dictatorial regimes act as censors of the same. Persuasion, Peitho, reached the condition of a goddess for Greeks. In the ancient cultures of Greece and Rome, a long time before 700 BC, argument and reason held a key role in the poetry of Homer. The Greeks learnt to order discourse in such a way that it could achieve the desired effect. Rhetoric is a totally western phenomenon with the Greeks being the only ones to produce analytical and explanatory treaties with which they sought to discover the true basis of human communication (Murphy, 1983, 9–10). Gorgias stated that "the word is a powerful sovereign that, with a very small and indiscernible body, carries out divine works, since it can calm fears, take away sorrow, bring joy and increase mercy" (Gorgias, 1980: 12).

In the 21st century, the word "persuasion" is still relevant and remains in the society of knowledge – Stanford University founded the Persuasive Technology Lab. Its founder and principal, B.J. Fogg – one of the gurus in the development of new technologies – coined the phrase *captology*, an acronym for "computers as persuasive technologies", which would later evolve towards *Behaviour Design*. These terms give their names to a new field of science which studies the persuasive interactions of subjects with users and how ICT can help to improve people's habits. Their research has confirmed that "the more users can identify with the product, the more likely they will be persuaded to change their attitudes or behavior in ways the product suggests" (Fogg, 2002: 99).

Cicero, in his book *De Inventione* wrote that "some unknown man acknowledged the power of intelligence and eloquence and, using both of them, created a society dedicated to the common good – a society based on justice and not physical force" (Murphy, 1983: 145). It would be in the context of Roman politics where they would witness the appearance and development of two terms of power with interesting connotations for this piece of work: *potestas* and *auctoritas*. These are key concepts for the functioning of *civitas* or citizens' rights. The concept of *potestas* is defined by the qualities of force and leadership. *Auctoritas* has to do with social recognition and the justification of the exercise of power, be it in the public or private sphere. It is not essential for sustaining power since by the use of coercion it may remain outside the recognition of the others (Royo, 1997: 31), but it does complement it and they form a pair which has endured until today with the natural evolution of the meaning of the terms (Morales, 2020).

The historical progress of western societies has led to the need for legitimization by the community. In that context, the media act as intermediaries between power and individuals. The concept of the public sphere set out by Jürgen Habermas is related to the boom of the press and other spaces for public exchange which appeared during the 18th and 19th centuries (Habermas, 1982). If, in the last century, Marshall McLuhan defined the media as technological extensions of humanity, in our day certain technological tools, such as smartphones, have ceased to be mere extensions to become technological prostheses which are taken as second nature inasmuch as they are permanently connected to us and so would appear to serve as additional bodily functions, allowing the individual a social connectivity which is both constant and instantaneous (Wu, 2016). Clearly, internet has modified the role of intermediaries in areas such as the marketplace and information, and it has also opened up new paths for deliberative democracy. As Karl Popper or even Jürgen Habermas remind us, reason is developed using dialogue, discussing the moral principles that are the basis for our law. Consequently, the legitimacy of the law, at the end of the day, depends on an express agreement between governors and society.

Joseph Nye and Steven Lukes identify three dimensions of power. The first, getting someone to do something which does not feature as one of their priorities; the second, the ability to establish an agenda as to what is decided; and the third, and most subtle, the capacity to model people's primary preferences in such a way that they do not even realize that their choices are the consequence of the exercising of power by another beforehand – this is, undoubtedly, a fundamental aspect in the field of public relations. It is obvious that the second and third dimensions are based on the control of knowledge and information which is of great interest for the subject being studied in this piece of work. Francis Bacon stated that knowledge is power and Michel Foucault reversed the idea to hold that power determines what is considered knowledge (Garton, 2017:47–48).

## 5.2 The business of persuasion and modern advertising

Since the appearance of the first daily newspapers around the beginning of the 18th century, models of advertising and paid adverts have come to light. However, one of the differences between that and modern-day advertising is that it treated advertising as a type of news, undoubtedly because it was considered of interest for its readers. Current historical research into advertising does not allow us to tackle the influence of the Industrial Revolution with a great degree of accuracy, among other reasons, because most studies have reversed their point of view and over-looked the beginnings. Significantly in the United Kingdom, manufacturers and sellers trusted it to distinguish their products and increase consumer demand.

From 1830 on, there was an acceleration in economic progress and a significant migration of people towards cities. Around that time, in New York, the most important daily newspaper was *The Morning Courier and New York Enquirer* with a readership of 2,600 in a city of 300,000 inhabitants. Its price was 6 cents, a luxury item for the working class and its target market was the city's business and political elite, the same as the rest of its competitors. Its potential influence did not reach most of the population and its contents were not appealing for the average reader. The 23-year-old, Benjamin H. Day, owner of a printer, felt he could see an opportunity in this situation and started publishing one on his own, *The New York Sun*, bringing in a new information business model which still remains today. With neither political intent nor any great amount of capital to back him, he started selling newspapers at an affordable price for the general public – 1 cent. The sale of newspapers did not guarantee the profitability of the business, but the advertising income generated from marketing would lead to a profit (Wu, 2016). This was how the mass production of cheap newspapers, referred to as the "penny press" began, with a simple, direct and sensationalist style (Goodman, 2010).

In the remainder of the 19th century, the press began a business with considerable political and social influence. One of the most illustrious examples is William Randolph Hearts who has been immortalized for using the media as a political instrument able to generate scandals and manipulate information to favour his own commercial interests. Before the fake news of today, there was yellow news. The term "yellow journalism" surfaced during the journalistic battle between the *New York World*, of Joseph Pulitzer, and the *New York Journal*, of William Randolph Hearst, from 1895 to 1898.

Nowadays the term "digital press" has become something like a pleonasm, with paper giving way to online editions seeking to increase the number of visitors with the same passion as in years gone by, either for free or paying. Many of them preserve that direct and sensationalist style, as witnessed in the management of their social networks, which have been turned into a new social area for debate and the forming of public opinion (Papacharissi, 2010). Its incorporation into this preexisting public sphere builds a hybrid system of communication where traditional media and digital platforms meet (Chadwick, 2013). As such, there is a double gatekeeper system, shared between the media – at the time of publishing – and the contact with users on social networks when they decide to "share them" (Singer, 2014). This participation on social networks may be considered a psycho-social variable of citizen involvement since the evaluations of the latter can affect political decision-making, thanks to their ability to generate commonly held opinion in society (Klesner, 2003). We should not, however, overlook the different motivational dimensions when analysing these virtual communities, among which the entertainment factor appears to stand out with the belonging culture outweighing deliberation (Igartua & Rodríguez-de-Dios, 2016).

In an information ecosystem where the habits of use force producers to adapt constantly, the traditional media use digital technologies intensively, primarily as a mechanism for self-promotion of its offers and distribution of its own contents, applying the logic of propaganda leading to social influence based on viralization (de Aguilera & Casero-Ripollés, 2018:7–10). Although the economic profitability of these practices can be questioned, the search for virality or contagion that increases the dissemination of their news, and consequently of their influence, is unquestionable. Income is the key to business, but trust is the determining value of interactions, since citizens not only satisfy their need for information with their consumption, they also enjoy its transmission and their public judgement (Baraybar, Arrufat, & Rubira, 2021: 10).

Many of the historians of advertising acknowledge Volney Palmer as the first business selling advertising space in the USA. Founded in Philadelphia in 1841, it saw the term "advertising agency" being used for the first time in 1850, as a reference to the agents who paid the newspaper – not the advertiser – on a commission basis for sales. Over time, the newly created agencies were obliged to offer additional services of wording and graphic design for free.

Under the influence of the economic paradigm of Fordism and Taylorism, advertising activity began to take root as a systematic and organized activity. Studies were carried out about it and how to obtain the greatest possible influence with the messages in its audiences moving away from its intuitive nature. William Smith wrote the first treaty on advertising in 1863: *Advertise, How? When? Where?* That being the case, an anonymous piece of work *A Guide to Advertisers* had appeared beforehand, with a certain degree of success, since in 1852 it already boasted three editions (Eguizabal, 2011: 225). In 1895, Oscar Herzberg published the article *Human Nature as a Factor in Advertising*, in which he suggested the power of advertising was a method for influencing the human mind and behaviour. Earnest Elmo Calkins, a pioneer in thinking about mass marketing, stated at the beginning of the last century in his book *Modern Advertising*:

> Napoleon who sneered at England's commercialism said that four hostile newspapers were more to be dreaded than a thousand bayonets. Here is the real reason for our commercial supremacy. Napoleon sneered at shopkeeping but bowed to the power of press. America has forged from her shopkeeping the most wonderful in the world. The shop and the newspaper joined forces and the result is modern advertising.
>
> (Calkins, 1905:3)

The First World War, which has gone down in history as the Great War, was surprising for its intensity and marked a modern concept of combat. Among other reasons, it was for the use of recent technical innovations in the field of armaments, such as machine guns, tanks or chemical weapons. It was also true in terms of persuasive communication by incorporating significant innovations such as the cinema, with the fascination for the general public of watching moving pictures, and advertising hoardings which, even today, are still part of our collective memory. The poster by James Montgomery Flag, in which Uncle Sam – the personification of the USA – points with his index finger and a serious gesture towards the public inviting them to enlist at the nearest office with the slogan "I want you for U.S. Army" is part of the history of advertising and reached such a level of impact that it was used again for the Second World War. It is clearly inspired by the one created by Alfred Leete who used the British War Minister, Lord Kitchener in the foreground and the phrase "Your country needs you".

The emerging advertising industry, in the service of governments, revealed the influence that an organized mass campaign could have on public opinion and behaviour. The days when advertising was perceived as a shady business which generated suspicion was now a thing of the past. A new period began which was characterized by, among other things, businesses becoming more technical and expanding. The situation of the USA as a world power helps explain why western nations imitated its economics and politics. That scenario favoured the new organizational concept of advertising agencies and public relations, following the US management model which would spread throughout Europe and South America.

The radio became the most characteristic medium of that period, forging a close link between the medium and the advertiser. In that regard, it is worth mentioning the series, known as "soap operas", so called because the sponsors of the programmes were soap manufacturers; Procter & Gamble invented the *soap opera* as a vehicle for their adverts (Swasy, 1993). The economic expansion of the 1920s and the new ways of hired purchasing made it popular with listeners. At the beginning, only the companies that made receivers and broadcasters could overcome the problems of funding. In England, the creation of the public service (BBC) in 1926, and the charging of a fee for the receiver would solve the problem. In the USA, the introduction of sponsors in programmes, normally featuring in the name of the programme itself, or being mentioned during the show, became its source of income, since audiences preferred this alternative to having to pay to listen. The considerable coverage and consumption, added to the interest of advertisers for investing in the medium, paved the way for the golden age of the radio. It even enjoyed good economic health during the depression of 1929, in a similar way to cinema or popular literature, thanks to its offer of escapism acting as an outlet for depressed citizens. Nowadays, the broadcasting of audible content via streaming, known as "broadcasts", using different devices has risen significantly in Spain in recent times.

Before the end of the Great War, the US President, Theodore Roosevelt, had employed the famous Texan publicist, Albert D. Lasker, to work with the president of the National Republican Committee, Will Hays, to relaunch the party. This was a clear sign of the belief in the value and competence of advertising and PR professionals in this context, which sociologists defined as the society of masses.

Lasker was, without doubt, one of the pioneers in political communication consulting and storytelling which is so in vogue nowadays, by using the persuasive effects of narrative for the radio and, later, television.

Since those days, the activity of public relations has been closely linked to lobbies with a view to influencing the legitimate representatives. They are also known as "pressure groups" or "interest groups" and seek to exert influence on the political and legislative decision-making process. Normally, political processes are virtually impossible to understand for the public; the lobby group carries out an informative and didactic role either in favour or against, depending upon the particular interests which, at times, do not coincide with those of general interest. Currently, in the European Union, in Brussels, some 500 multi-national companies and over 1,500 business associations have offices and there is also a considerable number of lawyers, consultants, and PR agencies, working for companies and all types of organizations (Hass & Sander, 2019: 7).

Advertising as an activity which was closely linked to the economy needed to extend its methods, faced with the need to reduce the business uncertainty regarding its effects. In the period between the two World Wars, new approaches to marketing began to appear and new theories about persuasive communication appeared. This would imply a shift towards psychology leading to the so-called "scientific advertising". By way of illustration, we will briefly mention two of the most representative figures of the period: Edward Bernays and Claude C. Hopkins.

Edward Bernays is, without doubt, one of the pioneers of public relations, a term which appeared in the book he published in 1923, *Crystallizing Public Opinion*. In it, he carries out a theoretical analysis of the activity, its link with social sciences and methodological needs. He gives his own vision of public opinion from the point of view of public relations, to try to reach the psyché of the general public using individual and group analysis. His fundamental ideas are still considered relevant, one century later (Bernays, 1923). The same occurs with his work, *Propaganda*, published in 1927, in which he structures the actions of public relations using a reflection stemming from the successful realization of PR campaigns, in both the private and public fields, which led to social and economic recognition (Bernays, 2010).

Claude C. Hopkins, who represents the rationalist vision of advertising, sets out the strategic proposal of advertising which stems from the features of the product, and consumers' needs. His book, *Scientific Advertising*, from 1923, introduces the concept of *Reason Why*, the carefully designed adverts of Hopkins, highlight the unique qualities of the product and the reasons why they should be acquired (Hopkins, 1923). The *Unique Selling Proposition* (*USP*), defended by Roser Reeves, represented the continuation of those theories.

During the Second World War, advertising was, in fact, a minor part of the propaganda machine which used all the persuasive means of communication. Once it ended, there was a period of austerity in Europe which affected the sector of agencies. The arrival of US companies and the internationalization of the market brought new communication needs. In the 1950s, the main US publicity agencies adopted a strategy of international expansion, helped by the tendency of American companies to use the same agency that they worked with in the domestic market in the rest of the world. In the following decade, the take-overs and mergers of the companies in the sector became a general trend, beginning a process of geographical concentration in the USA in two centres: New York and Chicago. There began the creation of large commercial communication groups, which bring together different specialist, independent companies, under a single brand, with a view to providing the client with different services – public relations, direct marketing, and so on, in a coordinated way.

The first agency that appeared on the London and New York stock exchanges was Ogilvy & Mather, which went public in 1966, with a turnover of 150 million dollars, having doubled their turnover in four years. Between 1960 and 1971, US agencies opened 291 offices or branches as opposed to the 59 which had opened in the previous 45 years. From then on, there would only be business for small national agencies which offered their own particular creativity and a highly customized service for their different clients as they could not compete in terms of the profitable management and planning of their investments in the media.

However, it would be in the 1980s when the creation of the large financial holding groups would begin and continue until today, displaying features which are typical of an oligopolistic market. This led to two relevant transformations: under a single holding, services can be provided to competing companies, but the profit stays in the same head office; and the use of financial markets – principally in the Stock Exchanges of New York, London, Paris or Tokyo – as a means of funding growth which would modify traditional styles of business management which had been the most common in the sector until then. The concentration in advertising macro-groups is due to the need to grow and increase profits to preserve their position in the Stock Exchange. Giving the stock-holder profit and confidence has become the number one objective, abandoning the idea which had been considered fundamental in previous decades, bearing in mind that it is a service business: the creative product, customer service and care of personnel.

This process began with the Saatchi brothers who considered it strategic for the survival of any successful business and to reach a position of relevance in the USA. It was a policy which was followed by its financial director Martin Sorrell, who, for decades has been the maximum executive of WPP. Among the world's largest holdings there are two from the USA, Omnicon and Interpublic; one British, WPP; another French, Publicis; and, finally, the Japanese Dentsu.

## 5.3 The business of digital marketing

If the expansion of persuasive communication agencies had an obvious boosting effect on mass media, in particular television, the arrival of internet has transformed, and still brings about highly significant changes in the business. More than half the income of US agencies of any discipline related to commercial communication comes from the digital market; income which has doubled in the period 2009–2018. However, the new panorama means it is impossible to forecast the same profit level which the traditional advertising business used to boast. According to the magazine, *e-Marketer*, Amazon grew in its advertising business by 52.5 per cent last year, increasing its share in the US digital advertising market to above

10 per cent, for the first time, establishing its position as the third publisher in terms of income per advert in companies it owns, such as Amazon Fire TV, Twitch and IMDb TV (e-Marketer, 2021).

Seventy per cent of investment in US digital advertising is shared between three companies: Google with a 28.9 per cent market share, Facebook accounting for 25.2 per cent and Amazon, 10.3 per cent; the remaining 37 per cent of advertising investment is shared among other agents. Consequently, we could talk about a digital *triopoloy* of advertising. In this trident, we do not find any communication group – it appears they did not know how to, or could not, join in the change, despite the fact that, in theory, they had a favourable position.

In general terms, we can identify some of the factors which have turned the technological market into a winner in the business of influence. They achieve economies of scale and have the backing of brands which consumers view as solid and household, in many cases over a long term. This brand value attracts talent to their organizations. The effects of direct networks – those associated with the increase in use of the good – and indirect ones (the ones that boost the use of other, complementary goods, for example the upsurge of new applications) – are also relevant, as are the costs of change and hurdles.

The market dominance of these three competitors provides many benefits for consumers and companies. The philosophy of governments' regulatory policies, as set out in their laws, seeks to guarantee free competition between companies as a formula for guaranteeing citizens better value for money for goods and services. This idea is questioned when we consider platforms. By way of example, Google offers consumers a service for which they do not have to pay and advertisers have a new communication tool which did not exist in the past. Current anti-monopoly laws look favourably on competition, taking into account consumers' short-term interests rather than the medium- and long-term health of the market and other stakeholders. Naturally, problems arise for understanding the architecture of power as built by companies in the 21st century, and their corresponding legislation.

The so-called "cognitive capitalism" is based on a change in the logical accumulation of tangible capital to intangible assets. These intangible assets – the brand, the ability to innovate or the flexibility to adapt to new environments – are impossible to measure using normal accounting metrics. We are aware of the ability to add value but, at the same time, we know it cannot be measured accurately. A brand's value or the ability to innovate are not the direct result of investment or measurable productive factors. Facebook extends this definition to what some researchers call "lived intangibles". During the second half of the 20th century, the consolidation of the mass communication media as intermediaries between power and society, boosted by the arrival of television which in the space of a few decades became a household phenomenon, forced a new internal organization and advertising gave up its informative nature turning into an industry of persuasion. Its priority would no longer be the product but rather the consumer, a consequence of which was the relevance of the brand as conceived in the mind of the consumer – in their imagination. These were theories which went beyond the strict definition of Ford's consumption norm (Aglietta, 1978). Social networks and media platforms opened new opportunities for the evaluation of these intangibles, making it possible to go one step beyond by providing a way of granting a universal value to people's experiences, whether they were consumers or not.

The platform market economy values the search above profits – a strategy which investors appear to have rewarded. In addition, online platforms act as critical intermediaries, becoming involved in all lines of the business. In this way, they are in a position to be able to control the basic infrastructure which their rivals depend on. This situation could also allow a platform to exploit the information gathered about the companies that use the services to undermine them as competitors.

Google and Facebook appear to fulfil the "winner takes all" thinking in the market of platforms although there are some who dispute that opinion. The argument is that whilst they do dominate the market for information searches and social networks, respectively, they must share the advertising market between themselves and other communication media (Evans & Schmalensee, 2016). However, they overlook the fact that the media are not homogeneous; advertisers invest money through different channels with different targets. Google totally dominates search-based advertising whereas Facebook has a dominant participation – and a tendency to grow – in online display advertising, especially for mobile phones. With limited marketing budgets, they compete in the same way as all consumer goods and services compete indirectly for consumers' spending. However, the reality is that advertisers have no substitutes with the same scale and reach – that may be one of the reasons why, despite questionable aspects such as audience figures and campaign result fraud, they continue to use them. The columnist Mark Ritson described this digital duopoly as the greatest problem faced by marketing in the UK in 2016 and his short-term predictions were not very promising (Ritson, 2017).

Fake activity is a threat for the whole business model – any commercial advertising relationship requires a reliable source of measurement, or at least one which is universally recognized by all the players involved, to facilitate the exchange between messages to the target public and money. Lack of clarity and mistrust will make the client likely to spend less money and the potential profit for the platform could be reduced. Fraudulent activity has reached considerable proportions: fake users, false statistics or bots (those algorithms which generate connections on social networks automatically and create false hits in order to make campaign objectives have been met or exceeded). Most studies compute human activity at less than 60 per cent of all activity on internet, the remaining 40 per cent being fake and generated by robots or humans. In 2018, Facebook itself admitted that its measurement of viewing time for each video could, in some cases, have been over-estimated by as much as 60–80% (Patino, 2020: 102–103). It seems paradoxical that even YouTube, whose mother company is Google, has created technology-based tools to detect fake audiences of robots pretending to b per cent humans; machine against machine.

In spite of these serious problems, the figures for advertising spending shown above clearly reveal that marketing professionals do trust in its advantages. Social networks like software, platforms and online media attempt to make it easier to communicate, relate and exchange content between users. Consequently, the main social networks – Twitter, Facebook, YouTube or LinkedIn – have become relationship builders and an ideal instrument for companies to connect with their potential clients. Nowadays, media are classified as "traditional" and "non-traditional". The latter, as opposed to the former, allow users to use Social Networking Services (SNS) to keep in touch with allied groups and freely exchange information about their experiences with brands. This means the purchasing experience based on the decisions of others posted on social networks is shared almost instantaneously and influences future purchasing decisions of other group members.

The experiment carried out by the sociologist Matthew J. Salganik, revealed that the success of individual creative work depends, to a large extent, on how it is perceived by the rest of the group. They created an artificial platform of online music with all new songs in such a way that none of the listeners had heard any of them before. For the experiment, the participants were divided into two groups. The first had an individual experience whereas the second could see which songs the others were downloading based on a popularity ranking. The researchers found that each person developed their own set of results but the results were more homogeneous among those who knew the preferences expressed by the other listeners (Shiller, 2021: 94).

It is clear that platforms permit easy access to any information in an easy and instantaneous way, taking part in the endless decisions which the human being is constantly making. However, there is also the social aspect related to the theories of comparison set out by Leon Festinger – comparison of our abilities with those of others – and with social fear. This last concept explains the fear someone feels for missing something which others have access to and the fear of being omitted due to oversight, known by the acronym FOMO (Fear of Missing Out). The enthusiasm and energy which can be observed in debates about all kinds of topics on social networks underlines the deep need for community and exchange of ideas which people possess. "New ICTs are not necessarily producing 'new' citizens but they do provide for new citizen practices"(Hermes, 2006: 306).

On the other hand, different research studies have concluded that Facebook's advertising model successfully mixes brand equity, brand image and purchase intention, by linking people's interest for information about the product and its brand, with the possibility of establishing dialogues with other buyers and expressing their opinions and experiences. Consequently, social networks have become an almost free tool which is able to simulate word of mouth and generate a relationship of trust through influencers who serve as a contact node with their fans or followers to achieve positive commercial or brand results. It's an adaptation of the model of communication flow in two steps as set out by Lazarsfeld. On its way to the public, the message is filtered by the influencer who plays a transcendental intermediary role as a decodifier and opinion leader for their group, bringing understanding, credibility and trust.

It is true that the number of followers is considered one of the most important variables when it comes to choosing, although there are other important qualitative factors. The relationship between the influencer and their follower is not necessarily affected even when the latter admits that the content may be a paid advert (Dhanesh & Duthler, 2019). The rise of this practice has led to the publishing of classifications so that the advertiser can choose the design of campaigns more correctly. Gross and Wangenhein have identified four types which, even though the dynamic of constant change of social networks means any classification may suffer inaccuracies, helps to reduce uncertainty: snoopers, informers, entertainers and infotainers. Snoopers create their own content, following their own insight, and are individualistic and active. Informers use the exchange of knowledge and experience. They are well-informed and follow the information about the issues that interest them. Similar to snoopers, they are active and individualistic. The priority of entertainers is for people to enjoy their network. They are less individualistic, being aware that entertainment has more appeal than knowledge and the need to coincide with the tastes of the community. Infotainers share knowledge and experiences, providing people with information and education. At the same time, they are not against entertainment as long as it does not distract from focusing on the subjects being considered. Each influencer begins as a snooper or an informer and later evolves – either consciously or unconsciously – as a reaction to the comments of their audience (Gross & Wangenheim, 2018).

Any online media planning agency needs to reach agreements or become a partner of the main worldwide paid social supports. They provide strategic consulting services, campaign operations, data intelligence or integration and personalized technological development. Unlike traditional media agencies, which used to have strong bargaining power with the media thanks to their financial situation and a considerable control over the advertisers' investment budget, the situation of dependence has cut profit margins per operation. They evangelize among their potential clients about the opportunities and profitability of their investment in Social Media, carrying out a significant commercial role for platforms. Their argument revolves around the reach of their campaigns thanks to the high number of internet users and the time they spend on the different networks, allowing them to design complementary campaigns as they normally belong to the same mother company. Another of their main arguments has to do with segmentation when it comes to targeting specific audiences. Their premise is that it will be easier to find a specific individual than a socio-demographic segment with uncertain interest. In traditional media, they try to position themselves correctly so that, with a bit of luck, the audience will see them. However, with digital media the promise is to find the right group of people in a specific context; in other words, to show the right advert to the right person at the right time. The creation of an online advertising mix increases effectiveness by using a combination of the specifics and strengths of each of the platforms.

## 5.4 How to better understand consumer thinking

The work of Peter Drucker, one of the greatest minds of management theory, has as one of its key axes, knowing the consumer. The product or service must adjust to their needs and, as such, it sells itself. In an ideal scenario, marketing must lead to a consumer who is willing to buy. All that remains is to make the good or service available to them. In the same way that production and logistics professionals are responsible for managing supply, heads of marketing are responsible for managing demand in order to meet the targets set out by the organization, acting on the volume, timing and composition of the same. It is a management process which begins with product design phase and ends with ensuring brand loyalty.

The problem is that it is not easy to discover how consumers behave. As the great publicist David Ogilvy said, "consumers don't think how they feel, don't say what they think and don't do what they say" (Ogilvy, 1983). The fundamental principle of conventional market research is based on the possibility of asking people questions and that what they say will be true. The limitations of verbal statements and unawareness of what we really feel make it difficult, at times, to understand our own emotions. Consumer behaviour is a reflection of the complex processes of the brain which provoke all human action. Consequently, social psychologists never cease to explore the ways in which we are unaware of what really makes up our behaviour and the extent to which that contradicts the image we have of ourselves (Graves, 2011: 41). Advertisers are more and more aware that most human decisions are intuitive, automatic and are often taken without any conscious control (Matukin, Ohme and Boshoff, 2016). Herbert Simon, a pioneer in the study of the resources used during the decision-making process, showed that sometimes we prefer the simplest option to be able to argue how we reached that decision more easily and justify our choice to others.

A wide variety of measurement techniques and instruments are used to better understand consumer behaviour and the effectiveness of advertising messages, even though they all have certain limitations and biases. Another factor to be taken into account is linked to the deficiencies when analysing motivations and processes related to the how and why of consumer decision-making.

Data science could be defined as the discipline which combines statistics, scientific methods and data analysis in order to extract useful information. It seeks to identify patterns of behaviour and generate knowledge which, among other things, makes it possible to reduce uncertainty in decision-making and detect new trends. The year 1962 could be considered its beginning, with J.W. Tukey, famous for developing complex algorithms and his diagram, *Box Plot*, even though it was not until a decade later that Peter Naur coined the phrase which is used today. However, its antecedents go back to the 9th century in the person of the Persian mathematician, geographer and astronomer Al Juarismi, whose name when converted to Latin, Algorithmi, has given its name to one of the terms, algorithm, which when applied to the business of platforms, is interpreted as the mathematical formula which unites the economic interests of searchers, personal information and advertisers. In layman's terms, and talking about social networks, we understand an algorithm to be a set of programming rules which govern the appearance and spread of publications. Its design, therefore, will mean certain publications will appear more or less and will determine to whom and when they will be shown.

When in a world-famous garage, Menlo Park, Larry Page and Segey Brin developed the algorithm known as Page Rank – the driving force behind Google's search results – they showed its effectiveness for classifying the enormous amount of data on internet but, at the same time, the ability to prioritize granted it a power to shape our knowledge and produce results by suggesting they could classify, filter, search, prioritize or recommend information.

Data, by definition, speaks of actions which happened in the past since it is impossible to register that which has not happened yet. The models which are built, irrespective of the complexity obtained by the breakthroughs of information science and the enormous amount of data that can be processed, will be able to reduce risks thanks to more accurate results, but they will always reproduce that which has already been. The ability to predict, in the light of unexpected events – black swans – those phenomena with no precedent although with the benefit of hindsight they could be rationalized, continues to recommend moderate expectations.

Alan Turing defended the theory that machines would eventually be able to think for themselves. Machine learning, or the construction of analytical models using data analysis which makes it possible to identify patterns or models automatically, presents us with a dynamic for action which appears aseptic, following on from the European Cartesian tradition which states that everything can be measured, even though human participation is essential for the working of digital platforms. Behind the thinking of Turing lies a search to find out how the human mind works in order to copy it. But, can we really describe a human being in terms of numbers?

The problem is not in the algorithms but rather in the personal biases of individuals and society, itself, which is constantly undergoing change. Today's data do not necessarily have to coincide with tomorrow's and society itself includes its own biases at all times in its construction of reality. Algorithms, like viruses, can cause wide-scale biases in a very short time. The award-winning documentary, *Coded Bias* (2020), directed by Shalini Kantayya, is a reflection on the supposed neutrality of the technological world. It illustrates the works of the researcher from MIT, Joy Boulamwini, creator of the association *Algorithmic Justice League* whose aim is to raise society's awareness of the impact of artificial intelligence. Her research has identified sexist and racist bias in algorithms of facial recognition for those with darker skin.

Creators of algorithms tend to reproduce their own environment and the ideas thereof. From an intellectual point of view, developers tend to create endogamic groups. Undoubtedly, their IT know-how is high but they are lacking in other fields and they are biased in favour of their own discipline. For example, when it comes to formulating theories, their choice may be connected to those proposals which are easier to program or they may accept as valid those proposals which come from other sciences which are questioned or obsolete. Above all, multidisciplinary working groups must be created for those projects which have to do with aspects that add intangible value to organizations.

The reality is that it is impossible to observe human attitudes with the same accuracy as used by scientists studying molecules with electronic microscopes. The promise of being able to measure the influence of actions or communications with total accuracy has not yet been fulfilled. It is true that a large quantity of real-time data, obtained using the available IT analysis tools, may give the impression that there is total control of the spread of actions and the possibility of obtaining relevant quantitative information may exist. Of the nearly 46,000 million dollars spent on market research worldwide, 81 per cent is spent on quantitative research (Baños, Baraybar & Rajas, 2020). That figure allows us to detect a sense of truth about the data upon which decisions at organizations are taken, without knowing how they were obtained and what errors they may contain. This is even more the case when they are not supported by rigorous qualitative research which helps us understand the motivation behind the behaviour which they reflect.

## 5.5 Final thoughts

The winner of the Nobel Prize for Economics in 1978, Herbert Alexander Simon, warned that in a world which is rich in information, grabbing the attention of a potential audience acquires relevant significance (Simon, 1971). Based on this idea, it can be deduced that a wealth of information creates poverty of attention and a need to designate efficient attention within the excess of information. Moreover, being over-informed does not mean better documented or having a greater critical capacity. For an approach to understanding the attraction which users feel towards digital platforms and their ability to catch the attention, we must use psychology. That is also true for the study of momentary satisfaction which algorithms provide when they make lightning recommendations about user tastes or the imperious need to always be connected to our favourite networks, or having our smartphone as a sign of our personal identity, particularly with young people. Unquestionably a fundamental part of the digital economy, as evidenced in everyday life, depends on capturing attention and time.

Digitalization has brought about a cultural transformation and its impact affects all areas of the company: from the way in which we communicate and relate with interest groups, the management of operational processes, the experience and interaction with clients or the business model itself. The complexity of brand management has increased in the face of more demanding clients with more chance of buying offers instantly and expressing their opinion on social networks. The points of contact multiply, and the complexity of coordinating efficiently makes it necessary to adapt to this new environment. In order to construct the messages (what is known as "storytelling"), it is essential for organizations to have their purpose always present. Storytelling is an idea for generating content in the process of building and managing the brand, based on the creation of products, services and experiences which are perceived as being of tangible value for society. Targets must be clear, specific and in line with the organization's purposes. They may vary from creating awareness, improving engagement or raising the traffic of the owned media.

The digital transformation of any corporation is a common attitude involving all its members. By means of a transversal, transparent and honest effort we can talk about true cultural changes. We live in an environment which is totally interconnected, one tweet away from our audiences, which are at the centre of the conversation and no longer occupy the role of mere observers. Twitter, more than a social network must be considered a platform of content which takes on different meanings depending on its use, be it as a means of communication, a source of information... Social networks are a tool so that the consumer can share information about products and services that they use and, consequently, they can impact the reputation of the company.

The *Trust Barometer*, a worldwide report carried out for the last two decades by the public relations firm, Edelman, for measuring the level of trust which society has in institutions, revealed in its 2021 edition an "epidemic" of misinformation and distrust all over the world. This crisis affects governments in particular but also other types of institutions such as companies, NGOs and the media. Without a reliable source of leadership to follow, people do not know where to obtain information they can trust, nor from whom. Social networks (35 per cent) and owned media (41 per cent) are the least trusted although even traditional media (53 per cent) have experienced a significant fall in the level of trust worldwide (Edelman Trust Barometer, 2021).

Digital platforms have a key role to play and one which they must assume with social responsibility if they are to survive. If money is the currency of transactions, trust is the currency of interactions. Trust is the pillar of relationship marketing, enabling an organization to take responsible risks and recover from any errors committed. It is a must to have greater transparency in management, and the ability to implement measuring tools which are not susceptible to opaqueness, agreed on by the players in the market, and guarantee user privacy. Regarding the latter, new initiatives have appeared, for example one run by the Association of National Advertisers (ANA) or another by the audience measurement company, Comscore, to check the virtual person's identification (VID), which helps cross-media measurement. The VID project seeks to find metrics of reach and frequency of TV and digital audiences. This prototype has as its goal to find more transparent information, thus restoring essential measuring metrics of an advertising campaign and guaranteeing user privacy.

The serious health pandemic has clearly revealed the need for reliable information as an instrument to influence, raise awareness and educate the population. Conspiracy theories and misinformation schemes are a great risk in our societies. A greater dependence on social networks and other platforms, which facilitate access to a multitude of sources under the guise of alternative information, has once again shown their capacity for spreading information contrary to official discourses and which, on occasion, is misleading or simply false. That is a worrying scenario given its potential for influencing part of public opinion, thus destabilizing the connection between society and politics.

The different means of payment do not boast the same acceptance in all countries. Digital subscriptions to a single brand is the most common format, however, in Norway, the printed-digital packages have been shown to be successful and, in the USA, paid news aggregators are quite popular, thanks to Apple News +. As far as the reasons to explain the payment go, identifying with one editorial line or one particular journalist, and the quality of the content are some of the most used arguments.

It remains to be seen which of the business models will dominate but it is clear that the formulas for payment must look for ways to generate customer loyalty and commitment, by means of direct communication with subscribers and the regular use of podcasts. Whilst the model of advertising revenue is predominant, information companies will have to obey the investment decisions of advertisers and, consequently, their economic criteria.

The role of entertainment and the time which we spend on social networks must not be forgotten. That means that, in the quest for acceptance, intimacy may become a good. It surprises no-one that, in an attempt to attract audiences who are hungry for sensationalism, it is becoming more and more difficult to discern what is reality and what is fiction. The main danger is that reality will be transformed into something less believable than the fabled, viral content which is consumed worldwide. Umberto Eco warned of the risk of social networks becoming the loudspeaker of those "idiots" who have always been around but, nowadays, are more difficult to silence.

To sum up, going back to the ideas we set out at the beginning of this study, influence and persuasion are an essential part of the building of society in western culture. The ends for which they are used and the tools involved are another issue. As Professor Jorge Lozano reminded us: all political activity must be based on persuasion,

> because although it may be a violent thought, that does not mean that it doesn't oppose violence. Rather than falling for a pantheism of Persuasion, I am persuaded that Persuasion is inevitable.
>
> (Lozano, 2012:131)

## References

Aglietta, M. (1978). Fases de la expansión del capital de EE, UU. *New Left Review*, 110, 17–28.

de Aguilera, M., & Casero-Ripollés, A. (2018). ¿Tecnologías para la transformación? Los medios sociales ante el cambio político y social. *Icono 14*, 16 (1), 1–21. DOI: 10.7195/ri14.v16i1.1162

Baños, M., Baraybar, A., & Rajas, M. (2020). The application of neuromarketing techniques in the Spanish advertising industry: Weaknesses and opportunities for development. *Frontiers in Psychology*, 11, 1–14. https://doi.org/10.3389/fpsyg.2020.02175

Baraybar, A., Arrufat, S., & Rubira, R., (2021). Public information, traditional media and social networks during the COVID-19 crisis in Spain. *Sustainability*, 13, 1–14. https://doi.org/10.3390/su13126534

Bernays, E. L. (1923). *Crystallizing public opinion*. New York: D. Appleton and Company.

Bernays, E. L. (2010). *Propaganda*. Santa Cruz de Tenerife. Melusina.

Calkins, E. E. (1905). *Modern advertising*. New York: D. Appleton and Company.

Chadwick, A. (2013). *The hybrid media system: Politics and power*. Oxford. Oxford University Press.

Dahl, R. A. (1957). The concept of power. *Behaviorial Science*, 2 (3), 201–215.

Dhanesh, G. S., & Duthler, S. (2019). Relationship management through social media influencers: Effects of followers awareness of paid endorsement. *Public Relations Review*, 45 (3), 1–13. https://doi.org/10.1016/j.pubrev.2019.03.002

Edelman (2021). Edelman trust barometer 2021. Access July, 07, 2021. https://www.edelman.com/trust/2021-trust-barometer

Eguizabal, R. (2011). *Historia de la publicidad* (2nd ed.). Fragua. Madrid.

E-Marketer (2021). Amazon´s share of the US digital ad market surpassed 10% in 2020. 6, April. https://www.emarketer.com/content/amazon-s-share-of-us-digital-ad-market-surpassed-10-2020. (Accessed July, 07, 2021).

Emerson, R. M. (1962). Power-dependence realtions. *American Sociological Review*, 27 (1), 31–41.

Evans, D. S., & Schmalensee R. (2016). *Matchmakers: The new economics of multisided platforms*. Boston. Harvard Business Review Press.

Fogg, B. J. (2002). *Persuasive technology: Using Computers to change what we think and do*. Morgan Kaufmann/Elseiver. San Diego.

Garton, T. (2017). *Libertad de palabra. Diez principios para un mundo conectado*. Barcelona. Tusquets Editores.

Goodman, M. (2010). *The sun and the moon: The Remarkable True Account of Hoaxers, Showmen, Dueling Journalists, and Lunar Man-Bats in Nineteenth-Century New York*. New York. Basic Books.

Gorgias (1980). *Fragmentos de Gorgias de Leontini*. México, Universidad Nacional Autónoma de México. Version of Pedro Tapia Zúñiga.

Graves, P. (2011). *¿Por qué consumimos?* Barcelona. Urano.

Gros, J., & von Wangenheim, F. (2018). The big four of influencer marketing. A typology of influencers. *Marketing Review St. Gallen*, 2, 30–38.

Habermas, J. (1982). *Historia y crítica de la opinión pública: la transformación estructural de la vida pública*. Barcelona. Gustavo Gili.

Hass, T., & Sander, H. (2019). The European car lobby. A critical analysis of the impact of the automotive industry. *Bruselas, Rosa Luxemburg Stiftung*. 1–32. DOI: 10.13140/RG.2.2.20746.41921

Hermes, J. (2006). Citizenship in the age of the internet. *European Journal of Communication*, 21, 295–309. DOI: 10.1177/0267323106066634

Hopkins. C. C. (1923). *Scientific advertising*. New York. Crown Publishers Inc.

Igartua, J. J., & Rodríguez-de-Dios, I. (2016). Correlatos motivacionales del uso y la satisfacción con Facebook en jóvenes españoles. *Cuadernos.info*, 38, 107–119. https://dx.doi.org/10.7764/cdi.38.848

Kantayya, S. (2020). *Coded Bias* (Film). 7th Empire Media.

Klesner, J. (2003). Political attitudes, social capital, and political participation: The United States and Mexico compared. *Estudios Mexicanos*, 19 (1), 29–63.

Lozano, J. (2012). *Persuasión. Estrategias del creer*. Bilbao. Universidad del País Vasco.

MacMillan, I. (1978). *Strategy formulation: Political concepts*. Minnesota. West Publishing, St. Paul.

Matukin, M., Ohme, R, & Boshoff, C. (2016). Toward a better understanding of advertising stimuli processing exploring the link between consumers' eye fixation and their subconscious responses. *Journal of Advertising Research*. 56 (2), 205–216. https://doi.org/10.2501/JAR-2016-017

Morales, J. (2020). Los conceptos de auctoritas y potestas durante la época moderna. *Bajo Palabra*, 24, 337–358. https://doi.org/10.15366/bp.2020.24.017

Murphy, J. J. (1983). *Sinopsis Histórica de la Retórica Clásica*. Madrid. Gredos.

Naím, M. (2013). *El fin del poder*. Barcelona. Debate.

Ogilvy, D. (1983). *Ogilvy y la publicidad*. Barcelona. Ediciones Folio.

Papacharissi, Z. A. (2010). *A private sphere. Democracy in a digital age*. Cambridge, Cambridge Polity Press.

Patino, B. (2020). *La civilización de la memoria de pez*. Madrid. Alianza Editorial.

Ritson, M. (2017). Why you should fear the digital dupoly. *MarketingWeek*. https://www.marketingweek.com/ritson-digital-duopoly-2018/ (Access May, 28, 2021).

Royo, J. M. (1997). *Palabras con poder.* Madrid, Marcial Pons Ediciones Jurídicas y Sociales.

Shiller, R. J. (2021). *Narrativas económicas. Cómo las fake news y las historias virales afectan la marcha de la economía.* Barcelona. Deusto.

Simon, H. A., 1971. Designing organizations for an information-rich world. In *Computers, communications and the public interest*, ed. M. Greenberger, 37–72. Baltimore. Johns Hopkins Press.

Singer, J. B., 2014. User-generated visibility: Secondary gatekeeping in a shared media space. *New Media & Society*, 16 (1), 55–73. DOI:10.1177/1461444813477833

Swasy, A. (1993). *Soap opera. The inside story of procter & gamble.* New York. Random House.

Wu, T., (2016). *The attention merchants.* New York. Alfred A. Knopf.

# 6 Influencer marketing dynamics

## The roles of social engagement, trust, and influence

*Sylvia Chan-Olmsted and Hyehyun Julia Kim*

## 6.1 Introduction

Influencer marketing has reshaped people's understanding of advertising practices. In traditional advertising, the source and intent of the message was clear. The brand intended to sell its product and the message was delivered to consumers through mass media channels. Over time, technological advancements gave rise to diversification of media channels and creation of new media platforms that innovated advertising message dissemination. Influencer marketing is a marketing practice that seized the door of opportunities brought about by proliferation of social media. As the name suggests, the practice markets influence by capitalizing on key individuals' persuasive power over their social network. The key individuals, known as social media influencers, or simply influencers, wield a disproportionate amount of influence over two generation groups: Generation Z and Millennials. Generation Z, those born 1997 onward, and Millennials, those born between 1981 and 1996 (Dimock, 2019), are major target audiences for brands collaborating with influencers and are also most receptive toward influencer marketing. According to Google, 70 percent of YouTube's teenage users report feeling stronger connection to YouTubers than to traditional celebrities, while 40 percent of millennial users mirror similar sentiments in relation to their relationship with YouTubers over their friends (O'Neil-Hart & Blumenstein, 2016).

Generation Z and Millennials possess significant purchasing power in the retail industry. A report by Morgan Stanley (2019) states that the two generational cohorts' spending power is on track to outspend the Baby Boomers as Boomers outgrow their prime working years and make less income. Sixty percent of those between 18 to 34 years of age, the primary age group for Generation Z and Millennials, report having been influenced by a digital content creator in their purchase decision (Influencer Intelligence, 2019). Taking into account the purchase power of these age groups and their digital media consumption behavior, it comes as no surprise that the influencer marketing industry is on its way to becoming a $15 billion-dollar industry by 2022.

Growth in influencer marketing has resulted in some visible shifts in the advertising industry. This shift is the most noticeable in advertising media mix, where a survey of 226 industry professionals reported an increased focus on social media and influencer marketing (Williamson, 2019). With growing reliance in the

DOI: 10.4324/9781003134176-7

marketing practice, advertisers are expected to spend more than 10 percent of their marketing budget toward influencer marketing. There are other companies, like Estée Lauder, who has committed 75 percent of their marketing budget toward of focusing on influencer marketing (Pearl, 2019). This growing proportion of digital marketing budget in a media mix, especially toward influencer marketing, helps to highlight the strong foothold that the practice is gaining in the advertising industry.

As a consequence of increasing focus on influencer marketing, social media platforms have introduced new features to further enhance influencer marketing practices for users and marketers. One notable feature is the launch of "Shop" function on Instagram, which allows users to shop a sponsored post and make purchases directly in the application (Droesch, 2019). This addition carries enormous implications. For Instagram, it helps the platform to establish itself as a comprehensive solution provider for those seeking influencer marketing needs. For brands, it gives them the opportunity to truly gauge effectiveness of sponsored posts and its return on investment. In addition, marketers are able to reduce frictions in consumer journeys by eliminating the hassle of downloading an app or being redirected to an external site to finalize their purchase. At large, consumers are still hesitant about adopting social commerce features, but recent survey paints an optimistic picture for future of social commerce adoption, with 31 percent of US consumers reportedly making purchases on social media (Droesch, 2019). By incorporating shopping features into sponsored posts, social media influencers are becoming a part of a consumer's decision journey, from awareness to purchase.

While the industry is growing at a rapid pace, a conceptual understanding of the underlying constructs that make influencer marketing successful are somewhat limited. Academic research has addressed influencer marketing from the perspectives of consumers (Sokolova & Kefi, 2019; Jin & Muqaddam, 2019; Lou & Yuan, 2019; Rasmussen, 2018), management, branding (Breves et al., 2019; Khamis et al., 2017), and platforms (Abidin, 2016). With the bulk of research dedicated toward understanding consumer perceptions, less attention has been paid toward understanding the underlying dynamics of influencer marketing practices and the antecedents of its success. In fact, research relevant to this topic often draw upon electronic word of mouth (eWOM) or celebrity endorsement literature which do not address the many unique characteristics of influencers on social media.

Some industry professionals attribute the success of influencer marketing to consumers' belief in the idea that influencers were a voice of trustworthiness and authenticity at a time when trust in traditional media was declining (Twomey, 2020). This premise can also be evidenced in a 2016 Twitter industry report, which shows that consumers' level of trust in influencers rivals that of their own friends (Swant, 2016). As such, it can be argued that trust and perceived intimacy were pivotal in the success of influencer marketing. Furthermore, studies have shown that the commercial effect of influencers is often affected by the relationship between them and the followers (Balaban & Mustăţea, 2019; Dhanesh & Duthler, 2019). Therefore, parasocial interactions in the form of digital engagement would play a role in the process of influencer marketing. In fact, it is the proposition of the authors that the "influence" in this context is largely affective.

Hence, the objective of this chapter is to address the underlying dynamics of influencer marketing from this perspective. In particular, it will discuss the roles of four emotion-laden factors: engagement, trust, authenticity, and relationship, as well as how they might collectively influence the effectiveness of influencer marketing.

## 6.2 Influencer marketing

### 6.2.1 Defining influencer marketing

Influencer marketing encompasses several concepts and ideas related to a fast-growing marketing practice. Although scholarly research has yet to reach a single definition for influencer marketing, several defining characteristics can be observed across the research field. Most definitions of influencer marketing seem to agree that, in essence, influencer marketing is about the marketing of influence centered around key individuals who have influence or persuasive power over their network (Lou & Yuan, 2019; Ranga & Sharma, 2014). The persuasive power can be in reference to awareness building (Brown & Hayes, 2008, as cited in Lou & Yuan, 2019; Ranga & Sharma, 2014) or increasing purchase intention (Jin et al., 2019; Knoll, 2016). Key individuals around which influencer marketing is centered on are called influencers, or more specifically, social media influencers (SMIs). SMIs can be largely categorized into four groups: blogger, YouTuber, celebrity, and Instagrammer. Of these, YouTubers and Instagrammers have become the most prominent form of SMIs. An estimated 50 million content creators are believed to be active on YouTube and among these, the most popular channel has over 126 million subscribers (Aslam, 2020b). On Instagram, there are an estimated 500,000 active SMIs (Aslam, 2020a).

Influencers can also be categorized by the number of followers (see Table 6.1). Even though many would assume that megainfluencers with over 1 million followers would wield the most expansive reach, it should be emphasized that number of followers is not an automatic indicator of the degree of persuasive power that can be exerted on their network. In contrast to the common belief that a large following leads to greater impact, industry insiders state that microinfluencers, those with up to 100,000 followers, have the greatest influence over their network due to their intimate engagement and authenticity (Enberg, 2018).

In the beauty and fashion industry, microinfluencers have proven to be the most effective tier of influencer types. At its core, influencer marketing embraces authenticity and engagement, but these elements are not as easily conveyed if the

*Table 6.1* Influencer Type Definition

| Influencer type | Size of following |
| --- | --- |
| Megainfluencer | > 1 million |
| Macroinfluencer | Between 100,000 & 1 million |
| Microinfluencer | Between 1,000 & 100,000 |
| Nanoinfluencer | < 1,000 |

Source: Influencer Marketing Hub.

influencer is speaking to millions of followers (Enberg, 2018). In other words, intimacy is often inversely related to the popularity of an influencer. This creates a paradoxical outcome and has strategic implications in terms of campaign goals and the appropriate choice of influencer types.

Influencers are at the core of influencer marketing and their influence is typically anchored by the content they create. Social media influencers are, first and foremost, content creators (de Veirman et al., 2017; Lou & Yuan, 2019) who typically have expertise in specific content (de Veirman et al., 2017; Lou & Yuan, 2019). Influencers share their specialized content, which may or may not be sponsored, along with snaps of their daily life (de Veirman et al., 2017), which heightens a sense of friendship or closeness experienced by the influencer's followers. Influencers drive influencer marketing by sharing details of daily, personal lives that sets them apart from traditional celebrities, making them more accessible, relatable, believable, and intimate to followers (Abidin, 2016). This also helps to strengthen the tie between the influencer and the followers as users are likely to feel an emotional connection with the influencers as they share their lives like close friends. In sum, SMIs are the "trusted tastemaker" (de Veirman et al., 2017) in their specialized area of content and consumers place trust in their opinions as an emotional bond is strengthened.

In general, the younger the consumer, the more receptive they tend to be toward influencer marketing. In the US and the UK, friends and influencers (e.g., Instagrammers, YouTubers, bloggers) were identified as top sources of influence among those six to 16 years of age (Droesch, 2019). The impact of social media influencers also runs deep among those over 16 years of age. A survey by Kantar found that 70 percent of those who fall under Generation Z follow at least one social media influencer (Williams, 2020), a finding also reflected in other industry reports which shows that teenagers are most likely to follow many, as opposed to at least one, social media influencers (The Morning Consult, 2019). Generation Z, combined with Millennials, show the highest receptivity toward influencer marketing, with 72 percent of survey respondents admitting to following at least one influencer. Beyond the two, younger generational cohorts, the older generations, specifically Generation X and Baby Boomers, also occupy substantial Internet presence and possess potential purchase power. Defined as those born between 1965 and 1980 for Generation X and between 1946 to 1964 for Baby Boomers (Dimock, 2019), these two generational cohorts are often overlooked in influencer marketing because marketers mistakenly assume that they are not heavy users of social media. However, surveys reveal that Generation X and Boomers spend about one to two hours on social media on a daily basis, with many consuming DIY tutorials on YouTube, and as a natural progression, following influencers, as well as TV celebrities and politicians (Tabor, 2019). The potential purchase power of these groups should not be overlooked and more attention should be brought to focusing on them as an untapped market with great potential.

Some studies have likened influencer marketing to a new generation of product placement (Jin & Muqaddam, 2019), while others have compared it to eWOM with influencers taking on the role of opinion leaders (de Veirman et al., 2017). A key assertion in opinion leadership is the leaders' ability to influence the social network around them, thus generating word of mouth that would have higher credibility than an advertiser's message. In other words, their messages are more persuasive, therefore more influential, than a message from an advertiser. Studies in influence have assumed that influence moves from top-down, from those with authority to those who place trust in the opinion of these figures (Keller & Berry, 2003). However, with the proliferation of social media and SMIs, a media system that relies on social networks, the direction of influence has become more horizontal, rather than vertical. Such change of influence direction also allows for more networked connections, personal interpretation, and, thus, the incorporation of affect and relationship.

Influencer marketing seems to deliver noticeable outcomes. Industry reports state that for every dollar spent on an influencer marketing campaign, brands can expect to earn anywhere between $5.20 (Influencer Marketing Hub, 2020) and $6.50 (Digital Marketing Institute, n.d.). Although there is no industry consensus on the precise ROI on influencer marketing, it is clear that brands are profiting from their influencer collaborations. In one industry example, Lord and Taylor, a US department store chain, partnered with 50 Instagrammers and *Nylon* magazine to promote their Design Lab clothing line. In the same day, 50 Instagrammers uploaded posts of themselves wearing the same dress, which was also featured on *Nylon*'s website. With the wide exposure the campaign generated, the same dress promptly sold out (Malcolm, 2016). The campaign generated priceless engagement for the brand by reaching an estimated 11.4 million Instagram users, 328,000 shares, likes, and comments (Federal Trade Commission, 2016). Although the brand violated Federal Trade Commission's (FTC) deceptive marketing mandate and faced a lawsuit from the organization, the campaign spoke volumes in regard to the power of influencer marketing and its impact on consumers' purchase decision.

Lord and Taylor's campaign is an example of a successful campaign that generated sales through wide exposure. However, success stories in influencer marketing can manifest at all levels of SMIs. Recognizing younger generations' caffeine needs and desire for socially active fast food chains, Dunkin' Donuts moved in a digitally savvy direction to enhance their communication with their new target audience by increasing their social presence (Wiltshire, 2018). To reach their audience, Dunkin' Donuts zeroed in on Instagram influencers who could genuinely engage young users. The brand collaborated with several influencers whose follower count ranged from 3,000 to 50,000 followers (Media Kix, 2019). From this range of influencers, the campaign showed that nanoinfluencers generated the highest engagement and reached over 1.13 million Instagram users. Dunkin' Donuts' campaign demonstrates the hidden potential of micro- and nanoinfluencers whose personalized posts evoke stronger intimacy and authenticity, leading to stronger engagement and relational outcomes not only with the influencer, but also with the brand.

Higher engagement and sales are clear benefits to brands during influencer marketing campaigns. However, what are its implications after a consumer logs out of the platform post engagement? According to Google, data show that in comparison to traditional celebrities, brand collaborations with YouTubers can raise brand familiarity by four times (Nazerali, 2017). The report demonstrates influencers' power to drive deeper involvement with their followers, giving brands the opportunity to speak to their customers on an emotionally deeper level. Another major advantage of working with influencers on YouTube is the flexibility of sponsored content. Brand-sponsored videos can range from product haul, vlogs (video blogs), product reviews, to how-to tutorial videos (Johnson, 2019). Moreover, since YouTubers' area of expertise varies greatly, options are endless for brands who wish to partner with popular YouTubers. One such example is popular YouTube channel, WhatsUpMoms, which now has 3.07 million subscribers. The most watched video has gathered 71 million views, earning Elle Walker, the YouTuber behind the channel, the title of number one parenting influencer in the United States (WhatsUpMoms, n.d.). In 2018, Walker's estimated worth was $1 million (Carter, 2018). In essence, Walker was successful because of her relatability and authenticity, which were combined with niche content delivered on an interactive platform that could scale her content. For brands, this could give them the opportunity to amplify their brand value through an authentic and relevant voice. As these cases show, influencer marketing, if done right, is becoming an attractive marketing strategy for many brands.

### 6.2.2  Platforms

Before we elaborate on the potential of influencer marketing due to the four affective aspects, we will first discuss the topic of platforms which shapes how an influencer delivers his/her content and connect with the followers. The platform issues also impact how brands might integrate influencers into their campaigns. Media platforms enable brand marketers various ways to communicate with target audiences. They act as a conduit of influence and work as an intermediary between brands and consumers. In the age of traditional media, mass communication channels, such as television and radio, were influential media channels and audiences tuned in to the media where advertising messages were delivered to them unidirectionally. However, as technological advancements reshaped how marketers deliver advertising messages, traditional media have given way to social media channels as the primary source of information (Lou & Yuan, 2019). In contrast to traditional media channels whose primary objective was to disseminate content, the focus of social media is on collaboration and distribution of content. The collaborative aspect of social media not only facilitates co-creation of content, but also allows for collective discussion and improvement of the content, truly making it a collaborative process.

Social media have many unique features that facilitate collaborative co-creation of content. Viral marketing has been a buzzword since social marketing became a widely employed strategy in digital marketing. In concept, viral marketing is similar to eWOM, and if done right, it can be a cost-efficient way for brands to promote products and services, possibly leading to purchase intention (Gunawan & Huarng, 2015). Social media's "share" feature gives users the opportunity to share others' content, while also giving users the chance to create their own, thus increasing a level of engagement previously unseen in traditional media. With its ability to easily amplify voices and opinions among users, advertisers' scope and scale of influence can be largely magnified (Subramani & Rajagopalan, 2003). Social media also provide ability to use rich media content, such as videos, to easily create, upload, and share with larger audiences (Koivisto & Mattila, 2018). As social media became a major communication channel, content created and diffused through rich media by users, also known as user generated content (UGC), became more ubiquitous and people seized the opportunity to market their niche product knowledge, eventually leading to influencer marketing. A computer-mediated environment provides many shortcuts for influencers' voices to be heard on a large scale. In addition to easily connecting users, giving influencers the power and reach to communicate with a wider audience, feedback occurs in real time, allowing people to enhance future strategies (Subramani & Rajagopalan, 2003). These characteristics have the power to intensify the reach and influence of those who are well-connected with a large following on social media, giving more persuasive power to influencers.

The inherent characteristics of different social media offer various benefits and experience to users. For instance, research has found that Facebook users primarily use the platform for maintaining, as opposed to forming, connections (Ellison et al., 2007), whereas the popular microblogging platform Twitter is beneficial for quick diffusion of information with its 140-character limit (Rinaldo et al., 2011). Social media, by nature, are dynamic and social media companies constantly compete with existing as well as new platforms, to gain a competitive edge in the market. One way to gain a competitive edge is to continue offering users enhanced experiences by introducing new features. As a leading influencer marketing platform, Instagram has adopted key features from various social media platforms to gain an upper hand in the market. When Snapchat launched in 2011, the new platform was predicted to pose a threat to Instagram's user base with its ability to allow users to upload short videos that disappeared after 24 hours. This was in direct contrast to Instagram, where users sought to capture and share the perfect moment that permanently remained on their feed, causing a mental burden on some users to upload an "Instagram-worthy" post every time they wanted to share their life (Wagner, 2018). For some, this led to decreased usage of the platform, posing an issue for Instagram. As a result, Instagram launched Instagram Stories in 2016 to incorporate Snapchat's lower pressure content sharing model to give users a similar experience to the one they attained from Snapchat (Constine, 2016). This new feature eased the pressure that many users felt to create the perfect post that not only blended in with their feed, but also told a cohesive story throughout the account.

In addition to Snapchat, a new platform emerged in the social media landscape that forced Instagram to launch a new feature to enhance user experience. Launched in 2017, TikTok's popularity skyrocketed among users under 30 years old, recording over 800 million monthly active users by 2020 (Iqbal, 2020). TikTok combines Snapchat's short video feature with Instagram's photo-enhancing and hashtag capabilities into one mobile application that enable users to consume and co-create scalable content through "TikTok challenges" that often go viral (Bump, 2019). To compete with this newcomer, Instagram launched "Instagram reels" in August 2020 which allow users to search for specific audio or scroll through longer format videos in the application. Instagram's adoption of new features that resemble other social media platforms illustrate the dynamic and fluid nature of the social media market. For marketers, this gives them the opportunity to continuously better interact with consumers in more engaging ways.

Each social media platform offers a different experience, therefore different benefits to their users. Because user experience is the key driver of social media consumption, it is crucial that social media companies keep enhancing and expanding their platforms to satisfy people's usage motivation. Even though each social media platform offers different experience to users, user satisfaction attained from social media platforms appear to be stable. User motivations for using social media vary from forming, maintaining, and organizing social connections to an active performance of their identity (Chi, 2011). This means that regardless of the type of platform, underlying reasons and motivations for why people use social media remain relatively stable. Social media are defined by its connectivity and interactivity features, which give users a new format to communicate with one another, and as a result, creating a "sphere of influence" that places social relationships at its core (Hanna et al., 2011). This sphere provided by social media, according to Hanna et al. (2011), is user-centric and dialogue focused. This suggests that user experience should be an essential element of social media marketing. Given that users are at the heart of social media marketing, it is important to understand users' experiences and outcomes derived from social media. Each social media is engineered differently to deliver a different user experience. In influencer marketing, YouTube and Instagram have been identified as key platforms for communicating with audiences.

Acquired by Google in 2006 (Sorkin & Peters, 2006), YouTube, a video sharing platform, is now the world's leading social media platform after Facebook (Pew Research Center, 2019), with over 2 billion monthly active users. YouTube's success can be attributed to the site's capability to serve as a platform for social network, which gave audiences an opportunity to become content creators who can gain fame. Moreover, it converges aspects of traditional entertainment and new media, while empowering users to "broadcast the self" through a new mode of self-promotion (Khan, 2017). According to a report by Pew Research Center (2019), approximately 73 percent of American adults are YouTube users and 51 percent of those users report using the platform on a daily basis. The platform also boasts a wide range of content types to match its massive number of users, making it an ideal media channel for marketers to promote their products. YouTube has been vital to the success of influencer marketing, giving rise to YouTube influencers, or simply "YouTubers," who create own content on YouTube, which are consumed by subscribers who follow the social media personalities (Xiao et al., 2018). As such, it is not surprising that YouTube, along with Instagram, is the platform of choice for influencer marketing and for those who wish to leverage the extensive influence of the social media influencer (Kádeková & Holienčinová, 2018).

Instagram, in contrast, offers users a different type of experience from YouTube. The proverbial phrase "pictures speak louder than words" has proven true for Instagram. As of 2018, Instagram's number of monthly active users has surpassed the 1 billion mark (Dhillon, 2018) and has generated over $20 billion dollars in advertising revenue in 2019 (Frier & Grant, 2020). The platform, with its image and video-enhancing features, is a one-stop shop for visual-oriented users who like to document their daily life (Lee et al., 2015). With e-shopping features directly integrated into its posts, it is no wonder that many US marketers allocate nearly 70 percent of their influencer marketing budget toward Instagram (Newberry, 2019). Academic literature also points out Instagram as the social media of choice for most social media influencers (Jin et al., 2019; Kádeková & Holienčinová, 2018). A major strength inherent in Instagram is the social aspect of the platform which allows users to build relationships with those who share similar interests (Lee et al., 2015). Photo-enhancing capabilities, in conjunction with the relationship-building aspect of the platform, helped to build Instagram as the backbone of influencer marketing's success.

## 6.3 Influence

### 6.3.1 Authentic identity / authenticity

Authenticity, in essence, denotes being true to oneself. Staying true, being faithful to the self implies fidelity to one's ideals, beliefs, and, more importantly, one's identity (Kristinsson, 2007). Human behavior guided by authenticity, behavior that adheres to one's principles and originality, is considered to be socially "good" behavior, whereas inconsistency between the self and behavior are considered to be "bad" behavior. Then, authentic behavior, stemming from a genuine, honest, and faithful place of the self, implies moral superiority to those who behave inauthentically (Wilt et al., 2019). The positive associations surrounding authenticity has cemented the concept as a principal idea in modern western culture (Kristinsson, 2007).

These ideals have also been extended to marketing and branding academic literature. In a world rife with uncertainties, consumers have been increasingly seeking authenticity as a way to alleviate their perceived uncertainty. The inherent need to reduce uncertainty extends to product consumption, making authenticity a major pillar in modern-day marketing (Brown et al., 2003). In present-day marketing, brands must convey authenticity through advertising messages and communication should be founded on genuineness and honesty. Conceptualized as "a subjective evaluation of genuineness ascribed to a brand by consumers" (Napoli et al., 2014, p. 1091), brand authenticity encompasses perceptions of truth, realness, and ingenuity. Authenticity, as a concept, has been adopted from various disciplines, therefore lacking a unified definition in marketing, but scholars conclude that authenticity is related to feelings of stability, consistency, individuality, trustfulness, keeping promises, genuineness, and credibility.

Marketing and authenticity embody an oxymoronic relationship because mass marketing techniques and advertising claims undermine attempts to appear authentic (Beverland & Luxton, 2005). Despite the difficulty that comes with authenticity appeals in marketing, as academic scholars have emphasized, authenticity is essential to modern-day marketing and must be embraced. Influencer marketing seemed to provide marketers with a solution to this challenge.

By collaborating with influencers, brands leverage not only the SMIs' influence over their social network, but also their authenticity (Kozlowska, 2019). Unfortunately, despite the clear benefits that authenticity brings to influencer marketing, cognitive concepts underlying how authenticity contributes to stronger relationship between consumers and SMIs requires more insight. Homophily and social identity are important concepts in the field of social identity that help to explain people's changing nature of identities and group formation in social context. An insight into these concepts can illuminate the underlying mechanisms of authenticity that make it a major cornerstone of influencer marketing.

Homophily operates on one simple principle: similarity breeds attraction. At its core, homophily dictates that connections between those who perceive one another as being similar to self are more likely to form a bond than those who are dissimilar (McPherson et al., 2001). Years of research in homophily show that people, as early as school children age, are likely to experience natural affinity to those with similar education, race, sex, age, intelligence, and values. According to Lazarsfeld and Merton (as cited in McPherson et al., 2001), there are two homophily types: status homophily and value homophily. Status homophily refers to demographic variables that divide social classes, whereas value homophily deals with cognitive dimensions that make up individual's orientation and identity, such as values, beliefs, and attitudes. A study of adolescents by Kandel (1978) helped to provide a clearer understanding of causality in homophily and relationship development. The findings indicated that negative behavior, like drug usage among adolescents, were more likely to be the effect of selecting relationships with those who already exhibit similarities, rather than an outcome of interpersonal influence within the group. In other words, the relationship formed because these similarities already existed. The implication behind this finding is that people naturally gravitate toward those who are similar to themselves, resulting in ties within a social network.

Building ties with those similar to the self can only occur in a social context. Humans live in a social world and amid the complexity of the social world, people take on different identities. Known as social identity, the concept exists as part of one's self-concept arising from one's recognition of membership to a group (Tajfel, 1974). In social identity, group membership, defined as in group versus out group, underlies social identity construction. In order to know what you are, you must have a sense of what you are not. This presupposition categorizes in group and out group in one's mind, aiding construction of one's social identity, enabling the individual to find his place in his social network (Tajfel, 1974). In the age of social media, in the form of follower/following count, one's social network is visible to members of in group, as well as out group. This visibility has also made it possible for others to evaluate who others align with in their social network. In other words, social identity has become more significant as people are defined in relation to others (Pan et al., 2017), making social identity a more salient feature of people's self-identity.

Communications research has well-documented the role of homophily in message sender-receiver relationships. Academic literature claims that homophily between the sender and receiver increases message receptivity and effectiveness (McCroskey et al., 1975). In other words, the perceived similarity is instrumental in conveying the message of a true, authentic identity. Taken in conjunction with social identity, these constructs can help to understand feelings of perceived closeness, similarity, and relatability that consumers feel toward social media influencers, strengthening the ties between the two parties and the feeling of "realness." Perceived belongingness to certain social groups can yield many benefits, such as protection of the group. Scholars state that importance of group membership can often be overlooked in favor of individual self, attributing less importance to collective identity (Gaertner et al., 1999 as cited in Ellemers et al., 2002). This finding demonstrates that one's social group membership can become a part of one's social identity.

In an influencer marketing context, it can be deduced that consumers perceive a sense of similarity and group membership with SMIs, as a result making their messages more persuasive and realistic. As seen in homophily, people select as friends those who display similarities to themselves. By relying on perceived similarity as an indicator of trust, people reduce risks that may entail formation of new social ties (Kossinets & Watts, 2009). A major proposition in influencer marketing, that influencers are regular people with honest opinions, can signify trust, reducing risks of forming social ties. This risk reduction can enable in-group membership, further strengthening the ties between the influencer and the follower. The founding principle of influencer marketing is that influencers are people like us. This relatability and intimacy also help to intensify the emotional connection between the influencers and followers. In short, perceived similarity helps consumers to see the evidence that the influencers they follow are genuine, and, thus, worth trusting.

Authenticity can be a double-edged sword for the influencer marketing industry. While the industry owes its success to influencers' authenticity stemming from being genuine (Pavlika, 2019), failure to disclose brand sponsorships has led to some influencers being labeled as inauthentic, resulting in backlash (Raedts, 2019). To combat such inauthenticity in the industry, the US FTC guidelines have been strictly enforced to disclose any sponsored relationship between the sponsored post and influencer (Federal Trade Commission, 2017). In an effort to ensure that the influencer marketing continues its upward trend, industry experts argue that in order for the industry to protect its "authenticity appeal," transparency must be the solution to the problem (Pavlika, 2019). On Instagram, when influencers upload a sponsored post, the underlying assumption is that the post is crafted with authenticity, infusing the sponsored post with stronger credibility (Childers et al., 2019). Industry professionals are also careful to note that enhanced authenticity and credibility stem from the nature of the relationship between influencers and consumers. In a traditional celebrity endorsement, celebrities endorse from the perspective of a brand, but in influencer marketing, the information is presented as the individual's personal opinion, which is delivered to those who actively follow the influencer. This can also instill and strengthen a sense of trust between the consumer and the brand via the relationship between the consumer and the influencer. Then, in order to arouse feelings of authenticity in influencer marketing, the marketing strategy must embody trust (Brown et al., 2003).

### 6.3.2 *Trust*

Importance of trust and satisfaction in relationship development has been well-recognized in marketing literature (Bloemer & Kasper, 1995; Delgado-Ballester & Munuera-Alemán, 2001; Hess & Story, 2005). In the early stages of trust in marketing research, scholars identified trust as being rooted in customer satisfaction, therefore leading many to believe that satisfaction, not trust, was a key determinant of consumer behavior (Bloemer & Kasper, 1995). Over time, however, scholars learned that although satisfaction is important, satisfaction derived from transactional relationship with a brand does not help brands to build ongoing, enduring relationships with consumers because it is not founded on trust (Hess & Story, 2005). Trust in a person is regarded as sense of security in another built on the assumption that the other person's actions are altruistically guided with best interest at heart (Chaudhuri & Holbrook, 2001). It also denotes upkeep of promises, therefore lowering any risk in development of relationship, resulting in a valuable relationship. Thus, in order to build a true relationship that extends beyond shallowness, functionality, and simple transactions, relationships must be built on trust.

Trust is inherent in all meaningful social interactions (Delgado-Ballester & Munuera-Alemán, 2001). It is a multidimensional construct and encompasses elements of reliability and brand intentions (Chaudhuri & Holbrook, 2001), commitment (Hess & Story, 2005; Morgan & Hunt, 1994), and credibility (Lee et al., 2011). Reliability is conceptualized as a brand's capacity to meet the consumers' needs, thus a performative element, whereas brand intentions is an affective and emotional dimension of trust (Chaudhuri & Holbrook, 2001). Commitment is integral to building ongoing relationships. Regardless of the relationship type, those in committed relationships will devote the highest level of effort to ensure longevity and security of the relationship (Morgan & Hunt, 1994). People value the relationship because the relationship creates value for them, thus increasing desire to invest efforts to preserve the relationship. Its emphasis on relationship preservation makes it a major pillar of relationship marketing. In today's complex and cluttered media environment, consumers need a way to evaluate credibility of the message source. Evaluating a source's credibility refers to evaluating its believability, underpinned by perceived trustworthiness and expertise of the source delivering the message (Hovland et al., 1953; Metzger & Flanagin, 2013). Prior to the digital age, message sources were limited to a select few, those characterized by formal education or relevant experiences which served as a credibility signifier (Metzger & Flanagin, 2013). Currently, in the digital age, many message sources do not come with such signifiers, making it difficult to build credibility, and, consequently, trust, between brands and consumers. However, riding on the quality of authenticity, certain influencers have a better chance of cultivating trust.

Dimensions of trust are especially important in uncertain situations because it mitigates the consumer's perceived risk and vulnerability posed by a situation (Chaudhuri & Holbrook, 2001). In consumption situations, reliability, brand intentions, commitment, and credibility operate together to help consumers evaluate the message source, potentially saving them from making regrettable choices. Traditionally, media channels acted as a trustworthy information source, but misinformation has given rise to media mistrust among consumers, causing confusion among marketers in selecting the best media channels to deliver their advertising messages. In this scenario, marketers had the opportunity to utilize social media influencers as an alternative media channel embodying trust. This new media channel had a voice that could speak directly to customers, which could lower resistance to a traditional form of advertising tactics and potentially build relationships. As such, trust is instrumental in relationship marketing, especially for building enduring relationships between consumers and brands.

In an industry built on authentic relationships, trust is vital to the relationship that consumers build with influencers as it leads to a stronger, enduring relationship between the consumer and brand. Industry reports have made a case for influencers who are like friends who provide authentic, honest opinions (Twomey, 2020), an opinion which has also been mirrored in academic research (Mudambi & Schuff, 2010). Recent data show that consumers trust influencers more than traditional celebrities (Chiang, 2018) and point to influencers as being a trustworthy information source in the purchase decision journey (Digital Marketing Institute, n.d.). Given the centrality of trust in building relationships, some industry cases help to highlight the unforeseen, negative impact that can shroud the practice when trust is violated. One such case is popular Instagrammer, Marissa Casey Fuchs, who uploaded a series of Instagram posts and stories of her trip around the world, which culminated in a surprise marriage proposal. The surprise proposal, as it turns out, had previously been pitched to numerous brands for sponsorship opportunities (Lorenz, 2019), which became evident when a pitch deck created by her boyfriend was released on the Internet. This prompted major backlash online, making consumers call them "sociopaths", and sarcastically wishing them well in their "farce" (Jennings, 2019). A dishonest and insincere campaign violated the trust Fuchs' followers placed in the influencer, causing many to question her authenticity.

Other examples also help to showcase the outcome of trust dissolution between influencers and followers. As a notorious example of an influencer marketing fail, Fyre Festival in the US came to be known as a cautionary tale for brands who collaborate with social media influencers. With a sweeping social media campaign promoting a luxury music festival with a chance to party with influencers, customers paid for tickets as high as $100,000 to attend a music festival (Baggs, 2019). However, event planning began to unravel as disorganization and time constraint overtook the event, resulting in a chaos where festival goers slept on the ground and ate sandwiches out of Styrofoam boxes. For those who invested time and money for a once-in-a-lifetime experience, the promise was not kept. Trust that the event organization would provide them with a luxury experience was broken. Furthermore, event organizers had leveraged the network and trust of influencers' followers, which also threatened the relationship between influencers and their followers. The festival resulted in a lawsuit against the organization, as well as few megainfluencers, such as Kendall Jenner, who promoted the event. As the events show, the negative impact lasted long after the event ended.

As influencer marketing continues to grow, more cautionary tales will emerge and brand marketers must take precautions to only make promises they can keep to maintain long-lasting relationships with consumers. As Brown et al. (2003) point out, a marketing strategy must embody trust in order to appear authentic. This implies that consumers trust SMIs because they perceive them to be authentic, suggesting that authenticity and trust are inextricably linked concepts in better understanding the impact of influencer marketing.

### 6.3.3 Engagement

Engagement has often been explored in organizational behavior literature to better predict financial performance. This body of research has shown that a better engaged workforce results in better performance with customers, which then results in higher customer satisfaction and loyalty. In the realm of organizational behavior, engagement has been widely researched, but in marketing literature, it is a relative newcomer (Hollebeek, 2011a). Hollebeek's (2014) review of engagement conceptualization across various disciplines shows that engagement arises out of two-way interaction between the subject (the consumer) and object (brand), is individual-specific, motivational, and context-dependent. In addition, engagement is dynamic in nature, meaning it can vary in strength and may also change over time. Other definitions in consumer literature also point out the importance of interactivity and co-creation of value (Brodie et al., 2011), as well as involvement (Hollebeek, 2011b) as key antecedents to engagement.

As its various conceptualizations show, engagement is multidimensional and is comprised of cognitive, emotional, and behavioral components (Hollebeek, 2011a, 2011b). High consumer brand engagement can yield many positive benefits for brands, such as higher brand performative outcomes, that is, increase in sales, word of mouth, and profitability (Nambisan & Baron, 2007). Simply put, strong consumer engagement will result in favorable outcomes in a brand's relationship-building efforts. In the digital sphere, engagement has especially been an important topic of discussion. One of the ways in which brands can build engagement is through facilitating consumer brand interactivity. Interactivity has long been touted as a major benefit of the Internet because of its ability to facilitate two-way communication not only between brand and consumers, but also between individual consumers (Goldfarb & Tucker, 2011). Moreover, studies show that higher interactivity, such as asking questions or inducing clicks through hyperlinks, can lead to more likes and comments on social media posts, leading to higher popularity (de Vries et al., 2012). Thus, two-way, active, interactive communication between consumer and brand is essential in effective engagement (Hollebeek, 2011a). Social media researchers also echo similar opinion by arguing that relationships rooted in strong interactivity between consumers and social media can also lead to stronger trust (Cheung et al., 2020; Dennis et al., 2009). In other words, engagement that enhances the emotional bond between influencers and followers is likely to contribute to the degree of influence.

YouTube and Instagram have unique features that make them ideal platforms for better engagement and influencer marketing. Namely, YouTube's like, subscribe, comment, and share features provide a space for users to not only engage with the creator, but also with other users (Khan, 2017). Similarly, Instagram's like and comment features create an environment in which users and creators can build relationships. One of the ways in which YouTube has been able to drive engagement among its users is due to the active participatory, rather than passive consumption, nature of the platform (Khan, 2017). This characteristic gives users an opportunity to become content consumers, as well as content creators, further reinforcing the horizontal flow of influence exhibited in social media.

One could argue the practice of influencer marketing and popularity of SMIs were built on social media's interactivity features. However, as influencer marketing becomes increasingly commonplace in today's marketing industry, today's marketers should try to unveil more effective ways to increase engagement that go beyond platform features, such as clicks and likes. Although likes and comments are an immediate and quantifiable gauge of a consumer's engagement, it does not do much to reveal the long-term, enduring impact of the engagement on relationship building. One of the defining features of influencer marketing is its ability to promote advertising messages under the guise of being non-promotional messages from authentic, genuine people who seamlessly integrate promotional content into their social media feed. Promotional messages woven into the lives of social media influencers is, in many ways, a form of storytelling, which has the power to stimulate human emotions, engage the audience more, thus increase the message's persuasiveness. These are essential elements of effective influencer marketing that should not be overlooked. The power of influencer marketing lies in crafting covert advertising messages, which are delivered by real-life people who tell authentic stories. Conveying authenticity through storytelling is not an easy task; however, if done right, it has the power to build affective engagement, giving marketers the opportunity to build enduring relationships with consumers.

### 6.3.4 Relationships

In the words of a 19-year-old avid social media user, a disingenuous or dishonest sponsored post could signal the end of a relationship with a social media influencer (Oriola, 2019). In the mind of this 19-year-old, sponsored social media posts pose no risk to the influencer's authenticity, leading her to justify the sponsorship as "everyone must make a living." This sentiment reflects much of the discussion already presented in this chapter regarding authenticity in influencer marketing. Consumer behavior research findings show that consumers who closely identify with brands activate their defensive response when the brand is under threat (Cheng et al., 2012; Lisjak et al., 2012). For these consumers, a threat to the brand is a threat to their identity and self-concept, which is likely to lead consumers to engage in mental processing to lessen the perceived threat to their self-concept. Simply put, the brand is the self and the self is the brand. This strong consumer brand relationship is the type of relationship that marketers strive to develop, but the road to such relationships is not always smooth. In the industry, one of the ways in which marketers try to achieve this relationship is through influencer marketing. A major objective for marketers who engage in influencer marketing is to leverage the influencer's authenticity to build a strong relationship founded on trust. In academia, the research objective boils down to identifying antecedents that help marketers to build better relationships with their consumers. One of these antecedents that has already been explored in influencer marketing research is parasocial interaction and relationship.

Parasocial relationship is not a new research topic when it comes to understanding people's relationships with others (Young, 2017). Parasocial relationship arises out of parasocial interaction, a conversational, interpersonal interaction that audiences develop with media figures during viewing (Horton & Richard Wohl, 1956). While media consumption takes place, viewers may begin to develop a sense of friend-like, interpersonal relationship with the media performer, which may continue to develop off-screen. During this time, post-exposure, the viewer evaluates and analyzes the media performer's actions and if the viewer accepts the performer's actions, the relationship is likely to continue off-screen, resulting in an enduring relationship, known as parasocial relationship (Rubin & McHugh, 1987). Although parasocial interaction and relationship are closely related concepts, parasocial researchers voice caution by pointing out that they are distinctively different concepts (Dibble, et al., 2016). In larger sense, both concepts refer to a psychological phenomenon that media audiences experience during and after media viewing. Parasocial research has been useful in advancing existing academic knowledge in why certain viewers express extreme sadness over the finale of TV series like *Friends* or build an enormous fan base centered around fictional characters, like Harry Potter. In marketing, studies show that parasocial interaction can result in an increase in likelihood of impulse purchase (Park & Lennon, 2004) and an increase in endorser credibility through self-disclosure and perceived friendship (Chung & Cho, 2014). In recent years, parasocial research has evolved from studying large screen media figures to online personalities that people interact with via smaller, personalized screens. The younger generation's media consumption behavior has largely contributed to this shift, along with rising popularity of social media and reality TV shows, such as *Keeping up with the Kardashians*.

Nowadays, social media influencers wield much power and influence over their following. In a digitally driven marketing environment, social media marketing research adopted an established body of parasocial research to extend existing literature in various research topics, such as celebrity endorsement (Chung & Cho, 2017; Rasmussen, 2018), electronic word of mouth and persuasion knowledge (Hwang & Zhang, 2018), and source credibility (Yuan & Lou, 2020). Another stream of fruitful parasocial research in influencer marketing has been around YouTube personalities or, simply, YouTubers. Development of parasocial interaction between YouTubers and viewers has been confirmed by Sokolova & Kefi (2019), and also by Rasmussen (2018). Chen (2016) and Kurtin et al. (2018) also showed that YouTube users also developed parasocial relationships with YouTube personalities.

Study of parasocial phenomenon in the digital age is a relevant topic of research as perceived closeness and intimacy is amplified through two-way interaction (Click et al., 2013). In the early stages of parasocial research, the direction of interaction was one-way, flowing from media figure to viewer. In the digital age, however, a line between real and imaginary cannot be as easily drawn since social media has made two-way interaction possible. Once deemed unapproachable figures, celebrities' own Instagram accounts became increasingly popular as they share details of their personal lives, closing the perceived gap between followers and the celebrities. In essence, SMIs are a channel through which brands communicate with their target audiences (Yuan & Lou, 2020). This communication channel is unique because it facilitates two-way interaction, which can enhance brands' messages. As boundaries between real and imaginary interpersonal relationships become more blurred and SMIs continue to become prominent public figures, SMI-centered parasocial interactions and relationship development could be a relevant topic of discussion in relationship marketing.

## 6.4  Path to influence

Influence is a vital component of decision making. According to Cialdini (2007), consumers tend to seek out mental shortcuts that ease the burden of decision making. One of the ways in which people ease this burden is through relying on stereotypes, such as "this brand must be worth using if this celebrity is endorsing it." In fact, it would not be an understatement to claim that the success of celebrity endorsement hinges on this key premise. This concept is also applicable to influencer marketing. In order to ease the mental burden of making a purchase decision, it can be posited that consumers are likely to rely on the opinion of online influencers. For example, with the number of followers and subscribers stated on SMIs social media accounts, consumers may use the follower number as an indicator of the influencer's credibility. From a marketer's standpoint, the number of followers is often used as an SMI identifier (de Veirman et al., 2017) and brands can cast a wider net via an influencer with a high follower count. However, scholars are careful to point out that a high follower count does not automatically guarantee marketing success and calls attention to the challenges of choosing the best influencer to suit communication objectives (Breves et al., 2019). In other words, simple exposure does not automatically equal influence and mass appeal does not equal persuasiveness. As discussed, the path to influence is complex and dynamic, impacted by the factors like engagement, trust, authenticity, and relationship.

Although influence is central to the practice of influencer marketing, the path of influence from an SMI to followers is not as clearly explicated. In public relations research, some attempt has been made to better understand the path to influence. Men and Tsai (2014) demonstrated that better engaged followers of organizations' social media pages reported a stronger relationship with the organization. Moreover, their findings suggest that higher authenticity, via transparency, leads to higher trust and mutual influence, resulting in higher commitment and satisfaction. Their results imply that path to influence may not necessarily be linear; in fact, influence may not be the outcome of a consumer-influencer relationship. Based on their findings, influence is a mediating variable on the path to stronger commitment and satisfaction. A major benefit of influencer marketing is higher authenticity and engagement, allowing consumers to take the mental shortcut they seek during brand consumption. In the path to influence, social media influencers can be the intermediary for influence through their authenticity and trust, leading to stronger relationship outcomes between consumers and brands.

## 6.5 Conclusion

Social media has changed the way brands reach their audiences. Prior to social media, advertising messages flowed from brands to consumers in a one-way communication, but the rise of social media platforms, like YouTube and Instagram, has made it possible for marketers and advertisers to communicate with consumers in new, innovative ways. One of these approaches has been through influencer marketing, a marketing strategy centered around key individuals with large social following, thus increasing the potential to reach wider audiences more effectively. There is ample evidence of the positive outcomes of influencer marketing; however, there is still much to learn about the underlying drivers of influencer marketing. In this changing marketing communication environment, brands must also be careful in considering the best method for executing influencer marketing campaigns. A major strength of social media lies in its ability to facilitate engagement, leading to co-creation of value (Brodie et al., 2011). Until now, marketers' main focus in influencer marketing has been on driving engagement and sales. However, as modern-day marketing has shifted toward relationship marketing (Morgan & Hunt, 1994), for influencer marketing to become a marketing staple, the practice will benefit from unearthing various ways to build stronger and long-lasting relationships with consumers.

As discussed in this chapter, authentic identity is the foundation of influencer marketing. It is centered around the idea that a person is true to oneself and does not conform to ideals that do not align with one's values (Kristinsson, 2007). Authentic identity has been the guiding principle in influencer marketing, with numerous industry experts identifying it as key variable in the successful outcome of influencer marketing. In spite of its importance, conceptual, academic understanding of the role of authentic identity, thus enabling marketers a methodological approach to influencer marketing, has yet to be accomplished. To compensate for such a shortcoming, this chapter explored homophily and social identity as possible antecedents to authentic identity. Homophily rests on the idea that similarity leads to attraction. Once this attraction is established, in-group membership can be formed, further reinforcing perceived likeness and similarity on which the homophily was founded. This membership also constructs one's social identity, helping to express an individual's identity in relation to others.

In addition to addressing the social context of influencer marketing, the chapter also focused on the individual, affective level of consumers' connection with social media influencers. Parasocial interaction and relationships have already been adopted as mediating the relationship between consumers and influencers. As the concept revolves around the idea of developing interpersonal relationships with media figures, the concept helps to tap into affective dimensions of what drives influence in influencer marketing. Enabled by the interactive features of social media, engagement is also a salient driver of success in influencer marketing. The different variables explored in this chapter, authenticity, parasocial interaction, and engagement help to instill a sense of trust in social media influencers. In a cluttered consumer marketplace, consumers need a signifier for credibility, expertise, and trustworthiness that help to reduce mental risks associated with brand consumption. For many consumers seeking ways to reduce the uncertainty, social media influencers can provide the trust that people need to feel safe about their decisions. With influencer marketing continuously growing and fast becoming a staple in digital marketing practices, understanding consumer motivations and outcomes of engaging with social media influencers will help to not only advance academic research in influencer marketing, but also provide marketers a more methodological approach to leveraging influence of social media influencers.

# References

Abidin, C. (2016). Visibility labour: Engaging with Influencers' fashion brands and# OOTD advertorial campaigns on Instagram. *Media International Australia*, 161(1), 86–100.

Aslam, S. (2020a). Instagram by the numbers: Stats, demographics & fun facts. *Omnicore*. https://www.omnicoreagency.com/instagram-statistics/#:~:text=There%20are%20 500%2C000%20active%20influencers,to%20reach%20%2414%20billion%20dollars

Aslam, S. (2020b). YouTube by the numbers: Stats. demographics & fun facts. *Omnicore*. https://www.omnicoreagency.com/youtube-statistics/#:~:text=Most%20popular%20 YouTube%20channel%20has,since%20Content%20ID%20was%20implemented

Baggs, M. (2019, January 18). Fyre festival: Inside the world's biggest festival flop. *BBC News*. https://www.bbc.com/news/newsbeat-46904445

Balaban, D.-C., & Mustăţea, M. (2019). Users' perspective on the credibility of social media influencers in Romania and Germany. *Romanian Journal of Communication and Public Relations*, 21(1), 31–46. https://www.ceeol.com/search/article-detail?id=801006

Beverland, M., & Luxton, S. (2005). Managing integrated marketing communication (IMC) through strategic decoupling: How luxury wine firms retain brand leadership while appearing to be wedded to the past. *Journal of Advertising*, 34(4), 103–116.

Bloemer, J. M., & Kasper, H. D. (1995). The complex relationship between consumer satisfaction and brand loyalty. *Journal of economic psychology*, 16(2), 311–329.

Breves, P. L., Liebers, N., Abt, M., & Kunze, A. (2019). The perceived fit between Instagram influencers and the endorsed brand: How influencer–brand fit affects source credibility and persuasive effectiveness. *Journal of Advertising Research*, 59(4), 440–454.

Brodie, R. J., Hollebeek, L. D., Jurić, B., & Ilić, A. (2011). Customer engagement: Conceptual domain, fundamental propositions, and implications for research. *Journal of service research*, 14(3), 252–271.

Brown, S., Kozinets, R. V., & Sherry, J. F. (2003). Teaching old brands new tricks: Retro branding and the revival of brand meaning. *Journal of Marketing*, 67(3), 19–33.

Bump, P. (2019). 5 new social media platforms marketers should watch in 2020. *Hubspot*. https://blog.hubspot.com/marketing/new-social-media

Carter, B. (2018, January 27). Elle walker net worth 2018. *Gazette Review*. https://gazetter-eview.com/2018/01/elle-walker-net-worth/

Chaudhuri, A., & Holbrook, M. B. (2001). The chain of effects from brand trust and brand affect to brand performance: The role of brand loyalty. *Journal of Marketing*, 65(2), 81–93.

Chen, C. P. (2016). Forming digital self and parasocial relationships on YouTube. *Journal of Consumer Culture*, 16(1), 232–254.

Cheng, S. Y., White, T. B., & Chaplin, L. N. (2012). The effects of self-brand connections on responses to brand failure: A new look at the consumer–brand relationship. *Journal of Consumer Psychology*, 22(2), 280–288.

Cheung, M. L., Pires, G., Rosenberger, P. J., & De Oliverira, M. J. (2020). Driving consumer–brand engagement and co-creation by brand interactivity. *Marketing Intelligence & Planning*, 38(4), 523–541.

Chi, H. H. (2011). Interactive digital advertising vs. virtual brand community: Exploratory study of user motivation and social media marketing responses in Taiwan. *Journal of Interactive Advertising*, 12(1), 44–61.

Chiang, J. Y. L. (2018, January 30). Influencer marketing latest trends & best practices: 2018 report. *Musefind*. https://blog.musefind.com/influencer-marketing-latest-trends-best-practices-2018-report-a508540ad625

Chung, S., & Cho, H. (2014). Parasocial relationship via reality TV and social media: Its implications for celebrity endorsement. *Proceedings of the ACM International Conference on Interactive Experiences for TV and Online Video*, 47–54.

Chung, S., & Cho, H. (2017). Fostering parasocial relationships with celebrities on social media: Implications for celebrity endorsement. *Psychology & Marketing*, 34(4), 481–495.

Cialdini, R. B. (2007). *Influence: The psychology of persuasion* (Vol. 55, p. 339). New York: Collins.

Click, M. A., Lee, H., & Holladay, H. W. (2013). Making monsters: Lady Gaga, fan identification, and social media. *Popular Music and Society*, 36(3), 360–379.

Constine, J. (2016). Instagram launches "Stories," a Snapchatty feature for imperfect sharing. *Tech Crunch*. https://techcrunch.com/2016/08/02/instagram-stories/?guccounter=1&guce_referrer=aHR0cHM6Ly93d3cuZ29vZ2xlLmNvbS8&guce_referrer_sig=AQAAAJrrfDDvkSQFME4HhEtAEDF8zNPe1KWy9_d7GV0w6SuJOV-Vp73RhEOWsVMDKcyjrk5Wz-ES6yY_H1gBvSnk56K0G5G0sYVS40-kTiqd7VYToW1dqjtN4O45fJLTbmSTnhqtqIm8HTRip-Pem0RPHtT0ftiEGw7h52v0_Lrk0dkCv

De Veirman, M., Cauberghe, V., & Hudders, L. (2017). Marketing through Instagram influencers: The impact of number of followers and product divergence on brand attitude. *International Journal of Advertising*, 36(5), 798–828.

De Vries, L., Gensler, S., & Leeflang, P. S. (2012). Popularity of brand posts on brand fan pages: An investigation of the effects of social media marketing. *Journal of Interactive Marketing*, 26(2), 83–91.

Delgado-Ballester, E., & Munuera-Alemán, J. L. (2001). Brand trust in the context of consumer loyalty. *European Journal of marketing*, 35(11), 1238–1258.

Dennis, C., Merrilees, B., Jayawardhena, C., & Tiu Wright, L. (2009), "E-consumer behaviour", *European Journal of Marketing*, 43(9/10), 1121–1139.

Dhanesh, G. S., & Duthler, G. (2019). Relationship management through social media influencers: Effects of followers' awareness of paid endorsement. Public Relations Review, 45(3). https://doi.org/10.1016/j.pubrev.2019.03.002

Dhillon, S. (2018). How Instagram is eating the world. *Forbes*. https://www.forbes.com/sites/valleyvoices/2018/06/25/how-instagram-is-eating-the-world/#740f9b223145

Dibble, J. L., Hartmann, T., & Rosaen, S. F. (2016). Parasocial interaction and parasocial relationship: Conceptual clarification and a critical assessment of measures. *Human Communication Research*, 42(1), 21–44.

Digital Marketing Institute (n.d.). 20 influencer marketing statistics that will Surprise You. *DMI Blog*. https://digitalmarketinginstitute.com/blog/20-influencer-marketing-statistics-that-will-surprise-you

Dimock, M. (2019). Defining generations: Where millennials and generation Z begins. *Pew Research Center*. https://www.pewresearch.org/fact-tank/2019/01/17/where-millennials-end-and-generation-z-begins/

Droesch, B. (2019, December 10). Influencers could help drive social commerce. *AdWeek*. https://www.emarketer.com/content/influencers-could-help-drive-social-commerce

Ellemers, N., Spears, R., & Doosje, B. (2002). Self and social identity. *Annual review of psychology*, 53(1), 161–186.

Ellison, N. B., Steinfield, C., & Lampe, C. (2007). The benefits of Facebook "friends:" Social capital and college students' use of online social network sites. *Journal of Computer-Mediated Communication*, 12(4), 1143–1168.

Enberg, J. (2018, July 31). Marketers around the world are banking on microinfluencers. Except in China, where macroinfluencers still dominate. *eMarketer*. https://www.emarketer.com/content/why-marketers-are-banking-on-microinfluencers

Federal Trade Commission. (2016). FTC's Lord & Taylor case: In native advertising, clear disclosure is always in style. https://www.ftc.gov/news-events/blogs/business-blog/2016/03/ftcs-lord-taylor-case-native-advertising-clear-disclosure

Federal Trade Commission. (2017). *Guides Concerning the Use of Endorsements and Testimonials in Advertising*. https://www.ftc.gov/sites/default/files/attachments/press-releases/ftc-publishes-final-guides-governing-endorsements-testimonials/091005revisedendorsementguides.pdf

Frier, S., & Grant, N. (2020). Instagram brings in more than a quarter of Facebook sales. *Bloomberg*. https://www.bloomberg.com/news/articles/2020-02-04/instagram-generates-more-than-a-quarter-of-facebook-s-sales

Goldfarb, A., & Tucker, C. (2011). Online display advertising: Targeting and obtrusiveness. *Marketing Science*, 30(30), 389–404.

Gunawan, D. D., & Huarng, K. H. (2015). Viral effects of social network and media on consumers' purchase intention. *Journal of Business Research*, 68(11), 2237–2241.

Hanna, R., Rohm, A., & Crittenden, V. L. (2011). We're all connected: The power of the social media ecosystem. *Business Horizons*, 54(3), 265–273.

Hess, J., & Story, J. (2005). Trust-based commitment: Multidimensional consumer-brand relationships. *Journal of Consumer Marketing*, 22(6), 313–322.

Hollebeek, L. (2011a). Exploring customer brand engagement: Definition and themes. *Journal of Strategic Marketing*, 19(7), 555–573.

Hollebeek, L. D. (2011b). Demystifying customer brand engagement: Exploring the loyalty nexus. *Journal of Marketing Management*, 27(7–8), 785–807.

Hollebeek, L. D., Glynn, M. S., & Brodie, R. J. (2014). Consumer brand engagement in social media: Conceptualization, scale development and validation. *Journal of Interactive Marketing*, 28(2), 149–165.

Horton, D., & Richard Wohl, R. (1956). Mass communication and para-social interaction: Observations on intimacy at a distance. *Psychiatry*, 19(3), 215–229.

Hovland, C. I., Janis, I. L., & Kelley, H. H. (1953). *Communication and persuasion: Psychological studies of opinion change*. New Haven: Yale University Press.

Hwang, K., & Zhang, Q. (2018). Influence of parasocial relationship between digital celebrities and their followers on followers' purchase and electronic word-of-mouth intentions, and persuasion knowledge. *Computers in Human Behavior*, 87, 155–173.

Influencer Intelligence (2019). What consumers think about influencer marketing. *Excellence in Marketing*. https://www.influencerintelligence.com/insights/24/What-Consumers-Think-About-Influencer-Marketing

Influencer Marketing Hub (2020, June 15). 80 influencer marketing statistics for 2020. *Influencer Marketing Hub*. https://influencermarketinghub.com/influencer-marketing-statistics/

Iqbal, M. (2020). TikTok revenue and usage statistics (2020). *Business of Apps*. https://www.businessofapps.com/data/tik-tok-statistics/

Jennings, R. (2019). This viral "surprise" proposal shows the less glamorous side of influencing. *Vox*. https://www.vox.com/the-goods/2019/6/20/18693440/fashion-ambitionist-proposal-marissa-casey-fuchs-engagement

Jin, S. V., & Muqaddam, A. (2019). Product placement 2.0: "Do brands need influencers, or do influencers need brands?". *Journal of Brand Management*, 26(5), 522–537.

Jin, S. V., Muqaddam, A., & Ryu, E. (2019). Instafamous and social media influencer marketing. *Marketing Intelligence & Planning*, 37(5), 567–579.

Johnson, M. (2019, March 14). Different types of YouTube influencer video content. *Power Digital Marketing*. https://powerdigitalmarketing.com/blog/different-types-of-youtube-influencer-video-content/#gref

Kandel, D. B. (1978). Homophily, selection, and socialization in adolescent friendships. *American Journal of Sociology*, 84(2), 427–436.

Keller, E., & Berry, J. (2003). *The influentials: One American in ten tells the other Nine how to vote, where to eat, and what to buy.* New York: The Free Press.

Khamis, S., Ang, L., & Welling, R. (2017). Self-branding, 'micro-celebrity' and the rise of Social Media Influencers. *Celebrity Studies*, 8(2), 191–208.

Khan, M. L. (2017). Social media engagement: What motivates user participation and consumption on YouTube?. *Computers in Human Behavior*, 66, 236–247.

Knoll, J. (2016). Advertising in social media: A review of empirical evidence. *International Journal of Advertising*, 35(2), 266–300.

Koivisto, E., & Mattila, P. (2018). Extending the luxury experience to social media–user-generated content co-creation in a branded event. *Journal of Business Research*, 117, 570–578.

Kossinets, G., & Watts, D. J. (2009). Origins of homophily in an evolving social network. *American Journal of Sociology*, 115(2), 405–450.

Kozlowska, H. (2019, June 1). Can influencers and authenticity ever be compatible? *Quartz*. https://qz.com/1632589/can-influencers-ever-be-authentic/

Kristinsson, S. (2007). Authenticity, identity, and fidelity to self. *Hommage à Wlodek. Philosophical Papers Dedicated to Wlodek Rabinowicz*, 1–32.

Kurtin, K. S., O'Brien, N., Roy, D., & Dam, L. (2018). The development of parasocial interaction relationships on YouTube. *The Journal of Social Media in Society*, 7(1), 233–252.

Lee, C., Kim, J., & Chan-Olmsted, S. (2011). Branded product information search on the web: The role of brand trust and credibility of online information sources. *Journal of Marketing Communications*, 17(5), 355–374.

Lee, E., Lee, J. A., Moon, J. H., & Sung, Y. (2015). Pictures speak louder than words: Motivations for using Instagram. *Cyberpsychology, Behavior, and Social Networking*, 18(9), 552–556.

Lisjak, M., Lee, A. Y., & Gardner, W. L. (2012). When a threat to the brand is a threat to the self: The importance of brand identification and implicit self-esteem in predicting defensiveness. *Personality and Social Psychology Bulletin*, 38(9), 1120–1132.

Lorenz, T. (2019, June). Welcome to the Era of branded engagements: An influencer's "surprise adventure" was apparently pitched to brands months before it even began. *The Atlantic*. https://www.theatlantic.com/technology/archive/2019/06/was-viral-proposal-staged/592141/

Lou, C., & Yuan, S. (2019). Influencer marketing: How message value and credibility affect consumer trust of branded content on social media. *Journal of Interactive Advertising*, 19(1), 58–73.

Malcolm, H. (2016, March 15). Lord & Taylor settles FTC charges over paid Instagram posts. *USA Today*. https://www.usatoday.com/story/money/2016/03/15/lord--taylor-settles-ftc-charges-over-paid-instagram-posts/81801972/

McCroskey, J. C., Richmond, V. P., & Daly, J. A. (1975). The development of a measure of perceived homophily in interpersonal communication. *Human Communication Research*, 1(4), 323–332.

McPherson, M., Smith-Lovin, L., & Cook, J. M. (2001). Birds of a feather: Homophily in social networks. *Annual review of sociology*, 27(1), 415–444.

Media Kix (2019). Case study: Dunkin' Donuts brews success with nano-influencers. *Media Kix.* https://mediakix.com/blog/dunkin-donuts-nano-influencer-marketing-case-study-instagram/

Men, L. R., & Tsai, W. H. S. (2014). Perceptual, attitudinal, and behavioral outcomes of organization–public engagement on corporate social networking sites. *Journal of Public Relations Research*, 26(5), 417–435.

Metzger, M. J., & Flanagin, A. J. (2013). Credibility and trust of information in online environments: The use of cognitive heuristics. *Journal of Pragmatics*, 59, 210–220.

Morgan, R. M., & Hunt, S. D. (1994). The commitment-trust theory of relationship marketing. *Journal of Marketing*, 58(3), 20–38.

Morgan Stanley (2019, August 16). How a 'Youth Boom' could shake up spending trend. https://www.morganstanley.com/ideas/gen-z-millennials-set-for-consumer-spending-increases

Morning Consult (2019, November). The influencer report: Engaging Gen Z and millennials. An in-depth guide to how younger Americans interact with the new class of cultural tastemakers. *Morning Consult.* https://morningconsult.com/influencer-report-engaging-gen-z-and-millennials/

Mudambi, S. M., & Schuff, D. (2010). What makes a helpful review? A study of customer reviews on Amazon.com. *MIS Q*, 34(1), 185–200.

Nambisan, S., & Baron, R. A. (2007). Interactions in virtual customer environments: Implications for product support and customer relationship management. *Journal of interactive marketing*, 21(2), 42–62.

Napoli, J., Dickinson, S. J., Beverland, M. B., & Farrelly, F. (2014). Measuring consumer-based brand authenticity. *Journal of Business Research*, 67(6), 1090–1098.

Nazerali, S. (2017, October). How YouTube influencers are rewriting the marketing rulebook. *Think with Google.* https://www.thinkwithgoogle.com/marketing-strategies/video/youtube-influencer-marketing-rulebook/

Newberry, C. (2019, October 22). 37 Instagram stats that matter to marketers in 2020. *Hootsuite.* https://blog.hootsuite.com/instagram-statistics/

O'Neil-Hart, C., & Blumenstein, H. (2016, July). Why YouTube stars are more influential than traditional celebrities. *Think with Google.* https://www.thinkwithgoogle.com/marketing-strategies/video/youtube-stars-influence/

Oriola, S. (2019, July 29). How is influencer market changing? *Quora.* https://www.quora.com/profile/Steve-Oriola

Pan, Z., Lu, Y., Wang, B., & Chau, P. (2017). Who do you think you are? Common and differential effects of social self-identity on social media usage. *Journal of Management and Information Systems*, 34(1), 71–101.

Park, J. H., & Lennon, S. J. (2004). Television apparel shopping: Impulse buying and parasocial interaction. *Clothing and Textiles Research Journal*, 22(3), 135–144.

Pavlika, H. (2019, July 23). Can a lack of authenticity kill influencer marketing? *Ad Age.* https://adage.com/article/industry-insights/can-lack-authenticity-kill-influencer-marketing/2185076#:~:text=Authenticity%20means%20giving%20the%20product%20or%20service%20context.&text=Authenticity%20comes%20from%20being%20genuine,personal%20brand%20they%20are%20creating

Pearl, D. (2019, August 23). 75% of Estée Lauder's marketing budget is going to digital—and influencers. *AdWeek.* https://www.adweek.com/brand-marketing/75-of-estee-lauders-marketing-budget-is-going-to-influencers/

Raedts, M. (2019, March 29). Taking a stand on authenticity in influencer marketing. *Forbes.* https://www.forbes.com/sites/forbesagencycouncil/2019/03/29/taking-a-stand-on-authenticity-in-influencer-marketing/#6c13fd487270

Ranga, M., & Sharma, D. (2014). Influencer marketing-a marketing tool in the age of social media. *Abhinav International Monthly Refereed Journal of Research in Management & Technology*, 3(8), 16–21.

Rasmussen, L. (2018). Parasocial interaction in the digital age: An examination of relationship building and the effectiveness of YouTube celebrities. *The Journal of Social Media in Society*, 7(1), 280–294.

Rinaldo, S. B., Tapp, S., & Laverie, D. A. (2011). Learning by tweeting: Using Twitter as a pedagogical tool. *Journal of Marketing Education*, 33(2), 193–203.

Rubin, R. B., & McHugh, M. P. (1987). Development of parasocial interaction relationships. *Journal of Broadcasting & Electronic Media*, 31(3), 279–292.

Sokolova, K., & Kefi, H. (2019). Instagram and YouTube bloggers promote it, why should I buy? How credibility and parasocial interaction influence purchase intentions. *Journal of Retailing and Consumer Services.*

Sorkin, A., & Peter, J. (2006). Google to acquire YouTube for $1.65 billion. *New York Times.* https://www.nytimes.com/2006/10/09/business/09cnd-deal.html

Subramani, M. R., & Rajagopalan, B. (2003). Knowledge-sharing and influence in online social networks via viral marketing. *Communications of the ACM*, 46(12), 300–307.

Swant, Marty (2016, May). Twitter says users now trust influencers nearly as much as their friends. *Adweek.* http://www.adweek.com/digital/twitter-saysusers-now-trust-influencers-nearly-much-their-friends171367/

Tabor, E. (2019, December 19). Can you really market to Gen X and baby boomers on social platforms? *Forbes.* https://www.forbes.com/sites/forbesagencycouncil/2019/12/19/can-you-really-market-to-gen-x-and-baby-boomers-on-social-platforms/#684150fa5741

Tajfel, H. (1974). Social identity and intergroup behaviour. *Information (International Social Science Council)*, 13(2), 65–93.

Twomey, K. (2020, January). Opinion: The dishonest and wasteful practice of influencer marketing. *Ad Age.* https://adage.com/article/opinion/opinion-dishonest-and-wasteful-practice-influencer-marketing/2227541

Wagner, K. (2018). 'Stories' was Instagram's smartest move yet. *The Vox.* https://www.vox.com/2018/8/8/17641256/instagram-stories-kevin-systrom-facebook-snapchat

WhatsUpMoms (n.d.). Retrieved from: https://whatsupmoms.com/about-us/

Williams, R. (2020, March 2). Gen Z relies on influencers for purchase decisions, Kantar says. *Mobile Marketer.* https://www.mobilemarketer.com/news/gen-z-relies-on-influencers-for-purchase-decisions-kantar-says/573264/

Williamson, D. A. (2019, March 5). Global influencer marketing 2019. What to know about spending, stories, fraud and microinfluencers. *eMarketer.* https://www.emarketer.com/content/global-influencer-marketing-2019

Wilt, J. A., Thomas, S., & McAdams, D. P. (2019). Authenticity and inauthenticity in narrative identity. *Heliyon*, 5(7), 1–13.

Wiltshire, E. (2018, October 18). Dunkin': A rebranding for the digital age. *Social Media Today.* https://www.socialmediatoday.com/news/dunkin-a-rebranding-for-the-digital-age/539844/

Young, K. (2017, June 14). Why influencer marketing works for Generation Z. *Global Web Index.* https://blog.globalwebindex.com/trends/influencer-marketing/

Yuan, S., & Lou, C. (2020). How social media influencers foster relationships with followers: The roles of source credibility and fairness in parasocial relationship and product interest. *Journal of Interactive Advertising*, 20(2), 133–147.

# 7 How Instagram and YouTube users share news

## Algorithms, monetization and visibility on social media

*Jonathon Hutchinson and Tim Dwyer*

## 7.1 Introduction

As the world makes its way through the COVID-19 pandemic, the increased reliance on networked media has become not only visible but critical infrastructure for our continued engagement with friends, family, colleagues, and our societies more broadly. This moment has also seen the arrival of new platforms of choice through the rise of TikTok during 2020, livestreaming through the likes of TwitchTV and to a lesser extent YouTube and Instagram, and the integration of video conferencing into everyday life through the Zoom platform. The sorts of content that has been shared across these networked, privately-owned platformed spaces has included everyday communication, cultural production, entertainment, and significantly news and information that describes and decodes the worlds that surround us. Yet the way in which these types of content is shared is not from a heterarchical perspective, with many seen and unseen intermediaries at play that both enable and inhibit the distribution of information. This chapter explores the actors and content items that constitute the flow of news especially across YouTube and Instagram, and the conditions under which it is shared.

In each of the platformed scenarios described above, we have observed the clear reintroduction of the delineation between social media users and social media content creators. The phenomenon that scholars had previously observed as holistic social media users that incorporated those who create content and those who use that content (Bruns, 2008; Manovich, 2001), including audiences (Hartley et al., 2013), has seen the demotic turn (Turner, 2010) take yet another shift in its evolutionary cycle. We are now observing an emerging moment in the development of cultural production and distribution from a new era of online content creators who are notably proficient in attracting large audiences to their diverse repertoire of content production, including news media. This sharpening of skills by newcomers to the online content creation space calibrates with the stalwarts of social media who continue to dominate the ratings game. Some key examples that reflect this visibility strategy include collaborations between YouTubers and self-proclaimed entrepreneurs Logan Paul and KSI, musicians and celebrities Machine Gun Kelly with Travis Barker from Blink 182, online gamer MrBeast who collaborated with 600 other YouTubers, and, in the Australian context,

DOI: 10.4324/9781003134176-8

activist and creator Senator Briggs who partnered with Tim Minchin to create content for a mixed audience (Briggs & Minchin, 2020). The online content creators on social media, both new and emerging, are evidence of how their skill sets are being developed to continually respond to technological, societal, and regulatory developments within this space, to ensure increased and sustainable visibility.

This shift in the characteristic of content creators has in part emerged through the affordances of the technology and regulation; but is also emerging as a result of new social media practices that assist in enacting content and user visibility. This can broadly be encapsulated in the phrase *platformization of cultural production* (Nieborg & Poell, 2018), which sees the processes of content creation align with the affordances of platforms. For example, content that is created by popular creators for YouTube is produced with the lure of monetization of attracting larger audiences. Similarly, on Instagram, the potential of having the 'swipe up' function on one's Reels aligns their content creator status with that of those who are able to garner large and engaged audiences. Twitter's recent introduction of a 'Super Followers' program enables users to charge a monthly fee for subscriber-only content; representing a more positive step along the platform's faltering and thus far unsuccessful product path towards their broader monetization goal. A study generating data from a trial of a handpicked cohort of 77 popular accounts suggests that demand is limited, leading one columnist to opine that the successive product and format experiments 'feels as if Twitter is throwing spaghetti on the wall to see what sticks' (Kim, 2021). Yet in these examples we are seeing that, alongside a broad range of instances across other social media platforms, content creators are following the predetermined conventions of these platforms that require them to create, perform, publish, and integrate with the broader platform-determined affordances. In many instances, and by making these further contributions to the functionality of platform affordances, these kinds of platform conventions are significantly automated to cater for the high volume of content that is submitted by content creators; all in an attempt to match content of interest with specific platform audiences.

Within platformization, social media automation has emerged as a significant process, and in many cases as a tool, to coordinate content and audiences, particularly through the use of bots. Content creators are often either integrating the use of automation through bots or are creating 'bot-friendly' content to ensure they make adjustments with this digital form of intermediation. This content production technique has been observed in many spaces, but especially in relation to politics and official government information. The integration of semi-automated bots in social media spaces has been credited with manipulating elections and creating opinions en masse for users (Assenmacher, et al., 2020). While media automation sits alongside the human intervention of content creation and manipulation, there remains a significant role for humans to intermediate conversations based on the design and implementation of these bots (Ford & Hutchinson, 2021). Bots, broadly defined, are the penultimate example of the integration of human with non-human actors that define how media is visible; and thereby also invisible, across the social media spaces we inhabit every day. Yet, while platformization and automation are in place, audience creation through content production remains a joust between those who create the media and those who digitally gatewatch the process – it is a constant negotiation *en plein milieu* between those who make the content and those who see the content.

The emerging field of algorithmic visibility practices has been observing this 'nudge' approach of the platform society for several years (Yeung, 2016). Scholars have noticed the gaming of visibility across platforms that incorporate the inherent politics of power within these spaces (Petre, Duffy & Hund, 2019; Flew, 2021). In terms of influence, Cotter (2018) notes this is a visibility *game* between influencers of social media content and the algorithms they constantly navigate. This is true of news media content, too, which is a distinctively important category of cultural production. In framing this approach as computational news discovery, Diakopolous (2020) notes that there is little left of the news production process that remains untouched by algorithms, including the editorial process. Through the lens of computational news discovery, he notes, 'the use of algorithms to orient editorial attention to potentially newsworthy events or information prior to publication' (p.947), highlighting the central role that algorithms play in content selection and visibility. The selection of content based on algorithms extends further toward broader editorial decision-making processes (Peterson-Salahuddin & Diakopolous, 2020), which in turn will influence how content is created to align with these increasingly automated processes.

The technological affordances and emerging online content production techniques briefly discussed in the introduction provide the backdrop against which users share news on Instagram and YouTube. In this chapter, we provide a detailed overview of the automated media environment that operates beyond the often-referenced work of bots as automatic media producers, and shift towards the holistic approach of the unseen infrastructures of digital intermediation (Hutchinson, 2021). We also highlight some examples of content production techniques that are engaged in by content creators in this space to 'game' these automated and algorithmic-driven social media environments. We then draw on two specific case studies in the Australian and United States contexts that demonstrate the significance of YouTube news producers and the kind of influence they have on audiences. Finally, we highlight how contemporary online content creation on these platforms plays into monetization, piracy, and fake news outside of the existing regulation markers.

## 7.2 Through Platformization Toward Popularity

Popular content emerges when it is shared amongst socially networked users in a viral mode, and whereas Dwyer and Martin (2019) suggest, the key marker is the 'rate, reach and wider significance of news media events on the internet and social media networks or platforms' (p. 258). These authors argue,

> Social media platforms need content to go viral – it's an important element of their business models to encourage people to boost content, and especially content which might signal widespread, commonly held tastes and interests.
>
> (p. 260)

Yet the rate of virality is fundamentally dependent on the visibility of that content in the first instance, which in turn relies on the platformization of our communication processes. It is through platformization and its embedded social media logics that content becomes valuable, visible and indeed shareable. According to Dwyer and Martin,

> News media visibility then accelerates and extends a story's spread, and gives it further legitimacy, ensuring further circulation beyond the original social networks. A loop like this ensures that there is a steady stream of virtual news media events making its way into the news feeds of any platform that uses algorithmic curation. So our choice of which events to share becomes a kind of 'best of' selection, influencing the velocity at which stories diffuse, and the overall reach into the myriad of internet-worked distribution platforms.
>
> (p. 260)

Platformization sits at the core of the impact and manipulation of social media platforms, becoming most obvious in the way that content is not only shared, but also how it is created, published, processed, and distributed. Platformization, according to Nieborg and Poell (2018, p. 4275) is, 'the penetration of economic and infrastructural extensions of online platforms into the web, affecting the production, distribution, and circulation of cultural content'. In these environments, content producers are at the whim of changes that are initiated by the platform providers, which are in a constant state of flux and determined by their business models and corporate directives. As Gillespie (2010) has noted, platforms are located at the intersection point of commerce, regulation, technology, and users, where often the focus on, or perhaps purpose of, the users is determined by the other aspects of commercially oriented platform providers. Arriagada and Ibáñez (2020) note that these sorts of platform disruptions for content creators can be defined in three ways: communicative styles, temporal acceleration, and negotiation with other network actors. They conclude that content creators are continually adapting their practices to accommodate these commercially evolving platform ecologies.

Content creators operating in this environment are then in turn accustomed to these sorts of platformization practices, which inadvertently direct the content they create, and the resultant visibility and consumption rates of their content. It then emerges that there are three stakeholder principal groups engaging in a synchronous content production and visibility dance: the audience, the platform, and the online content creator. Within this platformization moment, if any of these stakeholder groups changes or shifts, the other two stakeholder groups shift and change to accommodate the shift in cultural production approaches. To take a random example, should the audience indicate it wants more content that reflects the relationships between professional mixed martial arts (MMA) athletes and celebrities, the platform will shift to highlight that content over other celebrity or MMA-related material. Popular online content producers will notice this platform and audience shift – likely through their analytics – and will integrate MMA and celebrity into their content. This is typically achieved through the title of the work, the use of poster images or integrating meta-data such as hashtags and the like. Yet, this relationship between these three stakeholders groups can be further analysed to highlight the impact of platforms on content creation.

Content diversity, or lack thereof, as a result of platformization that integrates automation, can be observed on most social media platforms. It is especially evident through the process of cultural production that occurs frequently on the YouTube platform. For example, the relationship of the algorithm between the three stakeholder groups can be distinct and can emerge in significantly influential ways. If we examine the top video categories on YouTube as a case study to demonstrate the relationship operates, we can highlight why popular content creators may create the content that they do within the context of increased visibility. The top five categories of 2021 on YouTube are Gaming, Make-up & Beauty, Reviews & Unboxing, ASMR, and Vlogging. These are the YouTube categories that attract the most video contributions by content creators, and are also the same categories that receive the highest amounts of engagement (YouTube, 2021) – a direct correlation between production and consumption. This suggests that when content within these categories is visible, it is more likely to be shared based on the principles of platformization. Yet, while there is a relationship between production and consumption in this dynamic of cultural production, the question of temporality arises: did the online content creators making the videos for the category make these the most popular, or was it the audiences who were exposed to the content that made them the most popular categories? How does this production and consumption relationship impact on media diversity, and to what extent is that a problem for our societies that engage with this material?

These dynamics are a key problem of digital intermediation (Hutchinson, 2021); where digital intermediation is a framework to describe the non-human actors facilitating the process of cultural production and its distribution. Here, the unseen technological infrastructures of platforms, databases, algorithms, and automation are the most prominent reasons why some content becomes more visible than other content. Digital intermediation integrates the technological affordances of platforms and popularizes content of their audiences. For example, digital intermediation is the reason why certain content appears in the 'Up Next' or 'For You' recommendation systems of platforms. It is in this scenario that we can locate this visibility mechanisms of popular content which drives the top categories of YouTube. It is the digital intermediation process that should make us pause and consider; does the platform sense that online content creators are wanting to produce content that matches with make-up tutorials, or that the audiences are interested in learning how to do a specific style of make-up? Why does certain content in the vlogging category attract significantly more viewing time, while other material attracts hardly any views? In many ways, there seems to be a causality conversation underway between audiences, content creators, and algorithms.

This digital intermediation problem is the exact scenario the YouTuber *Verisatium* highlighted in his video, 'My video went viral. Here's why' (4,202,899 views). In this video, he talks about his viral video 'Why are 96,000,000 black balls on this reservoir?' (74,181,238 views), and why this video was pushed in front of more viewers by the YouTube platform over the many other videos he has produced for the platform. In the video, he explains that because of the high level of content that is published to the platform, approximately 500 hours every minute (YouTube, 2020), users are essentially 'ignorant' to most of the content on the platform, suggesting there is too much content available on the platform for any single person to consume. As a result of this saturation of media content, the YouTube algorithm is in place to help users navigate the catalogue of extensive content by tailoring their interests to the content that is published on YouTube. He also explains the presence of three stakeholders, albeit not in the digital interme- diation framework – the audience, the content creators and the algorithm – and describes how they are consistently chasing each other to discern what the other two stakeholders are interested in. Finally, in a McLuhanesque tone, *Veritasium* suggests that in fact the algorithm becomes the content that both creators and audiences are watching. Both digital intermediation and *Veritasium's* empirical experience both demonstrate how platformization and popularization play an integral role in how content is made visible, consumed by audiences and shared amongst their networks.

With an understanding of how automated navigation operates on social media platforms, digital intermediation and the algorithm as content indicates that pop- ular content is the common characteristic for increased visibility. Popular content then accedes to the wishes of the algorithm to make it visible, and in so doing, identifying it as shareable. As a content producer approaching any social media platform, they would certainly employ a strategy that identifies the popular areas of media and bring it into line with their own cultural production in that particular arena. This is certainly the case for the consistently growing genre of *news* YouTubers who are incorporating traditional journalism techniques into their YouTube channels. We will return to this significant area in detail in the latter parts of this chapter, but it is useful to understand how single person media approaches are embodying this cultural production technique as a key strategy in their every- day professional lives.

## 7.3  Cultural Intermediaries, Influence, and Visibility

In the original Bourdieu (1984) sense, cultural intermediaries are those individuals located within the cultural production space, as agents to transfer knowledge and calibrate cultural understandings. Cultural intermediaries excel at translating cul- tural media texts for broader audiences, for example highlighting the significance of the opera to a folk music fan or describing the societal significance of pop cul- ture to someone opposed to this art form. They operate at the boundaries of cultural production which increases the significance of the creative industries, con- tribute to the market effectiveness of those industries operating within the creative industries, and champion the individual roles that emerge within these spaces. The creative industries from this perspective have much to offer to a broader society in which they operate. Cultural intermediaries increase the plasticity of cultural participants by enabling multiple stakeholders to participate in societies by acknowledging, understanding, and speaking through specific media texts.

Cultural intermediaries have also been articulated in a number of other ways within the creative industries. In each instance they have taken on translation roles within advertising and marketing (Kelly, 2014), fashion (Skov, 2014), journalism (Smith Maguire & Mathews, 2012), and hospitality (Ocejo, 2014). Other scholars have argued for the role of the cultural intermediary to move beyond the market-based operator (Negus, 2010) and towards a socially engaged agent as a 'third wave cultural intermediary' (Perry et al., 2015, p. 724). In the latest iteration of the concept of cultural intermediaries, Hutchinson (2017) moves into the networked communication arena to highlight how they can adopt the characteristics of those highlighted by previous scholars, while at the same time operate as influential agents amongst large and niche audiences across a number of social media platforms.

Into this networked media context, cultural intermediaries work as the central agents of communication within emerging media ecosystems that are in most instances platform specific. For example, a social influencer will produce content for a number of platforms because their audiences are present across several of them for specific purposes: TikTok for short videos, Twitter for text-based conversations, and Facebook for commerce are but a few examples of why content is presented differently for each platform, from the same content creator. This suggests that a cultural intermediary as a social influencer will create material for the same moment to suit Instagram, YouTube, Snapchat, the podcast, the magazine, the Netflix series and so on and so forth. The cultural intermediary here can be labelled as a digital first personality (Hutchinson, 2019) to suggest they build their status as a social influencer first, and then develop their celebrity status second. In building a paratext persona, social media enables users to create a public identity to increase their exposure for increased social and economic capital. This has been previously thought of through the lens of persona studies, which 'describes the wider practice of constructing and constituting forms of public identity, with celebrities providing some of the most visible, performative and pedagogic examples of the practice' (Marshall et al., 2019, p. 289). In the persona studies context, we begin to understand how digital content creation can be organized and monetized.

Abidin (2016), highlights the platform specific practice through the lens of influencer studies, by arguing that:

> Influencers are everyday, ordinary Internet users who accumulate a relatively large following on blogs and social media through the textual and visual narration of their personal lives and lifestyles, engage with their following in digital and physical spaces, and monetise their following by integrating "advertorials" into their blog or social media posts.
>
> (Abidin, 2016, p. 1)

Here, Abidin draws on the work of Senft (2013) and Marwick (2013) around the concepts of microcelebrity, digital traces, and visibility. Senft notes microcelebrity is 'a new style of online performance in which people employ webcams, video, audio, blogs, and social networking sites to "amp up" their popularity among readers, viewers and those to whom they are linked online' (Senft, 2013: 25). In this sense, influencers are using the affordances of social media to produce a specific style of media and address a niche audience to continue to grow their popularity, while increasing their remuneration potential. Marwick locates this type of activity in the attention economy, which she notes, 'treats visibility as status, [and] makes it important for anyone who hopes to succeed in the technology industry to live at least somewhat in the public eye' (2013: 143). Coupled with the work of Ferdinands (2016) on social media exposure, cultural intermediaries who operate as influencers draw on social media networks to become visible, yet rely on their fellow influencers to increase their exposure levels and further capitalize on their social and economic value.

In her evidence as a witness before the UK's House of Commons' Digital, Culture, Sport and Media Committee reference on 'Influencer Culture', Abidin set out to provide the Committee with some details linking platforms, influencer culture, scale and visibility, noting,

> We also need to remember that many influencers these days are not very visible to us. We need to think about the under-the-radar platforms, TikTok algorithms that do not show you exactly what is out there. Lots of subscription-only models where you need to pay to access this content. Lots of closed messaging groups that can fit between 1,000 and 4,000 people and have lots of influential people that the major news outlets don't even know about because they are all gated communities. To respond to the question, in terms of scalability, we need to consider what platform we are looking at. For a small-scale subscription platform, someone with 1,000 influences may be a mega-influencer because everyone in that space listens and responds to them. If you are on a more public platform like YouTube, surely you need to be somewhere 1 million and above to be considered one of the mega-influencers. Likewise, we have to scale for genre and scale for country. On the topic of money, anyone who earns an income is an influencer, so if you are earning a couple of dollars for a post as an aspirational person making your way there, you are an influencer. If you are one of those guys who has your hand in every genre, any pot of money, earning tens of millions of dollars, that also makes you an influencer, but perhaps something to offer the crew that we have here is looking at one of the newest platforms on TikTok.

Abidin's evidence also provided the Committee members with a useful take on the term 'influencer' itself. She noted:

> What is really packed into the word 'influencer'? We are implying that it is not just a person creating content but they are relying on their personal selves as a brand. They are showing their lives and having to put their lifestyles out there in order to gain a following, which is so different from a content creator who is only working on games and focused on something external to them.

Our research has revealed a similar cultural intermediary framework in terms of *personal selves as brand* within the South Korean Mukbang phenomena as one example of online content creators who have pioneered online content creation techniques for other creators, such as the news creators in this chapter. The South Korean BJs (Broadcast Jockeys) embody the cultural intermediary role to explain the joy and satisfaction they experience through broadcasting their eating experiences. They engage social networks to amplify their popularity, collaborate with other Mukbang influencers to increase their visibility, and ultimately influence their increasingly large audiences. Their hyper-visibility amongst their peers suggests they have a successful media career and are also demonstrating their digital first personality, to fluidly move between platforms to engage their temporal and transient audiences.

### 7.3.1 Mukbang BJs as Influencers

To understand how BJs operate, it is useful to explain the process. Mukbang closely translates to English as *eating broadcast* and is simply slated as watching someone eat in front of their camera to which they broadcast across digital platforms. Its origins are to be found in Japanese culture, where eating alone was increasingly popular during the early 2000s. To break down the solo aspect of this, several restaurants opened to encourage individual eating, where customers could also watch videos of others eating, for example *Oshokuji no Jikan*, which broadcasts young women eating a number of dishes 'with you'. As this concept spread to South Korea, whose population are intensely culturally social people, incredibly active on internet-related communication, and also have a strong passion for food and eating, the BJs incorporated live chat into the eating alone experience (Figure 7.1).

There are multiple styles of Mukbang that have become popular in recent times from speed eating, to large quantity eating through to recent trends in ASMR (autonomous sensory meridian response) which focusses on the sounds of the content over everything else. In restaurants, BJs will set up their chosen food with the camera in front of them to frame the many plates of food, and then broadcast themselves eating and talking to the camera. The most popular platform for South Koreans is AfreecaTV.com which incorporates a live chat capacity, a donation

*Figure 7.1* Mukbang user broadcasting his noodle eating in Myeongdong.

functionality in the star balloon, which collectively enables the BJs to converse with the audience while generating an income. While the BJs are physically eating alone, they are connected to the world around them and are engaging in social practices with their audiences.

Our research fieldwork in Seoul in 2017 revealed that many people are engaging in Mukbang in recent times, with one interviewee noting 'everyone is doing it'. The more contemporary version of Mukbang was to add specializations to one skill set as a BJ, in a particular genre. Of the two BJs we interviewed, *Mino* specialized in Ramen (noodles) consumption, while *Yasikee* focused on speed consumption. The specialization of these online content producers is commensurate with the digital first personality traits previously highlighted and also connects with the broader acts demonstrated by content creators beyond the Mukbang genre. The interviewees spoke in terms of aligning their practice with the affordances of the platform, engaging in tactics that increase their visibility, and creating content consistently in a similar genre to engage their audiences.

Both BJs address their audience personally and engage them through 'challenges', which is a specific type of subgenre within Mukbang. Yet the broader *modus operandi* is to engage in conversation with users on the AfreecatTV platform, who will send the BJ 'star balloons', where the star balloon translates directly to funds being transferred to their accounts. A user determines how much money is associated within the star balloon, but they are typically less than AUD$50. The AfreecaTV platform has a tiered influencer model where the 'regular' BJs take 60 per cent of the star balloon, the 'best BJs' take 70 per cent of the star balloon, while 'partner' BJs take 80 per cent of the star balloon income. The BJs also make an income from product placement, endorsements from the restaurants in which they eat, and many of them also make their content available over Western social media platforms. Mino, pictured in Figure 7.2, also has a popular

*Figure 7.2* Mino (speed BJ) about to ingest his pork fillet challenge on the AfreecaTV platform.

YouTube channel (approximately 665,000 subscribers) and said he earns approximately US$7,000 per month. Both Mino and Yasikee are professional BJs and they note they 'live comfortably' and 'earn above the average monthly wage' (Personal Interview, 2017).

Mukbang BJs are a typical example of how single person media producers are a specific kind of online content creator that have a set of professional skills that enables them to navigate the consistently shifting affordances of highly commercial platforms. As noted earlier, the unseen infrastructures of their platforms change frequently, leaving the online content producers to adjust, pivot, and adapt their content production approach. In the Mukbang genre, several sub-genres have emerged which are a result of the digital intermediation and algorithmic media diversity problem that we have previously highlighted. As the audience interest shifts, for example to the increasing popularity of ASMR, so too do the Mukbang producers, which is then reflected by the platform algorithms. This clearly shows how cultural intermediaries are key agents of popular content, and social media influencers, who are able to create media that works within the technological affordances of the platforms for increased visibility.

## 7.4  Online Content Creators, Visibility, and Media Diversity

Before discussing news creators as a specific genre of online content creators, and using Mukbang BJs as a contemporary contextual backdrop, it is important to understand the digital and networked environment in which online cultural intermediaries operate. We have outlined that online content creators often work across multiple platforms and engage as cultural intermediaries to add value to the content they create, and to also demonstrate how cultural production inscribes particular values for broader audiences. However, this activity is to some extent blurred if the content creators do not construct audiences to have their content seen. To understand this from a content creator perspective, it is useful to explore the algorithmic visibility and digital intermediation literature.

Sophie Bishop in her 2019 *New Media & Society* article mounts an argument that online content creators are playing 'the visibility game'; suggesting that they adopt a series of navigation strategies to ensure their content is seen across commercial social media platforms. Through this research, Bishop is highlighting the broader observation that online content creators are hedging their careers, and therefore livelihoods, on commercial platforms that are opaque and can change how their content appears and to which audiences have little to no advanced warning notifications. In that sense, online content creators are consistently monitoring, negotiating, and adjusting (Petre, Duffy & Hund, 2019) to ensure their content remains relevant to the platform algorithm and does not become buried amongst the unconsumable amount of content on the YouTube platform especially (Bódo et al., 2019).

The concepts highlighted by the algorithmic visibility literature are an indication of the items that have contributed to the opportunities and challenges of digital intermediation (Hutchinson, 2021). Digital intermediation as a framework incorporates unseen technologies, institutions and automation, and impacts how cultural production is both created and used. Technologies include the physical technologies, such as cameras and the like, but also the platforms and databases that sort, store, and distribute content. Institutions are the unseen agents in cultural production that regulate, promote, encourage, and engage the activities that surround cultural production. Automation refers to the processes that are built on machine learning and artificial intelligence that promote some content while inhibiting another piece of content. Digital intermediation is multi-faceted in that it can both assist and hinder those who are involved in cultural production across digital media environments.

As outlined above, the contemporary media environments in which we find our digital selves is entirely saturated with media – YouTube has 720,000 hours of content uploaded every day (Oberlo, 2021), 83 per cent of TikTok's 1 billion monthly users regularly post videos (Wallaroo, 2021), over 1,000 photos are posted to Instagram every second (99 Firms, 2021), and Facebook remains constant as it generates 4 petabytes of data per day (Osman, 2021). While these are only a handful of social media platforms, the content creation and publishing numbers are staggering and reinforce the fact that no human will ever be able to watch, read, listen, and engage with all the content that is created and published. This is the point where visibility becomes a critical moment that digital intermediation attempts to address. Digital intermediation's automation aspect especially assists users in finding content that is relevant to their interests and that they, and the connections in their networks, are likely to find of interest. Digital intermediation also presents challenges, especially for media diversity.

While the conversations around filter bubbles and echo chambers have been problematized (Bruns, 2019; Margetts et al., 2021), digital intermediation implicitly suggests that there are limitations surrounding media diversity that are out of the control of the user. In the context of algorithms, Pasquale (2015) has previously argued that we live in a black-box society where we cannot understand how such technologies operate; algorithms that are biased and treat specific groups of users differently (Noble, 2018); and that algorithms are made by predominantly white, male programmers based in North America (Whittaker et al., 2018). However, the way in which automated publishing practices operate remain for the most part opaque, leaving content producers and audiences alike consistently renegotiating the terms of their engagement with the role of the algorithms for cultural production. The place of social media content production within platform media ecologies can be characterized as a narrative of economic dependency, controversy, contestation, and precarity for content creators and businesses alike. At the same time it is also apparent that there is a transitioning away from the earlier millennial 'libertarian' internet phase, towards a period of more active scrutiny and stronger, more interventionist forms of regulation (Flew, 2021). Self-regulation by social media platforms is now widely and roundly criticized as attempts are underway around the globe to rein in anti-social malinformation, and to hold platforms accountable, and indeed liable for this content. However, this is no easy task given the power of these platforms, and the reality that their wealth often surpasses that of smaller nation states.

## 7.5 News YouTubers Within Digital Intermediation

With digital intermediation providing a contextual backdrop, alongside algorithmic visibility and having looked at how our case study of Mukbang influencers has emerged as one form of cultural production shared on video sharing platforms, we can now turn our attention to YouTubers that focus on News production. To understand how news producers have positioned themselves alongside the platform affordances outlined above, we begin the analysis not by using the YouTube channels of established news providers but instead we are focussing on three specific case studies; they demonstrate important elements of the algorithmic visibility and digital intermediation affordances we have outlined.

The three case studies are *Philip DeFranco, H3 Podcast*, and *The Friendly Jordies*. The first two accounts, Philip DeFranco and H3 Podcast, are based in the United States, specifically Los Angeles, and offer a daily round-up of contemporary issues in the news cycle. While they both have a focus on more culturally specific items that are consistent with social media platforms more broadly, they are very much addressing the news cycle, engaging in journalistic practices, and following conventions that are typically associated with 'capital J' journalism. The third case study examines an Australian YouTuber, *The Friendly Jordies*, not only because he occupies similar terrain to the other two YouTuber News creators, but also because he has become somewhat of a central figure in national politics within the Australian commentariat because of his involvement with politics. In each case study, it will become clear how these news online content creators are adopting available platform affordances, while also engaging with public affairs journalism.

Philip DeFranco is 'an American news commentator and YouTube personality', where this Wikipedia (2021) definition demonstrates the role of a journalist in this YouTube space is augmenting a traditional journalistic role with that of a digital first personality. In fact, his catch cry is 'Sup ya beautiful bastards' followed by 'smash that like button to feed the algorithm gods' every time he starts a video to in one trademark rhetorical flourish welcome his fans back, but to also acknowledge the impact of the YouTube algorithm overtly on his channel, *The Philip DeFranco Show*. In fact, he is so hyper-aware of the algorithm that he often creates two videos for the day: the first is an algorithm-friendly video (safe poster image, clean video title, non-contentious material), and the second is the same video only with the more contentious material added, that DeFranco acknowledges the YouTube algorithm will bury but he directs his audience toward in spite of this inevitable impact from automated curation. He will direct his audience toward the second video in his first video, leveraging his own visibility to increase the views of the content that does not align with the YouTube algorithm. For DeFranco, his knowledge of the YouTube algorithm drives his approach toward content creation and news commentary (Figure 7.3).

While there are many takes on how to drive engagement to one's YouTube channel, including from the YouTube Creator blog, Hootsuite offers very useful insights into how to drive engagement on YouTube. They provide five steps:

1. Use effective thumbnail images for your video, with text;
2. Don't make the video about the creator, but about the interests of the audience;

*Figure 7.3* The Philip DeFranco Show YouTube page.

3.   React to trends, or be newsworthy;
4.   Collaborate with other creators; and
5.   Track the performance through metrics and analytics.

While these strategies are aimed at public relations and marketing campaigns, the key strategies can be seen through DeFranco's work. His thumbnail is consistently familiar and indicates who he will be talking about or with, complete with informative text and video titles. He covers content that is contemporary public affairs, and often engages with other collaborators to increase his audience size and engagement. Each of his videos are typically around the 15-minute mark, which aligns with the recommendations from YouTube for a suitable length for a video. According to SocialBlade, DeFranco is a B+ ranked YouTuber, with 6.32 million subscribers, 1.2 billion video views, 61st in their News Rank and earns approximately between $55,000 and $880,000 per year (Social Blade, 2021).

Ethan and Hila Klein are the personalities behind the *H3 Podcast* YouTube channel which has been steadily growing from the original channel, *H3H3 Productions*. The former channel was more in line with a satirical commentary on internet culture more broadly, but as the channel outgrew its audience, and Ethan and Hila were married, they joined forces and created the *H3 Podcast* channel. The newer channel remains a commentary channel for all things culture on the internet, but at the same time falls into the news category due to its focus on items that sit comfortably in the public affairs category. It has grown to include a cast of other voices and production crew who are all actively involved in the program, and who have also developed the live format of the current YouTube videos.

Again, the production crew are very sensitive to the impact of the YouTube algorithm, as are most YouTubers who base their income on the monetization of their channels. Like DeFranco, they negotiate the digital affordances that are part of the platform to ensure their videos remain relevant, searchable, and indeed visible. Building on the affordances of the YouTube platform, the YouTube Creator Blog advises:

> We recommend videos based on things such as: what your audience watches and doesn't watch, how much time they spend watching, what they like and dislike, if they mark a video as 'not interested', and on satisfaction surveys. So, rather than trying to find a secret code to these systems, focus instead on making videos that you think will resonate with your audience.
>
> (YouTube, 2021)

To that end, *H3 Podcast* regularly creates and posts videos that are proud of two hours in length, and which would gel with the metrics of their audience who must watch for the duration, and would be reflected in their channel metrics. Their most recent video at the time of writing had received over 1.3 million views, suggesting their production approach for YouTube is significantly more sophisticated than 'making videos [they] think will resonate with [their] audience'. *H3 Podcast* are a useful example of a news YouTube channel that has incorporated the technological *and* cultural affordances of the platform to produce a product that is of high cultural value with a large audience. It is at this point that the community building aspect of news YouTubers is most obvious, as they incorporate the input from their fan community into the content that is created for their audience. This affective labour feeds into the automated aspect of the algorithm in that it increases the 'what their audience likes' and 'how much time they spend on the video', as per the YouTube Creator recommendations. According to Social Blade, *H3 Podcast* is also a B+ ranked YouTuber with 3.05 million subscribers, 645 million video views, ranked 1,883 in their entertainment category ranking, and earns between $77,000 and $1.2 million per year (Figure 7.4).

To move away from Los Angeles centric news YouTubers, we now turn our focus to an Australian-based YouTuber, Jordan Shanks, who is the celebrity for *The Friendly Jordies* channel. This is a channel of particular interest to us not only because of its pirouetting around the technological and cultural affordances of the YouTube platform, but also its legal precarity in the Australian judicial system. To highlight the legal issues at play here, it is important to first understand the channel and its approach towards content creation and publication, and then we can highlight the legal tensions surrounding Shanks and his production team of *The Friendly Jordies* YouTube channel.

Like the *DeFranco* and *H3 Podcast* channels, *The Friendly Jordies* also demonstrate the sorts of traits that satisfy the algorithmic requirements around the visibility conundrum all YouTubers face. They have effective poster images, use video titles effectively, create videos in the most likely timeframes to appease their audiences, they talk about content that interests their core audience and other less addicted visitors, and they are also incorporating their metrics into the production of their content to increase the views of their work – in other words, they have a symbiotic relationship with the YouTube algorithm. But unlike the other two channels, *The Friendly Jordies* has built its following on comedy and pop cultural references *together with* political commentary and public affairs journalism. This makes it difficult to

*Figure 7.4* The H3 Podcast YouTube channel.

pigeonhole Shanks as an entertainer, online content creator, or journalist – each having their own set of content ruling systems.

According to his Wikipedia (2021) page, Shanks is 'an Australian political commentator, stand-up comedian and YouTuber'; thus reinforcing the blurring around which professional category embodies – a kind of hybrid political entertainer. On his path to local celebrity status, he supported his career through live stand-up comedy shows, but probably his greatest claim to fame arrived when he started his response style videos for *The Bachelorette* and *Married at First Sight* television series. Beyond these initial steps into celebrity, he has found a local point of notoriety in becoming a vocal political commentator, with a specific focus on the current New South Wales (NSW) incumbents, the conservative Liberal National Coalition party. As one of the key antagonists of the NSW government, he has spearheaded social media protest such as #koalakiller, which highlighted the lack of government support for forestry for koalas, and more recently the alleged corruption and misconduct by the leader of the National Party, John Barrilaro.

At the time of writing, the Premier of the NSW, Gladys Berejiklian, has recently resigned while under investigation for corruption charges, and John Barilaro has resigned from politics, also under a cloud of a potential scandal. In his public announcement of his retirement, Barilaro referenced the ongoing defamation case between he and Jordan Shanks. 'It's unbelievable that I have to defend myself from vile and racist attacks in a social media setting by individuals and a trillion dollar company like Google' (Seven News, 2021). Barilaro is in the midst of an ongoing defamation case with Shanks and his production team, as a result of their consistent pressure for the now retired politician to be accountable for actions while an active participant of the government (Figure 7.5).

*The Friendly Jordies* is listed as a B level YouTube channel according to data analytics group SocialBlade, with 578,000 subscribers, 149 million video views and approximately $22,000 to $366,000 yearly income. In all three instances of these news YouTubers, they are operating for visibility to reach their existing and new audiences. These content production strategies do not prioritize regulatory

*Figure 7.5* Jordan Shanks accuses John Barilaro of corruption while filming his YouTube video in his multi-million-dollar Airbnb.

measures, but instead are based on techniques that enable increased monetization of their content, given that their YouTube channels are the main source of income. This tends to indicate that regardless of the regulatory levers that are in place for online content producers, the monetization triggers of social media platforms are far more powerful as content production guidelines to sway conduct. In this light, we argue that an eclectic range of content, including fake, misleading, and illegal content, is created with visibility – where visibility has a direct relationship with monetization – as its core concern over any existing regulatory direction currently in place.

## 7.6 Conclusion

The twin pincers of cultural and digital intermediation have set in motion a separation of content producer and audience users. In this process, as we have shown in this chapter, online content creation takes place under these cultural intermediation auspices and visibility is the key driver for producers, which has a direct correlation to monetization. These intermediation dynamics account for how the non-human actors facilitate the process of cultural production and its distribution. Importantly, unseen technological infrastructures of platforms, databases, algorithms and automation foreground why some content becomes more visible than other content.

We have all witnessed how COVID-19 has exacerbated the conflict that arises between economic and social policies within and between nations. Quite rightly, many have observed an implicit correlation between the *pandemic* and the *infodemic*. The platform society is unavoidably now positioned at the centre of economic stability and enmeshed with emerging geopolitical relations (Van Dijck et al., 2018). Indeed, platformization and its algorithmic shape shifters are reordering critical media practices including public interest journalism, and, as we have discussed in this chapter, how it becomes visible to audiences.

Regardless of the forms of regulation design that are in place, or under development, including the combination of 'self-policing' and black letter law approaches, platforms are driving the content stream that is produced based on the relationship between algorithms, audiences, and content producers. Inevitably, the regulation of social media platforms is an unfolding debate that will see a continuing battle between the platforms, powerful elite groups, lawmakers in the US Congress and the European Union, and national competition and media regulators around the world.

# References

Abidin, C. (2016). "Aren't These Just Young, Rich Women Doing Vain Things Online?" Influencer Selfies as Subversive Frivolity. *Social Media + Society*, *2*(23), 1–17.

Arriagada, A., & Ibáñez, F. (2020). "You Need At Least One Picture Daily, if Not, You're Dead": Content Creators and Platform Evolution in the Social Media Ecology. *Social Media + Society*. doi:10.1177/2056305120944624

Assenmacher, D., Clever, L., Frischlich, L., Quandt, T., Trautmann, H., & Grimme, C. (2020). Demystifying Social Bots: On the Intelligence of Automated Social Media Actors. *Social Media + Society*. doi:10.1177/2056305120939264

Bishop, S. (2019). Managing Visibility on YouTube through Algorithmic Gossip. *New Media & Society*, *21*(11), 2589–2606.

Bodó, B., Helberger, N., Eskens, S., & Möller, J. (2019). Interested in Diversity. *Digital Journalism*, *7*(2), 206–229.

Bourdieu, P. (1984). *A Social Critique of the Judgement of Taste* (1st ed.). London: Routledge.

Bruns, A. (2008). *Blogs, Wikipedia, Second Life and Beyond: From Production to Produsage*. New York: Peter Lang.

Bruns, A. (2019). *Are Filter Bubbles Real?* Cambridge: Polity.

Cotter, K. (2018). Playing the visibility game: How digital influencers and algorithms negotiate influence on Instagram. *New Media & Society*, *21*(4), 895–913.

Diakopolous, N. (2020). Computational News Discovery: Towards Design Considerations for Editorial Orientation Algorithms in Journalism. *Digital Journalism*, *8*(7), 945–967.

Dwyer, T., and Martin, F. (2019). Understanding Viral News Sharing, in Martin, F. and Dwyer, T. (Eds.), *Sharing News Online: Commendary Cultures and Social Media News Ecologies* (pp. 257–283). Cham: Palgrave Macmillan.

Ferdinands, B. (2016). *Drink this Tea and Look Like Me*. (Honours). Sydney: University of Sydney.

Flew, T. (2021) *Regulating Platforms*. Cambridge: Polity.

Ford, H., & Hutchinson, J. (2021). Newsbots That Mediate Journalist and Audience Relationships. In N. Thurman, S. C. Lewis, & J. Kunert (Eds.), *Algorithms, Automation, and News: New Directions in the Study of Computation and Journalism*. New York: Routledge.

Gillespie, T. (2010). The Politics of Platforms. *New Media and Society*, *12*(3), 347–364.

Hartley, J., Burgess, J., & Bruns, A. (2013). *A Companion to New Media Dynamics*. New York: Wiley.

Hutchinson, J. (2017). *Cultural Intermediation and Audience Participation in Media Organisations.* New York: Palgrave Macmillan.

Hutchinson, J. (2019). Digital First Personality: Automation and influence within evolving media ecologies. *Convergence: The International Journal of Research into New Media Technologies, Online First.* doi:10.1177/1354856519858921

Hutchinson, J. (2021). Digital Intermediation: Unseen Infrastructures for Cultural Production. *New Media & Society.* doi:10.1177/14614448211040247

Kelly, A. (2014). Advertising. In J. S. Maguire & J. Matthews (Eds.), *The Cultural Intermediaries Reader.* London: SAGE Publication Ltd.

Kim, T. (2021) Dorsey's Refresh of Twitter hasn't Convinced Anyone. *Australian, Financial Review,* 24 September.

Manovich, L. (2001). *The Language of New Media.* Cambridge, MA: MIT Press.

Margetts, H., Lehdonvirta, V., González-Bailón, S., Hutchinson, J., Bright, J., Nash, V., & Sutcliffe, D. (2021). The Internet and public policy: Future directions. *Policy & Internet, 13*(2), 1–23.

Marshall, P. D., Moore, C., & Barbour, K. (2019). *Persona Studies: An Introduction.* Washington, US: Wiley.

Marwick, A. (2013). *Status Update: Celebrity, Publicity, and Branding in the Social Media Age.* New York: Yale University Press.

Negus, K. (2010). The Work of Cultural Intermediaries and the Enduring Distance between Production and Consumption. *Cultural Studies, 16*(4), 501–515.

Nieborg, D. B., & Poell, T. (2018). The Platformization of Cultural Production: Theorizing the Contingent Cultural Commodity. *New Media & Society, 20*(11), 4275–4292.

Noble, S. U. (2018). *Algorithms of Oppression: How Search Engines Reinforce Racism.* New York: NYU Press.

Pasquale, F. (2015). *The Black Box Society: The Secret Algorithms that Control Money and Information.* Cambridge: MIT Press.

Perry, B., Smith, K., & Warren, S. (2015). Revealing and Revaluing Cultural Intermediaries in the 'Real' Creative City: Insights from a dairy keeping exercise. *European Journal of Cultural Studies, 18*(6), 724–740.

Personnal Interview (2017) Mukbang eaters Mino and Yasikee, Republic of Korea, 28 November.

Peterson-Salahuddin, C., & Diakopolous, N. (2020). Negotiated Autonomy: The Role of Social Media Algorithms in Editorial Decision Making. *Media and Communication, 8*(3), 27.

Petre, C., Duffy, B., & Hund, E. (2019). "Gaming the System": Platform Paternalism and the Politics of Algorithmic Visibility. *Social Media + Society, October–December 2019,* 1–12.

Senft, T. M. (2013). Microcelebrity and the Branded Self. In J. B. John Hartley, Axel Bruns (Ed.), *A Companion to New Media Dynamics* (pp. 346–354). New York: Wiley-Blackwell.

Seven News (2021) 'Deputy Premier John Barilaro announces resignation after Gladys Berejiklian stands down'. 4 October. https://7news.com.au/news/nsw/deputy-premier-john-barilaro-announces-resignation-after-gladys-berejiklian-stands-down-c-4141926

Skov, L. (2014). Cultural Intermediaries and Fashion. In J. S. Macguire & T. Miller (Eds.), *The Cultural Intermediaires Reader.* London: SAGE Publications Ltd.

Smith Maguire, J. & Mathews, J. (2012). Are we all Cultural Intermediaries Now? An Introduction to Cultural Intermediaires in Context. *European Journal of Cultural Studies, 15*(5), 551–562.

Social Blade (2021). https://socialblade.com

Turner, G. (2010). *Ordinary People and the Media: The Demotic Turn*. London: SAGE Publications Ltd.

UK House of Commons (2021). Digital, Culture, Media and Sport Committee. Oral Evidence on 'Influencer Culture'. 13 July. Dr. Crystal Abidin. UK Parliament. Transcript available at https://committees.parliament.uk/oralevidence/2552/html/

Van Dijck, J., Poell, T., & De Waal, M. (2018) *The Platform Society: Public Values in a Connective World*. New York: University of Oxford Press.

Whittaker, M., Crawford, K., Dobbe, R., Fried, G., Kaziunas, E., Mathur, V., ... Schwartz, O. (2018). *AI Now Report 2018*. Retrieved from New York: https://ainowinstitute.org/AI_Now_2018_Report.pdf

Yeung, K. (2016). 'Hypernudge': Big Data as a Mode of Regulation by Design. *Information Communication & Society*, *20*(1), 1–19.

# 8 A cross-pollination of fame?

## Star athletes and influencers on Instagram

*Emilio Fernández Peña, Natividad Ramajo*
*and Adolfo Nieto*

## 8.1 Introduction

Instagram was launched in October 2010 as a friendly, fun mobile app for sharing photos and applying various filters. Since its acquisition in April 2012 by Facebook, further business opportunities and complementarities have been explored (Rushe, 2012). Instagram has played on the simplicity of interconnection between it and Facebook and, having taken some characteristics from Twitter, has become a mixed social media platform situated between the latter two. The interaction and design features of Instagram mean that it has greater capacity to enhance its particularities (Quesenberry, 2019: 149–150). Since its acquisition, Instagram has been managed as an independent company. At the time, Facebook CEO Mark Zuckerberg highlighted Facebook users' interest in photo sharing: 'But providing the best photo sharing experience is one reason why so many people love Facebook and we knew it would be worth bringing these two companies together' (Rushe, 2012).

Instagram and its interface are about the moment. Instagram is associated with an ephemeral flow, in which interaction modes are simplified as much as possible and speed and simplicity are rewarded (Zulli, 2018: 143). Its interaction model initially revolved around high-quality photos, with videos being introduced at a later stage (Zulli, 2018).

Like all other social media platforms, it has quickly become a means of personal communication for sports personalities and a space where celebrities and athletes can promote products and services by building their personal brand. While Facebook remains the platform with the largest number of users, Instagram has experienced strong growth. With 1.2 billion users worldwide, it is now one of the most influential social media platforms (Chaffey, 2021). As noted by Lee et al. (2015), the qualities that make Instagram a particularly attractive platform are: the ease of interaction, the ability to observe the private lives of other people using an archive of images and videos as a tool, and the configuration of psychological mechanisms that allow us to escape from reality for a few moments. Miles (2014) also notes that content posted on Instagram tends to have a longer life span than that posted on other social media platforms because it is less conversation focused than Facebook and Twitter are.

DOI: 10.4324/9781003134176-9

People who post their photos on Instagram do so thinking about the glance of others, about how they are going to be decoded and seen: 'With the case of Instagram specifically, the glance is implicated in the name itself and interface design of the site' (Zulli, 2018: 140–141).

On social media, user-generated content (Jenkins, 2006) is the basis of a form of communication that gives rise to a new peer-to-peer language that is more direct and sincere. Shifting away from the old hierarchies of mass media, such communication essentially becomes a conversation (Locke et al., 2001).

This work focuses on sports stars and fashion Instagrammers. Both groups share the concept of celebrity as an element of audience attention-grabbing, making it easier to get followers on social media.

First, we will analyse how both groups engage and interact with the audience. Second, we will situate Instagram as a social media platform within communication strategy, and explore whether there are any complementarities between digital presences across platforms, between a personality's website and his or her presence on each of the platforms. In other words, we will examine whether there is a holistic vision of social media communication strategy, in which each different digital presence specialises in one type of content and one type of audience, and then transfers audiences to other platforms. We call this an integral strategy. It seeks complementarities and feedback between the different digital presences, which we refer to as 'cross-pollination' (Fernández Peña et al., 2011).

## 8.2 The complex, the systemic, and social media

To talk about the complex and the systemic is to talk about equivalent concepts (Capra, 1998). The systemic refers to things that are interrelated and interdependent, to something that functions as a whole. This holistic and linked vision of elements of reality in the area of science has the status of a theory, which has been variously called 'dynamic systems theory', 'complexity theory', 'non-linear dynamics', or 'network dynamics', among others (Capra, 1998). The most important property of systems is a pattern in the form of a network; 'if we see life, we see networks'[1] (Capra, 1998: 100). And the outstanding feature of any network is that its operation is non-linear, that is, it goes in all directions and offers feedback and self-regulation, which are the fundamental characteristics of a systemic vision. Another of its characteristics is self-organisation: 'A constant flow of matter and energy through the system is necessary for self-organisation to occur' (Capra 1998, 103). At the same time, the systemic is contextual, as individual elements of data become meaningful in the whole (Capra, 1998: 58). Elements are not considered separate, and 'the objects themselves are networks of relationships immersed in larger networks. For the systemic thinker, relationships take priority' (Capra, 1998: 58).

Internet-based digital media have that systemic, integral, interconnected vision of reality in their DNA. In this vision, the different parts interact to form a harmonious whole. This holistic, systemic vision was present in Tim Berners-Lee's idea for the design of the World Wide Web (Berners-Lee, 2000) and in Steve Jobs' inspiration for creating his Apple products (Isaacson, 2015), and is present in the operation of social media (Christakis & Fowler, 2011).

So, the history of the Internet and of the social media it has spawned is the history of the development of complex communication systems, each of which is based on the first Internet, a technological advancement that has gradually had new features added to the original architecture (Fernández Peña, 2016). The key concept is interconnection: non-linear, hierarchically egalitarian, network-based interconnection. The first Internet, ARPANET, expanded mainly from the 1980s and was based on the non-linear interconnection of computers forming nodes (Veà, 2013). The second major expansion occurred in 1993 with the advent of the World Wide Web. Based on the previous architecture of the Internet, it added multimedia capabilities, simplicity of use and the promotion of interconnected content through a system of hyperlinks (Berners-Lee, 2000). The third major development, which will be central to our work, is the interconnection between people through personal profiles. The outcome would be social media, which became available in the mid-2000s (Christakis & Fowler, 2011). Each of the previous developments formed the cornerstone of the next development. Thus, written in the genetic code of the first Internet and the World Wide Web is the subsequent development of its applications and commercial expansion.

## 8.3 The new and social media

Social media are territories of influence. Our friends influence us and we influence our friends in an influx of information that is not necessarily direct. Indeed, it can reach people who may not be directly connected with us, that is, they are indirectly connected through our friends (Christakis & Fowler, 2011).

In social life, the old or the traditional has always lost its power of attraction to the new, and the latter has been the raw material of the media's development since industrialisation (Fernández Peña, 2016). In his book *The Art of Worldly Wisdom* written in the 17th century, the Spanish writer Baltasar Gracián told us:

> 269 *Make use of the novelty of your position.* … Novelty pleases all because it is uncommon, taste is refreshed, and a brand new mediocrity is thought more of than accustomed excellence. Ability wears away by use and becomes old. However, know that the glory of novelty is short-lived: after four days respect is gone.
>
> (Gracián, 1892/1904: 162)

The new, novelty, is the raw material from which mass information is made, and it is what drives social media too. Information on paper, which became popular from the mid-19th century onwards, sells ephemeral news, whose etymological meaning contains the idea of the new. Journalistic information on paper was new until the next newspaper was published 24 hours later. After that, information based on novelty became a key piece of radio and television broadcasting until the 1980s, when entertainment became dominant in the audiovisual space (Postman, 2005). Social media base their ability to attract the audience's attention on a mix combining the novelty of user-generated content and the historical recovery of on-demand and always-interactive content (Jenkins et al., 2018).

Lipovetsky and Charles (2005) consider the taste for the new to be the driver of what he calls 'the logic of fashion'. People consume the new simply because of its novel character, the present is exalted and people disassociate themselves from tradition (Lipovetsky, 1991). This neophilic driver dominates the dynamics of posting on Instagram and on other social media. Following the logic of traditional journalistic culture, Instagram and other social media give prominence to the newest photos and stories. At the same time, consumer fashion, whose marketing formula has always been based on the new, is represented by the products that Instagrammers endorse. However, also produced on social media is a set of meanings that can be interpreted according to the logic of Bourdieu's distinction (2010), which focuses on the construction of consumption-based hierarchies, that is, on the capacity of consumer objects and, by extension, brands to distinguish between people. These two drivers, the logic of fashion and distinction, are present in an image-based medium like Instagram.

## 8.4 Fame, famous and celebrities: sport stars and fashion Instagrammers

Albeit with various nuances, fame and celebrity are close concepts. They are separate ones in the English-speaking world but not elsewhere, where other languages like Spanish are spoken. 'Famous' comes from the Latin *famosus*, and was incorporated into English in the Middle Ages through the influence of French. The word 'celebrity', which again came into the English language via France in the Middle Ages, began to be used much more from 1920 onwards as a result of the boom in mass media. From the outset, the concept of celebrity has been associated with audience interest (Lilti, 2017). In media societies, there has traditionally been a contrast between '"false-value" celebrity and deserved glory' (Wesolowski, 2020: 189). So, connected with these two concepts, we find others such as glory and reputation. 'Glory' is related to the attainment of goals that the average citizen would find hard to reach. It is associated with effort and talent and, for the purposes of our work, it is directly associated with sport and athletes. The second term, 'reputation', is a concept linked to the image people have of a person or a brand, that is, to the public image (Barclay, 2015). On the Internet, reputation has become fundamental (Madden & Smith, 2010).

Another concept surrounding fame is charisma. Since its modern articulation by Max Weber, it has been associated with what the German sociologist called 'inspirational leaders', be they political or religious. However, since the 1960s, charisma has also become associated with musicians, sports heroes, television stars, glamorous models and notorious rogues (Dickson, 2012: 764). This results in a transfer of the concept to personalities whose success is illuminated and increased by the social role of the mass media, and has reached new heights since the advent of social media.

Elite athletes base their success on talent, the competitive effort whose ultimate goal is to excel at what they do. The ethics of effort, the meritocracy of muscle versus the aristocracy of beauty. Dominating the attention economy always requires excellence. Professional excellence, but also excellence in the quality and selection of posts.

According to Sloterdijk (2012), in the 20th century and for the very first time, the culture of effort and self-improvement has been separated from religious practice. Until the modern age, the concept of asceticism, of exercise, was linked to the religious sacrifice practices of yogis, anchorites and hermits who devoted their lives to a god or gods. However, in the 19th century, it began to be associated with the modern concept of mass sports, whose emergence was linked to industrialisation (Ellul, 1963), the mass press and a new, broader world vision. The latter was a consequence of technical advances in the field of telecommunications such as the telephone, improvements in means of transport and the holding of universal expositions (Fernández Peña, 2016).

Asceticism, once exclusively religious, has since been transferred to people's day-to-day practices, and even more so to professional sport. According to Sloterdijk (2012), exercise had undergone a process of 'de-spiritualization of asceticism' (Sloterdijk, 2012: 94). That was how a new era began, an era in which sport is now a way of transforming people's lives, has a democratising capacity and is a promoter of social mobility, at least symbolically and momentarily.

The fame and celebrity associated with athletes is not a new phenomenon. In ancient Rome, Gaius Appuleius Diocles was one of the most famous and richest athletes. When he retired at the age of 42, after a long and successful career, he had earnt 35,863,120 sestertii, the equivalent of $15 billion today (Preskar, 2020).

Gaius Appuleius Diocles' successful career was based not only on his enormous talent, but also on an important strategic vision of distinction and a great sense of spectacle, and he became a master of drama (Preskar, 2020). In fact, he only won one-third of his races, but his huge sense of spectacle made him a favourite with the Roman audience.

Today, the social presence of sport, especially in the media, is unquestionable. That is why, among the world's 50 most followed influencers on Instagram, 11 are athletes, nine of whom are football players.

The processes of transnational connectivity have allowed elite athletes to engage with their audiences in an unprecedented way: via social media, they not only show their best sporting actions, but also the most intimate aspects of their private lives. And, at the same time, they promote products and brands, both their own and those of third parties. This tendency to publicly share aspects of their private lives is based on the fact that users identify with famous people or organisations when they perceive shared similarities (Soukup, 2006). Within the sporting context, these links occur with athletes, sports personalities or teams (Wann & Branscombe, 1993). Thus, 'fandom', defined as 'the regular, emotionally involved consumption of a given popular narrative or text' (Sandvoss, 2005: 8), implies evoking a shared sense of emotional attachment to a club or player (Abosag et al., 2012).

In order to enhance this connection, athletes need to develop their personal brand, that is, to do branding. A well-defined and well-managed personal brand increases their capital value because, if the associated feelings are positive, their brand messages have greater influence than those of competing brands (Hsieh & Li, 2008). An influencer is therefore understood as someone who reflects his or her personal brand (Markos et al., 2011), and who endeavours to get as much attention as possible. 'Authenticity', defined as 'the overall assessment of the credibility of a brand' (Jenkins et al., 2018: 95), becomes the main value judgment because a personal brand is now reaffirmed by convincing consumers of its inherent veracity (Hearn & Schoenhoff, 2016). For this purpose, competitive sport is an ideal framework as it shows 'real individuals participating in unpredictable contests'. Andrews and Jackson (2001) argue that this gives sport stars an important veneer of authenticity, which sets them apart from other celebrities from 'other, more explicitly manufactured, cultural realms' (Andrews & Jackson, 2001: 8). Thus, sport becomes an ideal showcase for the promotion of a personal brand because it receives massive media attention on a daily basis while generating opinion and conversation on social media. Using this global conduit, a sport star becomes a source of cultural identification, through which the dominant narratives, sensitivities and ideals are presented to popular culture (Rojek, 2006).

Generally speaking, football players become famous because of their sporting achievements and the public's interest in their off-pitch activities. Their brands therefore depend to a large extent on these two elements of their lives (Wu et al., 2012). It is about establishing a personal brand that includes the life stories, values, charisma, authenticity and truthfulness of the athlete in question (Cortsen, 2013). This has given rise to co-branding, that is, 'a public relationship between independent brands' (Seno & Lukas, 2007: 123). However, for these alliances to achieve the expected results, there must be some consistency between a product's and an athlete's image. There are a number of intangibles such as team, personal life, physical characteristics, level of success, age or reputation (Burton & Chadwick, 2008) that make athletes better or worse suited to certain products. Such coordination is essential because the value of the brand image that an athlete has managed to create of him or herself plays a decisive role in his or her economic and social standing.

This is known as 'impression management', which, as explained by Hasaan et al. (2018), is the process of controlling the impact we have on others (Leary & Kowalski, 1990). Thus, an athlete must pay attention to his or her gestures, clothing, appearance or way of speaking in order to improve self-representation and win others over (St. James, 2010). The physical condition of an athlete's body becomes relevant to a sports personal brand since it can be understood as a symbolic message about his or her own self-esteem (Lau et al. 2008), and it may even have an influence on how sexually attractive the athlete is to others (van Amsterdam et al., 2012 and Daniels, 2009).

However, the development of a personal brand needs more than that. Braunstein and Zhang (2005) identified professional trustworthiness, likeable personality, athletic expertise, social attractiveness and characteristic style as factors influencing the evolution of a sports personal brand. Personal charm, that is, an athlete's charisma and inspiring behaviour in other aspects of life beyond sport, can also generate followers (Cortsen 2013). Choi and Rifon (2007) have added genuineness, competence, excitement and sociability to the aforementioned personality traits.

Of course, sports talent is also a differential factor, to the extent that some fans acknowledge that they are more interested in seeing certain players' special skills than they are in seeing a team win (Theysohn et al., 2009). Kiefer (2014) also notes that good sports performances increase an athlete's market value. It is no coincidence that, of the nine most influential football players on Instagram, six are forwards. As Weiss (2001) showed, there is a positive relationship between scoring goals and achieving star player status.

The consequences of paying attention to all the factors mentioned above are, among others, that fans – by developing a positive perception of an athlete – tend to be more loyal to him or her. Such loyalty – understood as an emotional bond – tends to increase the intention to buy products and brands associated with that athlete (Hasaan et al., 2018).

Sports consumers with a strong attachment to a particular team or player are more likely to follow their social media accounts (Demirel & Erdogmus 2016), thus creating a virtuous circle between sports promotion, networking capabilities and their brand value. In addition, content linked to broadcasts of football matches usually gets the highest number of comments (Gallardo-Camacho et al., 2016), so using social media as a way of staying in touch with fans is, on the face of it, an unmissable opportunity for athletes. Even those who had refused to use them have ultimately yielded to the evidence that social media are an excellent tool for boosting brand image. Moreover, it has been proven that developing strong social connections can lead to better sports performances (Freeman et al., 2009). Some studies have shown that athletes who use social media during their competitions experience positive feelings of connection, relaxation and gratification (Hayes et al., 2019), since it can alleviate their nervousness, and messages of encouragement posted by fans can generate positive reinforcement.

## 8.5 Fashion influencers

Fashion influencers have seen the boundaries between their public and private lives become blurred. Also, the concept of meritocracy has ceased to be decisive and 'self-effort is replaced by self-sufficient uniqueness' (Hou, 2018: 551).

For commercial brands, having influencers promote their products and services on Instagram offers greater reliability and trust than other traditional forms of advertising. Consequently, Instagram influencers must appear authentic (van Driel & Dumitrica 2021; Hou, 2018). That compels them to maintain an ever shifting balance. They must appear authentic in relation to their audiences while managing to get enough followers to attract advertisers. One of the dangers of professionalisation is the standardisation of their content, which may lead to them being perceived as unauthentic. The challenge is to successfully overcome this difficulty (van Driel & Dumitrica, 2021).

Instagram fashion influencers offering a unique, original and distinct image are the ones with the highest number of followers, and they are considered opinion leaders capable of influencing others. Coupled with that is the public's perception that they are creative. This leads the followers of an account to interact with it, and they then go on to recommend the account to others. This recommendation process helps to raise the account's value (Casaló et al., 2020: 6).

Taking an ecological view of Instagram as a fashion showcase, Suh (2020) considers that the platform allows space and time to be transcended through social connection. Sharing fashion photos via this social media platform seeks to turn the fashion and styling of our everyday lives into a work of art: '(it) can be seen as festivals of everyday life. They act as mediators of recent desires' (Suh, 2020: 14).

A study of the main Spanish influencers, both male and female, concludes that reference to the fashion brand sponsoring them is more explicit among male influencers than it is among female influencers. The latter combine sponsored posts with posts that are aimed more at looking after their community (González Fernández & Martínez-Sanz, 2018: 435).

Furthermore, Instagram influencers with the highest number of followers are perceived as more desirable. Popular success catches the eye and attracts new followers. However, if an Instagrammer follows few accounts, he or she is perceived as undesirable (De Veirman et al., 2017).

In turn, social media have amplified the word-of-mouth (WOM) effect to such an extent that a new term has been created: *electronic word-of-mouth* (eWOM). eWOM is usually defined as 'any positive or negative statement made available to a multitude of people and institutions via the Internet' (Hennig et al., 2015: 39). While fashion influencers on social media are individuals with high levels of credibility as regards their followers (Jin and Ryu 2019), they often have considerable influence on the groups most likely to end up buying something (García-de-Frutos & Estrella-Ramón, 2021). This influence goes beyond the intention to buy: studies such as the one by Nash (2018) point out that it even has an impact on the very identity of fashion consumers.

Millennials, the demographic group born between the mid-1980s and early 2000s, and Generation Z, born between the mid-1990s and mid-2000s, are together responsible for $350 billion of spending in the United States alone. Generation Z alone already accounts for 40 per cent of global consumers (Amed et al., 2019). At the same time, those belonging to this generation are the ones that can easily see themselves becoming fashion opinion leaders and making it their profession (Schouten et al., 2020; Palfrey & Gasser, 2013). It is therefore logical for this new class of influencers to have become a powerful marketing tool, aware of its own mobilising and trending capabilities (Park & Kim, 2016). eWOM has the biggest impact when done by renowned personalities (Erkan & Evans 2018), hence the interest that brands have in becoming associated with them (Backaler, 2018 and Kim & Ko, 2012). However, the important role played by micro-influencers must not be overlooked. While it is true that users often feel more attracted to macro-influencers (those with more than 150,000 followers, as this influences the perception of their credibility and popularity) (Jin & Phua, 2014), a study by Pérez Curiel and Luque Ortiz (2018) revealed that, especially among women, micro-influencers are also relevant as they show products that are more affordable for consumers.

In any case, both large and small influencers should consider the effects of doing too many advertising campaigns because, when users recognise an Instagram post as advertising, they are more likely not to share it via eWOM (Evans et al. 2017).

Given that the attitude towards an influencer has proved to be a clear predictor of the intention to buy (Bergkvist et al., 2016), every influencer must pay attention to all the elements involved in the perception of their own image. In the case of fashion influencers, the way they dress plays a central role in their lives (O'Cass, 2004), so dressing fashionably becomes an especially important requirement.

## 8.6 Cross-pollination and engagement

In line with the notion of system applied to social media, in this work we propose the idea of cross-pollination (Fernández Peña et al., 2011; Fernández Peña, 2016: 192–193). Regarding social media strategy, we see it from the viewpoint of network marketing. In its holistic conception, this idea of cross-pollination integrates all the digital presences of an individual or organisation: website, YouTube channel, and Facebook, Instagram, Twitter and TikTok accounts. Thus, the idea of cross-pollination is a systemic, holistic, integral vision. Posts on Twitter or Instagram cannot be considered in isolation or separately. Instead, the entirety of an individual's or organisation's social media presences must be taken into account, seeking complementarities and feedback between them. This leads to specialisation in one type of content and one type of audience on the various social media platforms, and then drives traffic to others, for example, from Facebook or Instagram to an individual's or organisation's website.

In the case of the National Basketball Association, the specialisation of social media is as follows:

> YouTube: Best plays, such as Daily Top 10 and outstanding performances. Facebook: Mostly off-the-court, behind-the-scenes content, as well as images and graphics. Twitter: Live events and breaking news, including score updates and in-game highlights. Snapchat: Live events from beginning to end via photos and videos. Instagram: Used for in-game and post-game highlights.
>
> (Argüelles, 2018: 21)

Here, we can see that there are no overlaps; a strategy that pursues complementarities has been intentionally created, bearing in mind that each social media platform has its own audience and its own specificity as regards communicative characteristics (Quesenberry, 2019).

Relationships between social media accounts and websites are also present in this vision of cross-pollination. The World Wide Web has made it possible for us to have an interactive, user-friendly communication system that can be accessed from anywhere in the world, and has allowed content to be interconnected by hyperlink (Berners-Lee, 2000). However, because of its nature, an active attitude is required for users to access information. It is, in our view, a form of static communication (Fernández Peña, 2016). Social media are venues where people come to connect with others, view their profiles and comment on posted content, hence they are deemed more dynamic. Here, audience participation is spontaneous and is part of the DNA of the platforms themselves. From the viewpoint of marketing on social media, there is considerable potential for feedback between individual's and institutions' social media accounts and websites, the latter of which are only visited if there is express and sufficient interest. Proposed within this cross-pollination model is that social media platforms and YouTube have the capacity to drive traffic to websites, the latter being understood as static communication elements (Fernández Peña et al., 2011).

On the other hand, in this social media environment, defined by the lead role that users have in creating and distributing messages, the key term is 'engagement', which refers to the public's participation or to its level of involvement in posts published by a third party, be it an organisation, firm or individual (Fernández Peña, Ramajo, & Arauz, 2014). From the corporate marketing perspective, engagement is defined as 'a behavioral manifestation toward the brand or firm that goes beyond transactions' (Verhoef et al., 2010: 247), and includes 'all consumer-to-firm interactions and consumer-to-consumer communications about the brand' (Gummerus et al., 2012: 858). Within this context, engagement can be viewed as a cognitive and affective link to a brand or product that a website or application embodies (Mollen & Wilson, 2010). Thus, user engagement turns out to be one of the main objectives of any firm, organisation, institution or individual with a presence on Instagram and other social media platforms. By its very nature, Instagram elicits an active response from the public.

The engagement rate on Instagram is much higher than on other social media platforms. Specifically, this platform offers a 669 per cent higher engagement rate than Twitter and a 70 per cent higher one than Facebook. It is, therefore, the best platform for achieving organic engagement, that is, unpaid. This has to do with outstanding content (Ahmed, 2017).

An engagement strategy on Instagram requires a friendly relationship with the audience, which includes responding to direct questions, and good management of hashtags, which focuses on niches relevant to the target audience. Specifically, the addition of anywhere between five and 12 hashtags is recommended, 'following the acronym CLEEP, which stands for category, location, emotion, event and product'. It is also essential to pay attention to the look of an Instagram account: 'good lighting, composition and consistent design are important' (Quesenberry, 2019: 148–9).

## 8.7 Method

This work is a qualitative study of the accounts of the top 10 star athletes on Instagram and the top 10 fashion Instagrammers by number of followers. The accounts were monitored between 1 May and 10 July 2021. The posts that had the highest levels of audience participation, that is, the most engagement, and the type of pre-eminent content in each one were analysed, with special attention being paid to advertising content. In addition, the degree of cross-pollination between the various social media accounts and websites was observed. Specifically analysed were potential transferrals of content and audiences between the official website of each of the celebrities and their respective YouTube channels and Instagram, TikTok, Twitter and Facebook accounts (Tables 8.1 and 8.2).

*Table 8.1* Athletes analysed, and their Instagram accounts

| Athlete | Account | Country | Sport | No. of followers | Other accounts |
|---|---|---|---|---|---|
| Cristiano Ronaldo | @cristiano | Portugal | Football | 308,000,000 | YouTube, TikTok, Twitter, Facebook, website |
| Virat Kohli | @virat.kohli | India | Cricket | 132,000,000 | TikTok, Twitter, Facebook, website |
| James Rodríguez | @jamesdrodriguez10 | Colombia | Football | 46,700,000 | TikTok, Twitter, Facebook |
| LeBron James | @kingjames | United States | Basketball | 89,800,000 | YouTube, Twitter, Facebook, website |
| David Beckham | @davidbeckham | England | Football | 67,000,000 | TikTok, Facebook, website |
| Zlatan Ibrahimovic | @iamzlatanibrahimovic | Sweden | Football | 47,900,000 | Twitter, Facebook, website |
| Leo Messi | @leomessi | Argentina | Football | 224,000,000 | YouTube, Facebook, website |
| Ronaldinho | @ronaldinho | Brazil | Football | 55,900,000 | YouTube, TikTok, Twitter, Facebook, website |
| Marcelo | @marcelotwelve | Brazil | Football | 48,000,000 | YouTube, TikTok, Twitter, Facebook |
| Kylian Mbappé | @k.mbappe | France | Football | 53,400,000 | YouTube, Twitter, Facebook, website |

Source: Own compilation. Number of followers as of 30 June 2021.

## 8.8 Results and discussion

### 8.8.1 Star athletes and fashion Instagrammers: engagement and content flow without cross-pollination

The first observation was that the three athletes with the highest average engagement rates were also the ones with the highest number of followers at the time of the analysis, that is, Cristiano Ronaldo, Leo Messi and Virat Kohli. Beyond this

*Table 8.2* Fashion influencers analysed, and their Instagram accounts

| Influencer | Account | Country | No. of followers | Other accounts |
|---|---|---|---|---|
| Kylie Jenner | @kyliejenner | United States | 248,300,000 | YouTube, TikTok, Twitter, Facebook, website |
| Kim Kardashian | @kimkardashian | United States | 236,100,000 | YouTube, TikTok, Twitter, Facebook, website |
| Kendall Jenner | @kendalljenner | United States | 175,100,000 | YouTube, Twitter, website |
| Khloé Kardashian | @khloekardashian | United States | 165,000,000 | YouTube, Twitter, Facebook |
| Kourtney Kardashian | @kourtneykardash | United States | 132,600,000 | YouTube, TikTok, Twitter, Facebook, website |
| Gigi Hadid | @gigihadid | United States | 68,000,000 | YouTube, Twitter, Facebook |
| Huda Kattan | @hudabeauty | United States | 49,000,000 | YouTube, TikTok, Twitter, Facebook, website |
| Lele Pons | @leleepons | Venezuela/ United States | 44,700,000 | YouTube, TikTok, Twitter, Facebook, website |
| Bella Hadid | @bellahadid | United States | 44,100,000 | TikTok, Twitter, Facebook |
| Cara Delevingne | @caradelevingne | United Kingdom | 43,600,000 | YouTube, Twitter, Facebook |

Source: Own compilation. Number of followers as of 30 June 2021.

logical correlation, the case of French football player Kylian Mbappé stood out. With only 53 million followers, his content averaged around 2 million likes and comments. Mbappé was therefore the player with the best follower/engagement ratio out of all the athletes analysed. This indicates a very effective content strategy, based on the diversification of message types and the exclusion, as far as possible, of advertising posts. Paying attention to the content of posts to ensure that they do not become repetitive or monothematic is a key point in effective social media communication design (Geurin-Eagleman & Burch, 2016). By prioritising sports content – Mbappé is often seen in in athletic stances while playing for his club or the French national team – and not overlooking personal posts, which are often highly successful, he employs a diversified strategy that points to a closer connection with the audience. Earlier studies have concluded that putting 'behind-the-scenes' (BTS) content into posts on other social media platforms such as Facebook was beneficial to the athletes: 'athletes have the opportunity to cultivate stronger relationships with fans via the sharing of personal aspects of the athlete's life such as family or hobbies' (Geurin-Eagleman and Clavio, 2015: 331). Thus, Mbappé (and all the athletes analysed, to a greater or lesser extent) shared photos of himself in non-sporting contexts, posing with his father or brother while using Instagram as a platform to promote the fact that he had been on the cover of the French magazine *L'Obs*.

Although Cristiano Ronaldo, with an average of more than 6 million, was the athlete – out of those studied – with the highest total engagement rates, Mbappé managed to be twice as efficient as the Portuguese football player. As already mentioned, a differential factor of Mbappé's success might lie in limiting advertising content, that is, not using too much of it in his profile. Advertising posts were classified as being the least important factor in the development of an athlete's image (Lebel & Danylchuk, 2014); however, in the sample analysed, the explicit promotion of sponsors by athletes such as the Colombian James Rodríguez was overrepresented.

This study found that there was a tendency to post numerous messages revealing the athletes' most private sides: their homes, children, partners and family. For example, in the case of Leo Messi, his most successful post was a video in which his teammates congratulated him on his birthday. This post alone received 6 million likes and 120,000 comments. These results are consistent with studies (Geurin-Eagleman & Burch, 2016; Hambrick et al., 2010; Kassing & Sanderson, 2010 and Pegoraro, 2010) reaffirming that fans were more interested in athletes' personal lives than in their professional ones.

These posts were mostly photos (71 per cent), a far higher proportion than content posted in video format (29 per cent). The simplicity of posting one or two photos, often taken as selfies by athletes themselves, was the preferred option because it is cheaper and less time-consuming than making a video with high production costs. It was advertising that had the capacity to make such videos, using them mostly to communicate their messages.

Several of the most successful sports advertising posts, that is, the most popular ones with the fans, were those relating to their national teams. Thus, feelings of union, camaraderie and patriotism are values that followers seemed to favour, as observed in posts by Virat Kohli, posing with the entire Indian cricket team, or by Cristiano Ronaldo, posing with the Portuguese football team.

As for the content of non-sports posts, most sports stars tended to produce superficial, politically correct messages, staying away from controversial issues. From the sample selected in this work, basketball star LeBron James stood out for having a politically clear stance, unambiguously supporting the Democrat politician Joe Biden. His statements, urging his followers to vote for Biden and showing his solidarity with civil rights movements such as Black Lives Matter, stood apart from others because they were unusual and direct, and might have affected the view that fans on the opposite side of the political spectrum held of him. This is because people tend to choose media news aligned with their political opinions (Garrett, 2009) and might reject those personalities who are manifestly opposed to their ideas.

Regarding the fashion influencers, the first thing that stood out in our observation was the female dominance of the fashion world on Instagram, the opposite to what happens in sport, where the 10 most followed influencers were men. Instagram, therefore, has inherited the traditional dynamics of content segmentation: sport is a male environment and fashion is a female one. In addition, in the case of fashion, members of the Kardashian family undisputedly held the top five positions. Together, they have almost a billion followers, whereas the next five influencers together have 250 million followers, a figure similar to that achieved by Kylie Jenner, the member of this popular family with the most fans. Given these facts, talking about fashion on Instagram is clearly synonymous with the Kardashians.

The posting dynamics of the Kardashian sisters were very similar. From an image viewpoint, considerable attention had been paid to the content. Even when they posted selfies, they were fully planned; within their empire, nothing could be left to chance. The format they used the most was the photo, precisely because it makes it easier to achieve that image of sought-after perfection. They posted very few videos, and the ones that they did often coincided with the launch of their respective brand products (Ahmed, 2017). However, there was a small number of videos showing scenes of their everyday lives, with family, with friends or having fun.

The behaviour of other fashion Instagrammers was similar. Fundamentally, Instagram was a huge promotional showcase for them. All the analysed Instagrammers advertised various products, mostly related to the fashion world (luxury clothing brands, beauty products or accessories), although the members of the famous family also lent their image to alcoholic beverages. Advertising posts accounted for 35 per cent of the total analysed, exceeding the recommended limit as a proportion of all content. Some studies (Hambrick et al. 2010; Hambrick & Mahoney 2011) have found that advertising content usually accounts for 5–12 per cent of total posts. In this regard, the dynamics followed by Huda Kattan are worth highlighting. The influencer is the founder of the Huda Beauty cosmetic line. Her Instagram account, @hudabeauty, is dedicated exclusively to promoting and selling her products. Of the total posts analysed for this account, only one did not focus on her products. It was a video addressing her followers, in which she advocated banishing negative and offensive comments from social media.

As with the Kardashian sisters and the athletes analysed, the preferred posting format was the photo, one that is capable of prompting a higher number of audience reactions. However, there were some exceptions among these influencers too: Huda Kattan showed followers how to use her products and, to do so, videos – as tutorials – were the chosen format. The rest of the content analysed used either format depending on the purpose of the post: poses were in photo format, and the catwalk, scenes of everyday life and the tutorials mentioned above were mostly in video format. In figures, one-quarter of the content corresponded to videos (26 per cent) and the rest (74 per cent) to photos. These data are consistent with the fact that photos yield a higher degree of engagement on Instagram. Of all posts on Instagram, 86 per cent are photos. Content in this format gets the highest level of audience participation in the form of engagement. Photos generate 1.1 per cent engagement and videos 0.8 per cent. Therefore, 38 per cent more engagement is achieved with photos than with videos (Ahmed, 2017).

When almost 250 million followers are reached, the anticipated engagement in posts within another context must also attain unthinkable rates. In this sense, Kylie Jenner managed to get just over 15 million likes and comments by posting a photo with her partner. But, her sister Kendall, with 75 million fewer followers, surpassed 16 million interactions with a video showing her favourite relaxation techniques. In both cases, they were not advertising posts, but instead were linked to the stars' most private circle. This pattern held true for the other Instagrammers studied: the content that generated greater engagement was related to their respective private spheres, in which they showed themselves with their family or in everyday scenes. Another example of such interest was the video of Lele Pons greeting Daddy Yankee. This Venezuelan-American woman is known on social media for offering videos with a touch of humour. In particular, that video got more than 12 million likes and comments from a community of followers of just over 44 million. It therefore had the best ratio between number of followers and engagement achieved.

At the opposite end of the spectrum was content that achieved the least engagement, where we found promotional product posts, once again demonstrating that the audience is more interested in the personal sphere of Instagrammers and less so in their commercial activities. Take, for example, the post by Kylie Jenner launching her new bath products, which only achieved a million interactions, and compare it to the 15 million she got for a photo of her and her partner. Or the one by Kourtney Kardashian promoting her website on wellness, health, nutrition and styling, which did not manage to reach a million likes and comments. In this sense, as Hearn and Schoenhoff (2016) have already pointed out, celebrities can take advantage of social media to show themselves being 'themselves' with brands they are promoting around them, rather than posing with them in artificial advertisements.

In short, we can assert that the relationship between engagement achieved and content posted favours the private sphere side, which is consistent with the findings of Hou (2018). Little by little, that private sphere – an environment accessible to the few – is emerging into the public sphere, one where things are shared with a community of followers.

### 8.8.2 Cross-pollination as the integral management of digital presence

The absolute leader on Instagram and on other social media platforms was Cristiano Ronaldo, with more than 300 million followers of his Instagram account. However, he did not consider the website to be part of an integral communication system. In his case, and in the case of most athletes, there was no stratified content strategy adapted to social media and audiences. For example, most of them posted the same content on Instagram, Facebook and Twitter. The only social media platform on which they published specific content was TikTok, whose communicative characteristics limit the type of content that can be shown, which, in this case, must be fun, family scenes. Compared to Ronaldo, Messi had a more active website, a snapshot of his sporting and promotional activities, but he did not have accounts on TikTok or Twitter. In the case of Facebook and

Instagram, the interoperability between the two made the content posted on them the same. This overlap between content on Instagram and Facebook – and sometimes on Twitter – was observed in other athletes like Virat Kohli, LeBron James and Ibrahimovic. The absence of cross-pollination in the case of sports stars was striking when compared to the use of this strategy by sports organisations such as the NBA (Argüelles, 2018) or the Olympic Channel (Fernández Peña & Ramajo, 2021).

The athletes' websites were repositories of biographical content, whereas the Instagrammers' websites were commercially orientated and designed to sell products, as in the case of Kim Kardashian. However, there were some exceptions, Kendall Jenner being one of them, whose website was a predominantly audiovisual biographical platform. All the influencers repeatedly used Instagram as a personal photo and product promotion platform. Unlike the athletes, the Instagrammers were very active on YouTube, a social media platform for which exclusive content is created, in which they told the audience about the products they were promoting. Channel specialisation was observed to a greater extent among Instagrammers than it was among athletes: Website: e-Commerce; Instagram: Personal and product photos; YouTube: Videos with explanations; TikTok: Fun videos of products and family members. In the case of Kylie Jenner, a promotional feedback process on Twitter was observed, which was sometimes used to promote YouTube videos. The presence of these Instagrammers on Facebook was generally marginal, and their Instagram content was often repeated on it.

## 8.9 Conclusions

The athletes analysed can be situated within the general concept of being famous; they are people in whom a glory acquired through effort and talent has been deposited. A ubiquitous media presence resulting from their fame won through merit has also turned them into celebrities who are followed by millions of people worldwide. Although athletes devote some of their Instagram posts to their professional activities, it is within the realm of their private lives and of brand promotion that the worlds of athletes and fashion Instagrammers converge. The meritocracy of muscle and effort and the aristocracy of beauty therefore meet.

Sports careers and their projection in the media not only rely on athletic skills and triumphs but, in quite a few cases, are also complemented by a mastery of communication skills that goes beyond sport per se: aesthetic aspects, appropriate management, and the quest for synergies between them and social media communication resources and brand promotion, among others.

For sports stars and Instagrammers alike, the engagement generated by personal content, such as photos of them with their families or funny videos arising from once private situations, is higher than that of any other type of content, far exceeding the engagement achieved by promotional themes. Social media are an opportunity for a direct relationship with the audience. Private videos or BTS ones of sport or professional activities help to weave a kind of complicity with the audience, which can be exploited in order to achieve greater engagement in content sponsored by brands.

The concept of cross-pollination, which operates in companies and institutions such as the NBA or the Olympic Channel, does not occur in the case of sports personalities, and is observed only very marginally among the fashion Instagrammers. Since the communicative and interaction characteristics of Instagram, Facebook and Twitter are similar, the same content is quite often repeated across the three platforms with very few changes. Instagram is a mixed social media platform, with a combination of the communicative qualities of Facebook and Twitter. The cases analysed did not opt for the audience segmentation that each of the platforms would have allowed them to achieve, and specific content for a specific platform was only created in a few cases. This occurred when the communicative specificities of a platform required a different type of content. That was so for TikTok and YouTube.

For fashion influencers, advertising content accounted for more than 30 per cent of total content, whereas for a sports star like James Rodríguez, it accounted for 18 per cent, above the desirable limit and potentially leading to audience saturation.

The observed players exhibited a behaviour that is now common among sports stars: they combined mostly sports-related posts – showing themselves while performing training exercises, during matches or celebrating goals or victories with their teammates – with more personal, promotional and advertising-related messages. With audiences in their millions, promotional content allows athletes to give visibility to their own brands and products, especially sports clothes and footwear, and, as in the case of Cristiano Ronaldo, to hotels and colognes too.

Fashion Instagrammers follow a very similar dynamic. More than anyone else, they represent the paradigm of beauty and body worship. Through their image, they ensure that any brand of their own or a third party that they are able to promote becomes the one to which their legions of followers aspire. The smartphone screen becomes the mirror in which everyone looks, seeing a reflected image that many want to identify as their own.

In future works, we will address a number of challenges relating to cross-pollination on social media. One of them is to check whether this systemic strategy is implemented by large organisations, as opposed to the personal accounts of famous people or celebrities. The other challenge we have set ourselves is to create an analysis methodology, complemented by software that allows cross-pollination in the digital presences of an organisation, personality or brand to be analysed.

## Acknowledgements

This work was supported by the Ministry of Economy and Competitiveness of Spain for the CSO2015-69289-R project and the predoctoral grant BES-2016-078978 associated with it.

## Note

1  All quotes by Capra have been translated from Spanish.

## References

Abosag, I., Roper, S. & Hind, D. (2012). Examining the relationship between brand emotion and brand extension among supporters of professional football clubs. *European Journal of Marketing*, 46(9):1233–1251.

Ahmed, T. (2017). Instagram engagement rate is 70% higher than Facebook. *Locowise*, 14 March. https://locowise.com/blog/instagram-engagement-rate-is-higher-than-facebook (Accessed 2 July 2020).

Amed, I., Balchandani, A., Beltrami, M., Berg, A., Hedrich, S. & Rölkens, F. (2019). The influence of 'woke' consumers on fashion. https://www.mckinsey.com/industries/retail/our-insights/the-influence-of-woke-consumers-on-fashion (Accessed 1 July 2020).

Andrews, D.L. & Jackson, S.J. (2001). *Sport Stars: The Politics of Sporting Celebrity*. London: Routledge.

Argüelles, H. (2018). *NBA Global Media Distribution*. Power Point Presentation provided by the author.

Backaler, J. (2018). *Digital Influence. Case Studies: Influencer Marketing Best Practices from Around the World*. Cham: Palgrave Macmillan.

Barclay, P. (2015). Reputation. *The Handbook of Evolutionary Psychology*, 1–19.

Bergkvist, L., Hjalmarson, H. & Mägi, A. (2016). A new model of how celebrity endorsements work: Attitude toward the endorsement as a mediator of celebrity source and endorsement effects. *International Journal of Advertising*, 35(2):171–184. http://dx.doi.org/10.1080/02650487.2015.1024384

Berners-Lee, T. (2000). *Weaving the Web: The Original Design and Ultimate Destiny of the World Wide Web* (1st ed.). Harper Business.

Bordieu, P. (2010). *Distinction: A Social Critique of the Judgement of Taste* (UK ed.). London: Routledge.

Braunstein, J. & Zhang, J. (2005). Dimensions of athletic star power associated with generation Y sports consumption. *International Journal of Sports Marketing and Sponsorship*, 6:242–267.

Burton, N. & Chadwick, S. (2008). From Beckham to Ronaldo – Assessing the nature of football players brands. *Journal of Sponsorship*, 1(4):307–317.

Capra, F. (1998). *La trama de la vida. Una nueva perspectiva de los sistemas vivos*. Barcelona: Anagrama.

Casaló, L. V., Flavián, C. & Ibáñez-Sánchez, S. (2020). Influencers on Instagram: Antecedents and consequences of opinion leadership. *Journal of Business Research*, 117:510–519.

Chaffey, D. (2021). Global social media research summary 2021. https://www.smartinsights.com/social-media-marketing/social-media-strategy/new-global-social-media-research/

Choi, S. M. & Rifon, N. J. (2007). Who is the celebrity in advertising? Understanding dimensions of celebrity images. *The Journal of Popular Culture*, 40:304–324.

Christakis, N. & Fowler, J. (2011). *Connected: The Amazing Power of Social Networks and How They Shape Our Lives*. London: Harper Collins.

Cortsen, K. (2013). Annika Sörenstam – A hybrid personal sports brand. *Sport, Business and Management: An International Journal*, 3(1):37–62.

Daniels, E. (2009). Sex objects, athletes, and sexy athletes: How media representations of women athletes can impact adolescent girls and college women. *Journal of Adolescent Research*, 24:399–422.

De Veirman, M., Cauberghe, V. & Hudders, L. (2017). Marketing through Instagram influencers: The impact of number of followers and product divergence on brand attitude. *International Journal of Advertising*, 3(5):798–828.

Demirel, A. & Erdogmus, I. (2016). The impacts of fans' sincerity perceptions and social media usage on attitude toward sponsor. *Sport, Business and Management: An International Journal*, 6 (1):36–54.

Dickson, G. (2012). Charisma, Medieval and Modern. *Religions*, 3(3):763–789. DOI: 10.3390/rel3030763

Ellul, J. (1963). *The Technological Society*. New York: Vintage Books.

Erkan, I. & Evans, C. (2018). Social media or shopping websites? The influence of eWOM on consumers' online purchase intentions. *Journal of Marketing Communications*, 24(6):617–632.

Evans, N. J., Phua, J., Lim, J., and Jun, H. (2017). Disclosing Instagram influencer advertising: The effects of disclosure language on advertising recognition, attitudes, and behavioral intent. *Journal of Interactive Advertising*, 17(2):138–149.

Fernández Peña, E. (2016). *Juegos Olímpicos, Televisión y Redes Sociales*. Barcelona: UOC.

Fernández Peña, E., Arauz, M. & Sha, A. (2011). *Social networking and the Olympic Movement: Social media analysis, opportunities and trends. Report commissioned by the IOC*. http://ceo.uab.cat/es/b/social-networking-and-the-olympic-movement-social-media-analysis-opportunities-and-trends/

Fernández Peña, E. & Ramajo, N. (2021). Olympic Channel: Estrategia Digital y Contenidos. *Journal of Human Sport and Exercise*, 16:1. https://doi.org/10.14198/jhse.2021.16.Proc1.01

Fernández Peña, E., Ramajo, N. & Arauz, M. (2014). Social Media in the Olympic Games: Actors, Management and Participation. Sport and New Media. In A. Billings and M. Hardin (Eds.), *Routledge Handbook of Sport and New Media*, 153–164. London: Routledge.

Freeman, P., Rees, T. and Hardy, L. (2009). An intervention to increase social support and improve performance. *Journal of Applied Sport Psychology*, 21(2):186–200.

Gallardo-Camacho, J., Lavín, E. & Fernández-García, P. (2016). Los programas de televisión deportivos y su relación con la audiencia social en Twitter en España. *Revista Latina de Comunicación Social*, 71:272–286.

García-de-Frutos, N. & Estrella-Ramón, A. (2021). You absolutely (don't) need this! Examining differences on customer engagement components for (anti)haul youtubers' videos. *Journal of Research in Interactive Marketing*, 15(1):86–103. https://doi.org/10.1108/JRIM-11-2019-0181

Garrett, R. K. (2009). Echo chambers online? Politically motivated selective exposure among internet news users. *Journal of Computer-Mediated Communication*, 14:265–285.

Geurin-Eagleman, A. N. & Burch, L. M. 2016. Communicating via photographs: A gendered analysis of Olympic athletes' visual self-presentation on Instagram. *Sport Management Review*, 19:133–145.

Geurin-Eagleman, A. N. & Clavio, G. 2015. Utilizing social media as a marketing communication tool: An examination of mainstream and niche sport athletes' Facebook pages. *International Journal of Sport Management*, 16(2):316–334.

González Fernández, C. & Martínez-Sanz, R. 2018. Fashion influencers and Instagram. A quasi-perfect binomial. *Studies in Communication Sciences*, 18(2):425–437.

Gracián, B. (1892/1904). *The Art of Worldly Wisdom*. London: Macmillan.

Gummerus, J., Liljander, V., Weman, E. & Pihlström, M. 2012. Customer engagement in a Facebook brand community. *Management Research Review*, 35(9):857–877.

Hambrick, M. E. and Mahoney, T. Q. 2011. 'It's incredible – Trust me': Exploring the role of celebrity athletes as marketers in online social networks. *International Journal of Sport Management and Marketing*, 10:161–179.

Hambrick, M.E., Simmons, J.M., Greenhalgh, G. P. & Greenwell, C. T. 2010. Understanding professional athletes' use of Twitter: A content analysis of athlete tweets. *International Journal of Sport Communication*, 3:454–471.

Hasaan, A., Agyemang, K., Biscaia, R. & Kerem, K. 2018. A conceptual framework to understand the creation of athlete brand and its implications. *International Journal of Sport Management and Marketing*, 18(3):169–197.

Hayes, M., Filo, K., Riot, C. & Geurin, A. 2019. Athlete perceptions of social media benefits and challenges during major sport events. *International Journal of Sport Communication*, 12:1–33.

Hearn, A. & Schoenhoff, S. 2016. From Celebrity to Influencer. Tracing the Diffusion of Celebrity Value Across the Data Stream. In D. Marshall and S. Redmond (Eds.), *A Companion to Celebrity*. New York: Wiley.

Hennig, T. T., Wiertz, C. & Feldhaus, F. 2015. Does twitter matter? The impact of microblogging word of mouth on consumers' adoption of new movies. *Journal of the Academy of Marketing Science*, 43(3):375–394.

Hou M. 2018. Social media celebrity and the institutionalization of YouTube convergence. *The International Research Journal into New Media Technologies*. Online First: 1–20.

Hsieh, A. T. & Li, C. K. 2008. The moderating effect of brand image on public relations perception and customer loyalty. *Marketing Intelligence and Planning*, 26(1):26–42.

Isaacson, W. 2015. *Steve Jobs*. London: Abacus.

Jenkins, H. 2006. *Convergence Culture*. New York: New York University Press.

Jenkins, H., Ford, S. & Green, J. 2018. *Spreadable Media*. New York: New York University Press.

Jin, S. A. & Phua, J. 2014. Following celebrities' tweets about brands: The impact of Twitter-based electronic word-of-mouth on consumers' source credibility perception, buying intention, and social identification with celebrities. *Journal of Advertising*, 43(2):181–195.

Jin, S. V. & Ryu, E. 2019. Celebrity fashion brand endorsement in Facebook viral marketing and social commerce. *Journal of Fashion Marketing and Management*, 23(1):104–123.

Kassing, J. W. & Sanderson, J. 2010. Fan-athlete interaction and Twitter tweeting through the Giro: A case study. *International Journal of Sport Communication*, 3(1):113–128.

Kiefer, S. 2014. The impact of the Euro 2012 on popularity and market value of football players. *International Journal of Sport Finance*, 9(2):95–110.

Kim, A. J. & Ko, E. 2012. Do social media marketing activities enhance customer equity? An empirical study of luxury fashion brand. *Journal of Business Research*, 65(10):1480–1486. DOI: 10.1016/j.jbusres.2011.10.014

Lau, P., Cheung, M. & Ransdell, L. 2008. A structural equation model of the relationship between body perception and self-esteem: Global physical self-concept as the mediator. *Psychology of Sport and Exercise*, 9:493–509.

Leary, M. R. & Kowalski, R. M. 1990. Impression management: A literature review and two-component model. *Psychological Bulletin*, 107(1):34–47.

Lebel, K. & Danylchuk, K. 2014. Facing off on Twitter: A generation Y interpretation of professional athlete profile pictures. *International Journal of Sport Communication*, 7(3):317–336.

Lee, E., Lee, J., Moon, J. H. & Sung, Y. 2015. Pictures speak louder than words: Motivations for using Instagram. *Cyberpsychology, Behavior and Social Networking*, 18(9).

Lilti, A., 2017. *The Invention of Celebrity: 1750–1850*. Cambridge: Polity Press.

Lipovetsky, G. 1991. *Empire de l'éphémère*. Paris: Gallimard Education.

Lipovetsky, G. & Charles, S. 2005. *Hypermodern Times* (1st ed.). Cambridge: Polity Press.

Locke, C., Levine, R., Searls, D. & Weinberger, D. 2001. *The Cluetrain Manifesto: The End of Business as Usual* (Reprint ed.). New York: Basic Books.

Madden, M. & Smith, A. 2010. *Reputation Management and Social Media*. Washington, DC: Pew Internet and American Life Project. http://www.pewinternet.org/2010/05/26/reputation-management-and-social-media/ (Accessed 21 June 2021).

Markos, E., Labrecque, L. I. & Milne, G. R. 2011. Online personal branding: Processes, challenges, and implications. *Journal of Interactive Marketing*, 25(1):37–50.

Miles, J. G. 2014. *Instagram Power*. New York: McGraw Hill.

Mollen, A. & Wilson, H. 2010. Engagement, telepresence and interactivity in online consumer experience: Reconciling scholastic and managerial perspectives. *Journal of Business Research*, 63(9–10):919–925.

Nash, J. 2018. Exploring how social media platforms influence fashion consumer decisions in the UK retail sector. *Journal of Fashion Marketing and Management*, 23(1):82–103. DOI: 10.1108/JFMM-01-2018-0012

O'Cass, A. 2004. Fashion clothing consumption: Antecedents and consequences of fashion clothing involvement. *European Journal of Marketing*, 38(7):869–882. DOI: 10.1108/03090560410539294

Palfrey, J. & Gasser, U. 2013. *Born Digital: Understanding the First Generation of Digital Natives*. New York: Basic Books.

Park, H. & Kim, Y.-K. 2016. Proactive versus reactive apparel brands in sustainability: Influences on brand loyalty. *Journal of Retailing and Consumer Services*, 29:114–122.

Pegoraro, A. 2010. Look who's talking – athletes on Twitter: A case study. International *Journal of Sport Communication*, 3(4):501–514.

Pérez Curiel, C. & Luque Ortiz, S. 2018. El marketing de influencia en moda. Estudio del nuevo modelo de consumo en Instagram de los millennials universitarios. adComunica. *Revista Científica de Estrategias, Tendencias e Innovación en Comunicación*, 15:255–281. DOI: http://dx.doi.org/10.6035/2174-0992.2018.15.13

Postman, N. 2005. *Amusing Ourselves to Death: Public Discourse in the Age of Show Business* (20th anniv. Ed.). New York: Penguin Group.

Preskar, P. 2020. The highest-paid athlete of all time. *History of Yesterday*, 19 July 2020. https://historyofyesterday.com/the-highest-paid-athlete-of-all-time-4f40f9fc89f7 (Accessed 30 June 2021).

Quesenberry, K. A. 2019. *Social Media Strategy: Marketing, Advertising, and Public Relations in the Consumer Revolution (English Edition)* (2nd ed.). Lanham: Rowman and Littlefield Publishers.

Rojek, C. 2006. Sports celebrity and the civilizing process. *Sport in Society*, 9(4):674–690.

Rushe, D. 2012. Facebook spends $1 bn to get in mobile photo sharing frame: Instagram's huge price tag defies its profitless record App took just eight weeks to build and launch. *The Guardian*, 10 April 2012: 5.

Sandvoss, C. 2005. *Fans: The Mirror of Consumption*. Cambridge: Polity Press.

Schouten, A., Janssen, L. & Verspaget, M. 2020. Celebrity vs. Influencer endorsements in advertising: The role of identification, credibility, and Product-Endorser fit. *International Journal of Advertising*, 39(2):258–281, DOI: 10.1080/02650487.2019.1634898

Seno, D. & Lukas, B. 2007. The equity effect of product endorsement by celebrities. A conceptual framework from a co-branding perspective. *European Journal of Marketing*, 41:121–134.

Sloterdijk, P. 2012. *Has de cambiar tu vida*. Valencia: Pre-Textos.

Soukup, C. 2006. Hitching a ride on a star: Celebrity, fandom, and identification with the world wide web. *Southern Communication Journal*, 71:319–337.

St. James, M. 2010. Female sports celebrities targeting female teenagers: A content analysis of magazine advertising. *Journal of Business and Economics Research*, 8(1):1–13.

Suh, S. 2020. Fashion everydayness as a cultural revolution in social media platforms-focus on fashion Instagrammers. *Sustainability*, 12(5):1979.

Theysohn, S., Hinz, O., Nosworthy, S. & Kirchner, M. 2009. Official supporters clubs: The untapped potential of fan loyalty. *International Journal of Sports Marketing and Sponsorship*, 10(4):302–324.

van Amsterdam, N., Knoppers, A., & Jongmans, M. 2012. A picture is worth a thousand words: Constructing (non-)athletic bodies. *Journal of Youth Studies*, 15(3):293–309.

van Driel, L., & Dumitrica, D. 2021. Selling brands while staying "Authentic": The professionalization of Instagram influencers. *Convergence: The International Journal of Research into New Media Technologies*, 27(1):66–84.

Veà, A. 2013. *¿Cómo creamos Internet?*. Madrid: Atalaya.

Verhoef, P. C., Reinartz, W. J., & Krafft, M. 2010. Customer engagement as a new perspective in customer management, *Journal of Service Research*, 13(3):247–252.

Wann, D. L., & Branscombe, N. R. 1993. Sports fans: Measuring degree of identification with the team. *International Journal of Sport Psychology*, 24:1–17.

Weiss, O. 2001. Identity reinforcement in sport: Revisiting the symbolic interactionist legacy. *International Review for the Sociology of Sport*, 36(4):393–405.

Wesolowski, A. D. 2020. Beyond celebrity history: Towards the consolidation of fame studies. *Celebrity Studies*, 11(1):189–204.

Wu, S., Tsai, C. D., & Hung, C. 2012. Toward team or player? How trust, vicarious achievement motive, and identification affect fan loyalty. *Journal of Sport Management*, 26(2):177–191.

Zulli, D. 2018. Capitalizing on the look: Insights into the glance, attention economy and Instagram. *Critical Studies in Media Communication*, 35(2):137–150.

# 9 Crowd influences in branded communities

## The case of CrossFit

*Anne Morawietz, Adele Berndt and Tomas Müllern*

## 9.1 Introduction

Social media influencers have had a lasting effect on market communication and brand promotion practices. Recent research has indicated aspects associated with the functioning of influencer marketing and how individual influencers have become a powerful voice in creating brand awareness and brand loyalty (Abidin, 2016; Abidin & Ots, 2016; Enke & Borchers, 2019). Successful social media influencers turn into celebrities that act as endorsers of brands and products. The perceived credibility of the endorser can generate important marketing effects among consumers, for instance generating higher trust in the brand (Lou & Yuan, 2019), drawing consumer attention to the brand (Campbell & Farrell, 2020), and strengthening processes of identification with the brand (Feng et al., 2020). The growing literature on influencer marketing has focused much attention on the role of individual influencers and how they act as celebrity endorsers for specific brands. The consumer typically is given a relatively passive role in the social media influencer literature. In this chapter we draw on literature that describes consumers as active creators of value both on social media (online) and in the physical (offline) context, interacting actively with other consumers of the brand, the individual influencers as well as with the brand (Martínez-López et al., 2020).

Consumers, specifically when consuming online, are more active than previously (Kozinets, 1999), co-creating a range of experiences (Firat & Shultz, 1997). However, the emphasis has been on individual influencers who use self-presentation to attract followers and influence behaviour (Chae, 2018; Khamis et al., 2017; Lim et al., 2017) and not on the influencer dynamics that can be exerted by the crowd, both on other members of the brand community but also on other communities within the brand. In that way, we draw attention to the process of influencing, rather than focus on the individual influencer.

Brand communities, the "specialized, non-geographically bound community that is based on a structured set of social relations among admirers of a brand" (Muniz & O'Guinn, 2001 p. 412) which are increasingly the focus of research in marketing, specifically regarding the engagement and influence between members, highlighting the processes of influencing. This is specifically relevant where relationships exist between individual community members and with the brand itself (Ouwersloot & Odekerken-Schröder, 2008).

DOI: 10.4324/9781003134176-10

A context where these aspects are evident is CrossFit, a "lifestyle characterised by safe exercise and sound nutrition" which is available to people of differing fitness levels. CrossFit acknowledges the importance of both online and offline interaction between members of the community (CrossFit, n.d.-b). The devolved perspective of fitness allows for viewing CrossFit as member-driven, highlighting the importance of the individuals and their interaction with other community members to build the CrossFit brand (CrossFit, n.d.-a). Thus, we propose that influence exists between all members within a community the brand as well as a range of affiliated brands, and also exists between communities associated with the same brand, with CrossFit a suitable context for studying community (Blenkarn, 2018).

The basic definition of influencer marketing offered by the much-cited article by Lou and Yuan (2019) reads as follows: "a marketing strategy that uses the influence of key individuals or opinion leaders to drive consumers' brand awareness and/or their purchasing decisions". The traditional narrow focus on key individuals or opinion leaders does not apply to the empirical context of CrossFit which is more than just several key individuals. By extending this definition not only to individuals as influencers but to also include groups, it can be used to understand the role and importance of crowds as influencers within brand communities. With such an extended definition, influencer marketing becomes, even more, a co-created process where individuals engage with the community, for instance by sharing content, at the same time as they are influenced by others in the same community. We use the term crowd influencing to describe how the processes of influencing emerge in a brand community as seen in the CrossFit context, and that is not directly attributed to what is usually referred to as individual influencers. In a sense, the process of influencing is thus associated with being "freed" from the single influencer and becoming a part of the community, thereby also a community activity.

## 9.2 Purpose of the chapter

Previous brand community research has examined a range of products including cars and motorcycles (Cova & Cova, 2002; McAlexander et al., 2002), computers (Muniz & Schau, 2005) and consumer products such as Nutella (Cova & Pace, 2006) while Ouwersloot and Odekerken-Schröder (2008) investigated a board game community. Influencer research has not only tended to focus on online communities (Abidin, 2016), without extensive consideration of the offline community but has also focused on the effect of individual influencers (Khamis et al., 2017). With the relatively recent development of CrossFit, there has been limited published research into the community and well as the form and types of influences that exist within and between the various members of this community which functions both offline (in the box) and online (on social media).

Consequently, the chapter aims to provide a conceptual model that seeks to conceptualise and illustrate the nature of these dynamic influences based in the CrossFit context. In this chapter we use the case of CrossFit to describe the phenomena of crowd influencing (moving within and between online and offline communities and its members), the process, reason and outcome of influence and how it has contributed to make CrossFit a global success story through co-creation and a heightened sense of community, generating very strong brand loyalty.

### 9.2.1 The CrossFit context

People have always needed to connect with other people both for interaction and the shared commitment to or connection to a common purpose or goal such as positive personal change (Belger, 2012). People want to be healthy, which is associated with engaging in an exercise programme, such as running, cycling, or joining the gym. A rather recent additional option is CrossFit which is described as an exercise regime that not only provides a range of exercises but that also provides a supportive community where people work out together (Dawson, 2017 p. 364) but which has been also described as cult-like (Dawson, 2017; Rasczyk & Stephens, 2015).

CrossFit is a form of exercise that revolves around natural movements such as sitting down and standing up, running, lifting, throwing, climbing, jumping, pushing, and dragging. Those movements are natural to humankind, applicable to everyday life and they form the basis for the exercises that CrossFitters strive to master (CrossFit, n.d.-b). It is an intensive training that combines different types of exercises in various routines called WODs (Workouts of the Day). The training takes place with, for example, barbells, dumbbells, kettlebells, railings, climbing ropes, jump ropes, Roman rings, medicine balls, and other simple tools. CrossFit does not use machines. CrossFit practitioners rarely do the same routines during the same week or month but seek variety. In other words, CrossFit training is rather a philosophy and based on principles than an exact program or schedule (CrossFit, n.d.-b) to develop a level of fitness that adapts to any situation, encounter, task, or demand – no matter whether the individual is familiar with it or has never done it before (Belger, 2012).

CrossFit workouts mostly take place in affiliated gyms which are referred to as "boxes" which are usually situated in industrial areas. In contrast to many typical gyms, CrossFit is not a franchising organization. To run a CrossFit branded gym, the applicant must be at least a Level 1 Certificate holder, indicating that they have the necessary qualifications. Certification seminars are held several times a year around the world. In addition, proof of insurance is required from US applicants and insurance recommended elsewhere. The application requires three name proposals that include the word CrossFit whereby the "F" in CrossFit is always capitalized. Only the licensed name may be used. Each box must pay a yearly affiliation fee of US $3,000 to CrossFit LLC. Leader certificates must be renewed every five years (CF-L1 and CF-L2) and CrossFit affiliates can set their own rates.

Being a CrossFit affiliate entails the legal use of the CrossFit name, logo, and promotional materials, and the CrossFit Kids name. It also includes promotion from CrossFit.com and support from CrossFit, LLC on specific and general issues. While all affiliate gyms follow the CrossFit method, they vary tremendously in size, scope, style, and kind (Belger, 2012).

## 9.3 The CrossFit community

A CrossFit box is usually set up with minimal equipment, unlike a traditional gym that provides different kinds of machines such as rowing machines and exercise bicycles. While working out on these machines in the traditional gym, members can create virtual boundaries with others by watching TV or listening to music while using workout machines (Dawson, 2017). In contrast, CrossFitters on the other hand are not given the same chance to be anonymous, mentally and physically cutting themselves off as their group CrossFit training requires active participation. Thus, while many people join CrossFit to improve their general fitness (i.e., with self-focused fitness goals), the community emerges automatically through interaction. The value of the presence of other people makes CrossFitters push themselves and perform beyond their perceived limitations (Belger, 2012). Community and inclusivity are the cornerstones of CrossFit (Knapp, 2015b). Everybody is welcome and often new friendships are made. CrossFit does not discriminate against age, gender, race, religion, sexual orientation, or even fitness level.

To help travelling CrossFitters exercise while away from home, Greg Glassman introduced an online component in 2001 to add to the offline component, creating a website that provided daily workouts and allowed participants to keep track of their scores (Herz, 2015). CrossFit.com quickly attracted other fitness enthusiasts who liked the workouts and sharing their experiences (Heywood, 2015). The web-based component of CrossFit encourages a user-generated culture (Dawson, 2017). CrossFit owns and contributes to a range of different media channels, having a YouTube account and official Instagram, Twitter, Facebook accounts. CrossFit leverages a variety of messages to different platforms. While other sports often use their social media accounts as opportunities to sell products only 2 per cent of the messages were promotional (Kang et al., 2019). It also supports its members through its free journal, The CrossFit Journal (https://journal.crossfit.com) which provides daily workouts, articles, and videos. It facilitates community through constant dialogue and feedback with and among participants and observers (Knapp, 2015a).

Typical of brand communities (Dawson, 2017; Muniz & O'Guinn, 2001), CrossFit members share not only a common interest (Kozinets, 1999) in this instance exercise and nutrition but also the traditions and rituals which guide their behaviour in the community (Belger, 2012). Knowledge of the traditions and rituals enables community members to distinguish between insiders and outsiders, evidence through the use of unique terminology such as a "box" (gym), girls (benchmark workouts) or WODs (Gomillion, 2017; Pekkanen et al., 2017). Interaction does not only take place in the box through the provision of support to others (Dawson, 2017) but there are also opportunities to compete with other members across the world, for example, the CrossFit Games (Belger, 2012). The posting of achievements is also regularly undertaken as a form of inspiration to other members of the community.

To those used to working out in an isolated manner at traditional gyms (among strangers), these characteristics can be off-putting, supporting a view that CrossFit is less an exercise program than a cult (Dawson, 2017).

## 9.4 Developing a sense of community

The CrossFit community works as a support network for many and goes beyond the community found in a traditional gym. CrossFitters encourage and motivate each other in every class as they work toward their goals. For example, being the last one to finish a workout, one is likely to be surrounded by everyone else in the class, cheering them on. After each session, it is common to give everybody a high-five or fist-bump and congratulate them on a WOD well done. There is a lot of cheering and encouragement during a typical class which almost makes one forget that it is a competitive sport. Social connectedness and social capital positively impact physical and psychological health. The combination of the content of the CrossFit program and the process of how it is transmitted (group setting with shared fitness goals) leads to even greater positive effects (Belger, 2012), thus emphasizing the importance of engagement which is integral to the creation of the CrossFit community. Thus, beyond the health benefits of the workouts, nutrition, or lifestyle philosophy, CrossFit instils a sense of community and social belonging among its members that is rather rare in today's society.

Local box members do not only tend to know each other but may also socialize regularly outside of classes. There may be community-building activities and events like in-house competitions, holiday celebrations and "wedding WODs" for newly-wed couples. Barbeque and birthday celebrations make box members bond and may even extend the community as members bring friends or family. Moreover, it allows box owners to get to know the members more personally and for members to bond with each other. In addition, while members meet physically in the box, they are also interacting virtually (Belger, 2012), which reflects additional influencer effects. The interaction between members is not limited to the members of a box but includes interaction both nationally and internationally. There are currently 2.7 million followers on a range of social media where followers can share videos and posts which increases its brand exposure and gain new followers (Gomillion, 2017). This provides an opportunity for influence dynamics in both offline and online contexts due to the dual (hybrid) nature of the influence opportunities.

The feeling of belonging to a group and being important to others in that group has been described as sense of community (SOC), with members believing that they can reach their needs/goals through their shared commitment (McMillan & Chavis, 1986). There is a unique sense of community at CrossFit. Everyone knows each other, helps each other. CrossFitters share their commitment to the workout regime and share similar goals. They aim at overall fitness and to be able to face any physical challenge or task life throws at them. Member push through physical limits and experience a strong SOC (Knapp, 2015b).

McMillan and Chavis (1986) proposed four elements of SOC: membership, influence, integration and fulfilment of needs, and shared emotional connection which are relevant to communities, including the CrossFit community.

*Membership* describes the feeling of belonging or of sharing a sense of personal relatedness. Membership is distinguished through boundaries, emotional safety, a sense of belonging and identification, personal investment, and a common symbol. CrossFitters distinguish themselves from other gymgoers through their own language, rituals and practices as well as in the type of workouts offered. They are easily recognized when laying on the floor gasping for air after an intense workout. CrossFitters feel safe in their community. CrossFitters are generally very committed and spend a lot of time and effort (e.g., doing the WODs and sharing online) as well as money (e.g., membership fees). The explicit community-building mantra encouraged by CrossFit successfully creates greater levels of felt SOC than other mainstream gyms (Pickett et al., 2016).

The second element, *influence*, refers to the feeling that one matters and makes a difference to the group and reversely the group being important to its members. People find friendship and camaraderie at CrossFit. They feel they matter to the group when being cheered on at the end of a workout. Members hold each other accountable. It is not uncommon that other members may check-in if a member hasn't attended a workout for a while.

The third element, *integration and fulfilment of needs*, describes the belief of members that their needs will be satisfied through the resources of the community. Training workouts in a traditional gym can be isolating, requiring personal motivation. To achieve a SOC in CrossFit, WODs are structured to be simultaneously inclusive and supportive but physically intense and difficult (Pickett et al., 2016). Members feel they are supported by the community. They feel encouraged and motivated to keep going through tough workouts and provide moral and verbal support to others, pushing each other to perform better and faster. Members feel that the resources of the community such as the expertise of trained coaches, access to state-of-the-art equipment, and exercise programming (WODs) and the exchange with other fitness fanatics help them to meet their needs and strengthen their belief in themselves and their abilities. The free online CrossFit Journal facilitates and supports the community through constant dialogue and feedback with and among community members (Knapp, 2015a). In this way, they can attain their personal fitness goals.

Lastly, *shared emotional connection* describes the shared commitment and belief, the shared history, shared common places and shared experiences. Members usually introduce themselves to newcomers, socialize with each other outside of the box, and become invested in each other's success (Pickett et al., 2016). They complete the same workouts and share the suffering and exhaustion as well as the feelings of achievement, they share personal achievements (e.g., best times, highest weights) locally in the box where they do their workouts and online. The consistent organisation of workouts into classes (i.e., groups of members) likely enhances the quality of relationships and feelings of relatedness (Sibley & Bergman, 2018). The maintenance of social spaces stimulates a SOC which also heightens the perceived value of the service offering. The box is not only a place to work out but also a social space (Pickett et al., 2016).

*Conscious Identification* was added as a fifth dimension (Obst et al., 2002). CrossFitters identify consciously with the brand and generally like to talk about it, which results in it being described in religious terms (Dawson, 2017). For example, it has been stated that "[p]erhaps more than disciples of any other type of exercise, people who participate in CrossFit can't help being drawn to people who do the same" (Rubin, 2014). Identification goes beyond the local community that they know in person and includes the global community. When two CrossFitters meet, they instantly feel connected. So, when CrossFit was in a crisis due to racist comments of the previous CEO, this led to a huge internal struggle for many people associated with the brand. Their identification with the inclusive nature of the CrossFit brand led to their lack of identification with the comments made. Overall, previous research found that feelings of relatedness were found to be higher at CrossFit than what is typically seen in other gyms (Sibley & Bergman, 2018).

## 9.5 The importance of crowd influence: customer experiences and brand meaning

Customers are not only interested in the product or service, but also authentic experiences (Prahalad & Ramaswamy, 2000) and experiences with the organisation and its employees are fundamental to the creation of brand meaning (Brodie et al., 2009), the "evolving emotional and cognitive understanding attributed to a brand as a result of a socially negotiated process" (Tierney et al., 2016). The cognitive aspect uses brand artefacts to communicate the brand and emotional responses during and after consumption (Tierney et al., 2016). These meanings do not develop in isolation but within a market context among a range of stakeholders (Tierney et al., 2016). CrossFit's brand meaning includes beliefs regarding its values and purpose as well as its benefit and the emotions resulting from involvement in WODs. These are constructed within a social context that highlights the importance of fitness and health.

Customer experiences can facilitate a range of engagement behaviours on a range of brand engagement platforms. These platforms can be a digital or physical forum where the organisation and the customers connect, such as social media where a brand community can develop (Ramaswamy & Ozcan, 2016). The power of the CrossFit community (and the members on each other) drives the continued engagement with the brand, thus serving an important role for the brand. Customer activity on these platforms also results in the creation of communities that they build and control themselves (Prahalad & Ramaswamy, 2000).

## 9.6 The process of crowd influence

As argued above, the CrossFit community is very active in social media, and it excels in using a variety of channels to develop interaction between members and brand loyalty. A comprehensive study examined the use of social media in the CrossFit community on three platforms (Twitter, Facebook, and YouTube), and found extensive information-sharing activities of both organizational members (the Games and other events, the regions) and individual athletes about various events, training and competing in the sport. The platforms are used to create awareness of the sport and disseminate information to the members. High-profile athletes were both consuming CrossFit products and promoting the CrossFit brand (Kang, Rice, Hambrick & Choi, 2019). In the study, the social media messages repeatedly led to interaction and exhibited familiarity and unique relationships with each other. They were found to add value to the customer-CrossFit relationship and create a sense of community on several levels. A good example is the CrossFit Games, established in 2007 aiming to find the fittest man and woman on earth, that is, the Fittest on Earth™ who have clearly distinguished themselves from the rest of the participants. CrossFit uses social media to create a strong feeling of involvement for all members that are not able to take part or visit the games physically (this turned out to be a huge success during the Covid19 pandemic when the 2021 games were held).

Media coverage of the CrossFit Games has increased immensely since their beginning. In 2021 fans could follow the Games in several different ways: through live streams available through CrossFit's social media channels on Facebook, YouTube, and Twitch as well as updates on the CrossFit Games site. In addition, live broadcasting of events was available on CBS Sports Network and the Paramount+ service (CrossFit, 2021).

CrossFit uses social media to drive engagement and heighten anticipation among its members. Not only do they make the Games and other content available on Instagram and Twitter and their webpage, but they also link it directly to other channels such as Facebook and YouTube. Most importantly, they engage with the community and encourage members to participate in the Open, to comment, like, and share content that spreads the message even further to their friends and followers. The streaming of the live events gathers hundreds of thousands of viewers posting and reacting to the videos and allows for exponential organic fan growth. Building on the Games and to make them relevant to local members, CrossFit would, for example, post video with footage from actual CrossFit gyms, under the title "Now it's Your Turn," including a link to a map to find a local affiliate (Flying Cork, n.d.).

In 2021, CrossFit took consumer engagement at the NOBULL CrossFit Games to a new level with the 2021 Virtual games. This gave consumers the possibility to test their fitness parallel to the Games and compare their own abilities through a multiple workout challenge to other enthusiasts worldwide (https://crossfit.leaderboards.com/competitions/2021-crossfit-virtual-games/). This increases engagement with the broader CrossFit community, providing additional opportunities for interaction.

A further process of influencing is seen in attracting the contribution of the customer (Prahalad & Ramaswamy, 2004a, 2004b), in this case, CrossFit members. A successful strategy used by box owners and even used by headquarters is to crowd-source content from customers (members). Box owners may ask their members to geotag their workout posts to increase visibility. They may also repost members' posts. Affiliates also create their own content. They post their WODs and workout tips, share information about ongoing events such as Beginners' classes. Sometimes, affiliates also work with well-known individual influencers. This may be successful CrossFit athletes well-known and inspiring to the community or other workout gurus with many followers that may attract new customers. An example are sponsored posts that create brand awareness and traffic. Those may then also be reposted to leverage the followings of others.

The creation of unique culture can also serve as an influencing process both for CrossFit employees and members (Bailey et al., 2019). An essential part of the CrossFit identity is its own language and knowledge of the names and contents of the countless WODs distinguish CrossFitters from non-CrossFitters. Being new to the box (CrossFit gym) and doing their first WOD often leaves people feeling like they are in a different world as there are new terms, expressions, and words they probably never have heard before. Going beyond the literal meaning of a shared language is the shared experience that goes along with the execution of the challenging workouts and results in mutual connection and identification (Dawson, 2017). Over time, CrossFit has developed a very distinct, highly social, and "immersive" (Heywood, 2015) culture. Interactions do not only take place offline in the local box through shared workouts. CrossFitters are often also very active online. They share their experiences, achievements such as WOD times, workout photos and informative content publicly on social media such as Instagram posts, Tweets as well as videos on YouTube and Facebook with friends, family, and other followers. Content is also shared on affiliate websites.

## 9.7 The reason for crowd – co-creation of value

Value is a term used to describe that which comes about when consumers use a product or service. It is also known as value-in-use and the customer experience (value in the experience) (Grönroos & Gummerus, 2014; Helkkula et al., 2012). Value is derived from the interaction between the parties but is experienced subjectively (Echeverri & Skålén, 2011). It can be evaluated by the provider of a service (e.g., an influencer or affiliate owner) and by the customers themselves. How customers perceive the value associated with a product or service is important as customers decide which organisations they want to deal with and specifically how value will be created (Prahalad & Ramaswamy, 2004b).

Customer value is defined as the "overall assessment of the utility of a product based on the perceptions of what is received and what is given" (Zeithaml, 1988). CrossFit members attend their local box and do the WOD as they believe the utility or benefits they receive from these activities exceeds the efforts it requires from them. These benefits include physical, emotional, and social benefits such as improved mobility and social support.

Continued involvement over time with CrossFit will be due to the value that the customer perceives to get from taking part. The focus tends to be on positive value which keeps customers engaged with the organisation, yet it is acknowledged that value can also be eroded (Clark et al., 2020). Reduction (or erosion) of value is when the customer perceives that the benefits are declining and that continued involvement with the brand such as CrossFit is not desirable.

The changing perspective of the customer is that the customer can both describe and create value (Prahalad & Ramaswamy, 2004a). This changing perspective is shifting to include the creation of experiences and the associated interactions which is created between the organisation and the customer (Prahalad & Ramaswamy, 2004b). Customers are no longer viewed as passive recipients of the organisation's marketing activities. Active consumers can also serve as a source of competitive advantage (Prahalad & Ramaswamy, 2000). This is because the customer can co-create value with the organisation (Prahalad & Ramaswamy, 2004b). For this reason, box owners involve members in the development of box activities and provide opportunities for the increased involvement.

Co-creation is about the "joint creation of value by the company and the customer" (Prahalad & Ramaswamy, 2004b p. 7) which enables the customer to compile personal experiences. It means that value is created jointly and as a collaborative effort between stakeholders, suggesting customers are a resource for the organisation (Galvagno & Dalli, 2014).

Co-creation provides several opportunities for the organisation. They can interact with customers to develop new products and services and also give customers ways to engage with the organisation and other customers. For example, the organisation can create a social media page where this can take place or a website page to solicit inputs from customers as seen in the postings by members of the CrossFit community. This impact of co-creation is that the organisation has to change its product (or service delivery) process (Prahalad & Ramaswamy, 2004a), providing and managing ways in which interactions can take place across multiple channels (Ramaswamy & Ozcan, 2016).

Second, as the internet has increased the extent to which the consumers interact actively and directly with organisations, it means that they can initiate and control this communication across several platforms. Being active in the relationship with the organisation, customers are viewed as co-creators of value to experiences and brands as they are also collaborative with customers embedding their values into the brand (Ramaswamy & Ozcan, 2016).

Third, not only are customers able to influence the organisation (Prahalad & Ramaswamy, 2004b), they are also able to influence other customers (Prahalad & Ramaswamy, 2000 p. 80). This is seen in customers engaging in activities on social media by posting updates and photos to influence the viewer, engaging in specific leisure co-creational behaviours include collaborating, communicating, sharing, advising, and helping (Bianchi, 2019).

The willingness of customers to engage in co-creational activities can be viewed as a reflection of their engagement with the organisation, with benefits associated with higher levels. For example, higher levels of co-creation impact the brand experience (Nysveen & Pedersen, 2014), so if an organisation can develop and present a way for consumers to co-create, they can strengthen the brand experience.

Customers can also be viewed as competitors as they can use products to create value in unique ways and use them in ways that satisfy their needs, which may differ from what the organisation intends (Prahalad & Ramaswamy, 2000).

## 9.8 The outcome of crowd influence: Brand loyalty

While defined in different ways (Leckie et al., 2016), marketers agree on the importance of brand loyalty to both product and service organisations and their financial performance. For this reason, organisations invest effort in building strong brands as these brands have high brand loyalty (Kapferer, 2012). This is seen for CrossFit, described as the most well-known fitness brand (Togoh, 2020).

Loyalty is both behavioural and attitudinal in nature (Dick & Basu, 1994). The behavioural components refer to the actions (behaviours) of customers such as repeat purchase and recommendation behaviour (Keiningham et al., 2007). The attitudinal aspect reflects the commitment towards the brand and the intention to purchase the brand (Härtel & Russell-Bennett, 2010). For CrossFit, this means not only encouraging behaviours but also seeking to develop attitudinal loyalty towards the brand, so that during times of rest or injury, the members are eager to return to the box or share their experiences online. It has, however, been argued that it is possible for a consumer to buy a brand (i.e., exhibit behaviours) but have a negative attitude towards it as seen in situations where customers have little or no brand or product alternatives (Härtel & Russell-Bennett, 2010).

Loyalty is created by the brand features (Kapferer, 2012) and engagement with the organisation and its brands (Fernandes & Moreira, 2019). For CrossFit, the features of the brand such as the WODs and the CrossFit Games serve to create brand loyalty which is then shared on social media to influence others. Satisfaction is widely regarded as contributing to brand loyalty (Kaplan et al., 2015). Many product aspects can influence satisfaction, including the employees and the service quality offered to customers (Caruana, 2002). This means that CrossFit needs to provide continuous quality (e.g., quality WODs) as this impacts loyalty, which in turn impacts perceptions of future brand experiences, as reflected in Figure 9.1.

## 9.9 "Death by tweet" – When the community didn't stand behind leadership (Influencing leadership)

The effect of the community on the brand is not only seen in positive effects on the brand but can also be seen in the reactions and comments made during negative events or experiences with the brand. The success of the CrossFit brand was almost destroyed by a racist tweet by its founder following the death of George Floyd. The Institute for Health Metrics and Evaluation tweeted "Racism is a public health issue," and Glassman replied, "It's FLOYD-19." The CrossFit community reacted swiftly. Reebok, having been a long-time sponsor, decided not to renew its partnership with CrossFit HQ. Voices were quickly heard on Twitter calling for an end to the cooperation between sports brands and CrossFit (Lofranco, 2020). Several other sponsors also began to disassociate themselves from the brand. CrossFitters who had been proudly associating themselves with the brand for years started to step back.

Well-known CrossFit ambassadors such as the four-time winner of the CrossFit Games, Tia-Clair Toomey, voiced their disapproval of Glassman's tweet. She wrote

*Figure 9.1* The relationship between engagement and loyalty.

Adapted from Fernandes and Moreira (2019); Bloemer and Kasper (1995); Brakus et al. (2009).

that she was "incredibly saddened, disappointed and frustrated," and that her "future with CrossFit is unclear and depends on the direction of HQ." Rich Froning, another champion of the CrossFit Games, commented it was "impossible to stay loyal to leadership who make callous statements that alienate and divide in a time when unity is needed" (Togoh, 2020).

The CrossFit affiliated gyms were concerned about the impact on their business and reacted strongly. To make matters worse, when a long-time CrossFit gym owner wrote a lengthy letter to the CrossFit organization explaining why she would be changing the name of her gym and not renewing her affiliation with the organization, Glassman responded without remorse. Several affiliates around the world decided to change their name and not renew their affiliation considering those events.

Later, Glassman tweeted an apology explaining he made a mistake with his insensitive comment. But it wasn't enough to please the community he offended by betraying the core values the brand was supposed to represent. To limit the damage, Glassman finally acted and announced his resignation as CEO (Togoh, 2020).

He was succeeded as a CEO by Dave Castro who hoped to act in the interests of business partners, coaches, athletes, and other members as interim CEO. However, there is no distancing from the founder, as Castro explains he never wants to "lose sight of the mission Greg established for all of us" (CrossFit, 2020). Following the change in leadership, Reebok reports that it continues to feel connected to the CrossFit community (Lofranco, 2020). The CrossFit brand was then sold to Eric Roza who himself is dedicated to CrossFit. He ran his own tech company Datalogix for 12 years and even built a CrossFit gym for his employees. In 2015 he became the co-founder of another CrossFit box and has also been participating in the CrossFit Open. This incident clearly shows the impact and power of the crowd on the organisation and its activities.

## 9.10　Crowd influence – A conceptual model

We argue that the individual member of the crowd (in this chapter exemplified by the large following of CrossFit) plays a dual role in creating brand loyalty. First, the individual members contribute to a continuously increasing stream of relevant activity in the box, as described earlier in the chapter. They also contribute by posting online content. Even though each piece of content is a small contribution, the combined effect is substantial. Second, the individual member is also a consumer who is influenced by the content posted by the members. Social media influencers are often described as micro-endorsers (Lou & Yuan, 2019), microcelebrities (Belanche et al., 2021), and micro/nano influencers (Campbell & Farrell, 2020) and these concepts can also be used to describe the individual contribution to a brand community, such as CrossFit, but with the notable difference that the individual, in this case, acts as part of a crowd that endorses the brand. The individual is not an influencer in his/her own right but as a part of a crowd. At the same time, the crowd is dependent on the contributions of the single members of the community.

Can a crowd be an influencer/opinion leader? In a strict sense, a crowd is not an actor in the same way as an individual, and the study of crowds need to avoid reifying them. In a transferred sense, a crowd can be described in similar terms as individual influencers, having an impact on the consumers/members of the CrossFit community. We hypothesize that crowd influence draws its strength from the following principles.

### 9.10.1 Similarity

The literature on social media influencers has shown that consumers are drawn to influencers based on principles of perceived closeness to them (Jin et al., 2019). Although the influencer has gained the status of a celebrity, they typically appear as a common person that is easy to identify with. This factor of similarity is arguably even stronger in crowd influencing. In the case of CrossFit, similarity is an important part of the community, where the common language and practices facilitate the process of identification and a continued sense of belonging.

### 9.10.2 Credibility

The credibility of the brand and the expertise of the box leaders support this perception. Further, it is not only easy to identify with the fellow members of the CrossFit community, but the posts on social media also appear as credible, in the sense of both being *authentic* (it is easy to verify that a post is authentic through different markers that show, for instance, the location of an activity) and high on *expertise*. The CrossFit community is very active on social media, and it is very common to pass on information on different aspects of performing exercises. There is a strong informational value in sharing this kind of information (Feng et al., 2020; Lou & Yuan, 2019).

### 9.10.3 Influencer narratives

Based on the concept of transportation the narratives developed in co-created spaces put the individual member in a sacred space where they get absorbed into the world of CrossFit (Feng et al., 2020). The storytelling in individual posts is both easy to identify with and serves as a source of inspiration.

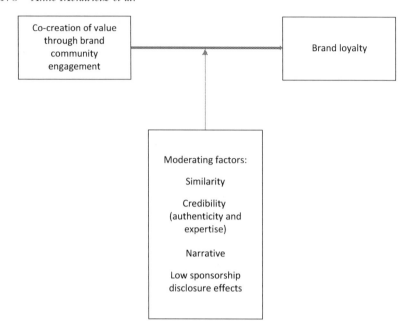

*Figure 9.2* Crowd influence – a conceptual model.

Source: adapted from Lou and Yuan (2019).

### 9.10.4 Low sponsorship disclosure effects

In the influencer marketing literature, the topic of disclosing commercial relations between the influencer and the endorsed brands is a contested topic. It is often assumed that hidden commercial relations can severely damage the reputation of the endorser and that disclosing whether a post is sponsored is an important prerequisite. Research on the effects of disclosing sponsorship information is inconclusive. Kim and Kim (2020) indicate a negative effect on product attitude, whereas Feng et al. (2020) found no significant effects on the dependent variables in their study. While this potentially does not explicitly form part of the interactive nature of community influence, the importance of sponsorship within the sport and for CrossFit is acknowledged (Pitch, 2019), resulting in its continued inclusion in the model.

Based on the different theoretical inputs described above, we propose the following tentative model as seen in Figure 9.2.

## 9.11 Conclusions and future research

This chapter started with exploring the idea that the influencing processes that have been observed concerning social media influencers can also be observed in settings where there is a more crowd-based pattern of sharing content online. We have used CrossFit as an example of the influence of the crowd on other community members and their willingness to engage in a range of behaviours. Further, the national and international influence of CrossFit members through social media has also been indicated. This is not to say that there are no individual influencers in the CrossFit field but, on the contrary, the power of the crowd in no way excludes the use of influencers in promoting CrossFit.

While this case has focused on the extensive community involvement in the building and support in the CrossFit context, some of these principles can also apply to other contexts. For example, community influence is part of both crowd-funding and product design. In the case of crowdfunding, the success of a project is dependent on the community (Mollick & Robb, 2016) while in product design, the designs are selected by community members (Katona, 2015). While this chapter has presented a conceptual model, the potential for testing this model in a range of contexts using both qualitative and quantitative methods is indicated. This includes both interviews and netnography which is particularly suitable to research in online communities (Kozinets, 2002).

Together with CrossFit, these contexts indicate the potential to research influence past that of the single influencer, supporting the need to extend the academic perspective of influencers.

# References

Abidin, C. (2016). "Aren't these just young, rich women doing vain things online?" Influencer selfies as subversive frivolity. *Social Media + Society*, 2(2), https://doi.org/10.1177/2056305116641342

Abidin, C., & Ots, M. (2016). Influencers tell all: Market-Driven and Democracy-Driven.

Bailey, B., Benson, A. J., & Bruner, M. W. (2019). Investigating the organisational culture of CrossFit. *International Journal of Sport and Exercise Psychology*, 17(3), 197–211.

Belanche, D., Casaló, L. V., Flavián, M., & Ibáñez-Sánchez, S. (2021). Understanding influencer marketing: The role of congruence between influencers, products and consumers. *Journal of Business Research*, 132, 186–195.

Belger, A. W. (2012). *The power of community CrossFit and the force of human connection*. Victory Belt Publishing Inc.

Bianchi, C. (2019). Value co-creation behaviours from customer-to-customer interactions (CCIs) in recreational social tango experiences. *Leisure Studies*, 38(5), 666–681.

Blenkarn, B. (2018). *Wanting to sweat together: The Relationship between Community and CrossFit*. Halifax, Nova Scotia: Dalhousie University.

Brodie, R. J., Whittome, J. R. M., & Brush, G. J. (2009). Investigating the service brand: A customer value perspective. *Journal of Business Research*, 62(3), 345–355. https://doi.org/10.1016/j.jbusres.2008.06.008

Campbell, C., & Farrell, J. R. (2020). More than meets the eye: The functional components underlying influencer marketing. *Business Horizons*, 63(4), 469–479.

Caruana, A. (2002). Service loyalty: The effects of service quality and the mediating role of customer satisfaction. *European Journal of Marketing*, 36(7/8), 811–828.

Chae, J. (2018). Explaining females' envy toward social media influencers. *Media Psychology*, 21(2), 246–262.

Clark, M. K., Lages, C. R., & Hollebeek, L. D. (2020). Friend or foe? Customer engagement's value-based effects on fellow customers and the firm. *Journal of Business Research*. https://doi.org/10.1108/JPBM-04-2020-2839

Cova, B., & Cova, V. (2002). Tribal marketing: The tribalisation of society and its impact on the conduct of marketing. *European Journal of Marketing, 36*(5/6), 595–620.

Cova, B., & Pace, S. (2006). Brand community of convenience products: New forms of customer empowerment – the case "my Nutella The Community". *European Journal of Marketing, 40*(9/10), 1087–1105.

CrossFit. (2020, 9 June). *Greg Glassman Retires.* CrossFit. Retrieved 2 July from https://www.crossfit.com/greg-glassman-retires

CrossFit. (2021, 4 June). *2021 NOBULL CrossFit Games return to CBS.* Retrieved 29 July from https://games.crossfit.com/article/2021-nobull-crossfit-games-returns-cbs/games

CrossFit. (n.d.-a). *About Affiliation.* Retrieved 29 July from https://www.crossfit.com/affiliate

CrossFit. (n.d.-b). *What is CrossFit?* Retrieved 29 July from https://www.crossfit.com/what-is-crossfit/

Dawson, M. C. (2017). CrossFit: Fitness cult or reinventive institution? *International Review for the Sociology of Sport, 52*(3), 361–379.

Dick, A. S., & Basu, K. (1994). Customer loyalty: Toward an integrated conceptual framework. *Journal of the Academy of Marketing Science, 22*(2), 99–113.

Echeverri, P., & Skålén, P. (2011). Co-creation and co-destruction: A practice-theory based study of interactive value formation. *Marketing Theory, 11*(3), 351–373.

Enke, N., & Borchers, N. S. (2019). Social media influencers in strategic communication: A conceptual framework for strategic social media influencer communication. *International Journal of Strategic Communication, 13*(4), 261–277.

Feng, Y., Chen, H., & Kong, Q. (2020). An expert with whom I can identify: The role of narratives in influencer marketing. *International Journal of Advertising,* 1–22.

Fernandes, T., & Moreira, M. (2019). Consumer brand engagement, satisfaction and brand loyalty: A comparative study between functional and emotional brand relationships. *Journal of Product & Brand Management, 28*(274–286).

Firat, A. F., & Shultz, C. J., II. (1997). From segmentation to fragmentation: Markets and marketing strategy in the postmodern era. *European Journal of Marketing, 31*(3–4), 183–207. https://doi.org/10.1108/EUM0000000004321

Flying Cork. (n.d.). *Social Media, Content Strategy and the CrossFit Games.* Retrieved 29 July from https://flyingcork.com/blog/social-media-content-strategy-crossfit-games/

Galvagno, M., & Dalli, D. (2014). Theory of value co-creation: A systematic literature review. *Managing Service Quality, 24*(6), 643–683.

Gomillion, S. (2017). *The success of CrossFit and its implications for businesses of all types* [Honors Thesis Projects, University of Tennessee]. https://trace.tennessee.edu/utk_chanhonoproj/2054

Grönroos, C., & Gummerus, J. (2014). The service revolution and its marketing implications: Service logic vs service-dominant logic. *Managing Service Quality: An International Journal, 24*(3), 206–229. https://doi.org/10.1108/msq-03-2014-0042

Härtel, C. E., & Russell-Bennett, R. (2010). Heart versus mind: The functions of emotional and cognitive loyalty. *Australasian Marketing Journal (AMJ), 18*(1), 1–7.

Helkkula, A., Kelleher, C., & Pihlström, M. (2012). Characterizing value as an experience: Implications for service researchers and managers. *Journal of Service Research, 15*(1), 59–75.

Herz, J. C. (2015). *Learning to breathe fire: The rise of CrossFit and the primal future of fitness.* Harmony.

Heywood, L. (2015). The CrossFit sensorium: Visuality, affect and immersive sport. *Paragraph, 38*(1), 20–36.

Jin, S. V., Muqaddam, A., & Ryu, E. (2019). Instafamous and social media influencer marketing. *Marketing Intelligence & Planning*, *37*(5), 567–579.

Kang, S. J., Rice, J. A., Hambrick, M. E., & Choi, C. (2019). CrossFit across three platforms: Using social media to navigate niche sport challenges. *Physical Culture and Sport*, *81*(1), 36–46.

Kapferer, J.-N. (2012). *The new strategic brand management advanced insights and strategic thinking* (5th ed.). Kogan Page.

Kaplan, M. D., Yildirim, C., Gulden, S., & Aktan, D. (2015). I love to hate you: Loyalty for disliked brands and the role of nostalgia. *Journal of Brand Management*, *22*(2), 136–153.

Katona, Z. (2015). Democracy in product design: Consumer participation and differentiation strategies. *Quantitative Marketing and Economics*, *13*(4), 359–394.

Keiningham, T. L., Cooil, B., Aksoy, L., Andreassen, T. W., & Weiner, J. (2007). The value of different customer satisfaction and loyalty metrics in predicting customer retention, recommendation, and share-of-wallet. *Managing Service Quality: An International Journal*, *17*(4), 361–384.

Khamis, S., Ang, L., & Welling, R. (2017). Self-branding, 'micro-celebrity' and the rise of Social Media Influencers. *Celebrity Studies*, *8*(2), 191–208.

Kim, D. Y., & Kim, H.-Y. (2020). Influencer advertising on social media: The multiple inference model on influencer-product congruence and sponsorship disclosure. *Journal of Business Research*. https://doi.org/10.1016/j.jbusres.2020.02.020

Knapp, B. A. (2015a). Gender representation in the CrossFit Journal: A content analysis. *Sport in Society*, *18*(6), 688–703.

Knapp, B. A. (2015b). Rx'd and shirtless: An examination of gender in a CrossFit box. *Women in Sport and Physical Activity Journal*, *23*(1), 42–53.

Kozinets, R. V. (1999). E-tribalized marketing?: The strategic implications of virtual communities of consumption. *European Management Journal*, *17*(3), 252–264.

Kozinets, R. V. (2002). The field behind the screen: Using netnography for marketing research in online communities. *Journal of marketing research*, *39*(1), 61–72.

Leckie, C., Nyadzayo, M. W., & Johnson, L. W. (2016). Antecedents of consumer brand engagement and brand loyalty. *Journal of Marketing Management*, *32*(5–6), 558–578.

Lim, X. J., Radzol, A. M., Cheah, J., & Wong, M. (2017). The impact of social media influencers on purchase intention and the mediation effect of customer attitude. *Asian Journal of Business Research*, *7*(2), 19–36.

Lofranco, J. (2020). *BREAKING: Reebok Cancels Future Games Negotiations*. Morning Chalk Up. Retrieved 20 May from https://morningchalkup.com/2020/06/07/breaking-reebok-cancels-future-games-negotiations/

Lou, C., & Yuan, S. (2019). Influencer marketing: How message value and credibility affect consumer trust of branded content on social media. *Journal of Interactive Advertising*, *19*(1), 58–73.

Martínez-López, F. J., Anaya-Sánchez, R., Fernández Giordano, M., & Lopez-Lopez, D. (2020). Behind influencer marketing: Key marketing decisions and their effects on followers' responses. *Journal of Marketing Management*, *36*(7–8), 579–607.

McAlexander, J. H., Schouten, J. W., & Koenig, H. F. (2002). Building brand community. *Journal of Marketing*, *66*(1), 38–54.

McMillan, D. W., & Chavis, D. M. (1986). Sense of community: A definition and theory. *Journal of Community Psychology*, *14*(1), 6–23.

Mollick, E., & Robb, A. (2016). Democratizing innovation and capital access: The role of crowdfunding. *California Management Review*, *58*(2), 72–87.

Muniz, A. M., & O'Guinn, T. C. (2001). Brand community. *Journal of Consumer Research, 27*(4), 412–432.

Muniz, A. M., & Schau, H. J. (2005). Religiosity in the abandoned Apple Newton brand community. *Journal of Consumer Research, 31*(4), 737–747.

Nysveen, H., & Pedersen, P. E. (2014). Influences of cocreation on brand experience. *International Journal of Market Research, 56*(6), 807–832.

Obst, P., Smith, S. G., & Zinkiewicz, L. (2002). An exploration of sense of community, Part 3: Dimensions and predictors of psychological sense of community in geographical communities. *Journal of Community Psychology, 30*(1), 119–133.

Ouwersloot, J., & Odekerken-Schröder, G. (2008). Who is who in brand communities – and why? *European Journal of Marketing, 42*(5-June), 571–585.

Pekkanen, A., Närvänen, E., & Tuominen, P. (2017). Elements of rituality in consumer tribes: The case of CrossFit. *Journal of Customer Behaviour, 16*(4), 353–370.

Pickett, A. C., Goldsmith, A., Damon, Z., & Walker, M. (2016). The influence of sense of community on the perceived value of physical activity: A cross-context analysis. *Leisure Sciences, 38*(3), 199–214.

Pitch. (2019). *The CrossFit Games: The Fight for the Biggest Brand on Earth*. Retrieved 19 July from https://www.pitch.co.uk/the-crossfit-games-the-fight-for-the-biggest-brand-on-earth/

Prahalad, C. K., & Ramaswamy, V. (2000). Co-opting customer competence. *Harvard Business Review, 78*(1), 79–90.

Prahalad, C. K., & Ramaswamy, V. (2004a). Co-creating unique value with customers. *Strategy & Leadership, 32*(3), 4–9.

Prahalad, C. K., & Ramaswamy, V. (2004b). Co-creation experiences: The next practice in value creation. *Journal of Interactive Marketing, 18*(3), 5–14.

Ramaswamy, V., & Ozcan, K. (2016). Brand value co-creation in a digitalized world: An integrative framework and research implications. *International Journal of Research in Marketing, 33*(1), 93–106.

Rasczyk, K., & Stephens, M. (2015). *Crossfit community, information community: Needs and behaviors*. San Jose State University.

Rubin, C. (2014). CrossFit flirting: Talk Burpee to me. *The New York Times, 8*

Sibley, B. A., & Bergman, S. M. (2018). What keeps athletes in the gym? Goals, psychological needs, and motivation of CrossFit™ participants. *International Journal of Sport and Exercise Psychology, 16*(5), 555–574.

Tierney, K. D., Karpen, I. O., & Westberg, K. (2016). Brand meaning cocreation: toward a conceptualization and research implications. *Journal of Service Theory and Practice, 26*(6), 911–932.

Togoh, I. (2020). *Reebok And Athletes Cut Ties With CrossFit Over Founder Greg Glassman's George Floyd Tweet*. Forbes. Retrieved 2 July from https://www.forbes.com/sites/isabeltogoh/2020/06/08/reebok-and-athletes-cut-ties-with-crossfit-over-founder-greg-glassmans-george-floyd-tweet/?sh=4c5c71a4c830

Zeithaml, V. A. (1988). Consumer perceptions of price, quality, and value: a means-end model and synthesis of evidence. *The Journal of Marketing*, 2–22.

# 10 Three key practices of image building in entrepreneurial identity work of freelance journalists

*Sven-Ove Horst and Toon Brouwers*

## 10.1 Introduction

This study focuses on better understanding the entrepreneurial journey of Dutch journalism students and practices of image building they face as part of their education and professional development. This study is practically relevant because the media and creative industries have become a significant driver of economic growth and innovation (Baker & Gielens, 2018; Hennekam & Bennett, 2016). Moreover, the contours of journalism education and practice are changing (Broersma & Singer, 2020; Singer & Broersma, 2020). An increasing number of technologies flatten the boundaries of what the media industry is (see e.g. Brems et al., 2017) and new organizations reimagine the function and conduct of media (Horst & Hitters, 2020; Khajeheian, 2020, 2021; Price Schultz & Jones, 2017). While this drives innovation and enables the institutionalization of new practices (Kosterich, 2019), it also challenges the status quo (Zboralska, 2017) and makes the professional development for media practitioners highly challenging.

To better understand this professional and entrepreneurial development, we build on the concept of identity work. Recent studies and reviews show that there is yet much to be learned about identity work (Bange et al., 2020; Brown, 2015, 2021; Brown & Coupland, 2015; Caza et al., 2018; Fachin & Langley, 2017; Oliver, 2015; Schultz et al., 2012; Winkler, 2018). *Identity work* is seen as the processes and practices in relating to others about creating, sustaining, and altering a person's self-identity – one's notion of who or how to be (Watson, 2008). Alvesson and Willmott (2002) explain that people are "continuously engaged in forming, repairing, maintaining, strengthening, or revising the constructions that are productive of [their] precarious sense of coherence and distinctiveness". This precariousness, transience, impermanence, and struggle of who and how to be is visible in the current conditions of the media and creative industries, and in the mediatization of many other modern forms of work and life (Albinsson, 2018; Baker & Gielens, 2018; Bergamini et al., 2017; Bhansing et al., 2018; Broersma & Singer, 2020; Broersma & Swart, 2021; Chen et al., 2018; Lange, 2017; Nielsen et al., 2018; Schediwy et al., 2018; Walzer, 2017; Werthes et al., 2018).

DOI: 10.4324/9781003134176-11

However, even though identity work is a growing discourse that is highly relevant for conceptualizing and understanding how people develop and make sense of themselves and others in a growingly mediatized context, there is little social constructionist research about how young media entrepreneurs develop their identity (Lewis, 2016; Nielsen & Gartner, 2017), and how social media affords creating, upholding, and forming their identity (Brems et al., 2017; Gandini, 2015), which may be seen as an everyday practice of identity work (Alvesson et al., 2008). Yet, this representation and communication about oneself and one's development is important because the self-employment of Dutch freelancers has grown significantly in the last years (Baker & Gielens, 2018). Moreover, this entrepreneurship is not always voluntary and is often driven by provisional jobs and part-time employment (Baker & Gielens, 2018; Wijngaarden, 2019). Therefore, this "push" towards entrepreneurship creates a need to grow our understanding and conceptualize how these journalists perform and reflect on their identity (Bhansing et al., 2020; Brown, 2017), and explore practices around identity work related to social media that students experience in their process of entrepreneurial development (Nielsen & Gartner, 2017). We began with a broad research question: *How do students of journalism reflect on the challenges of their professional development and perform identity work?*

This study contributes towards the field of identity work more broadly by describing and enriching our understanding of the management of image building practices on social media (Beech et al., 2012; Brown, 2015; Coupland & Brown, 2012), and builds a more nuanced conception of identity work in the media field more specifically (Bhansing et al., 2018; Lange, 2017; Nielsen & Gartner, 2017; Nielsen et al., 2018; Werthes et al., 2018). This way we add to the growing literature on media entrepreneurship (Achtenhagen, 2017; Ferrier, 2013; Horst, 2019; Horst & Hitters, 2020; Horst et al., 2019; Horst & Murschetz, 2019; Khajeheian, 2017; Sindik & Graybeal, 2017; Will et al., 2016; Zboralska, 2017), and specifically how processes and practices of journalistic development become more mediatized, and enacted on social media.

## 10.2 Theoretical background

### 10.2.1 Entrepreneurial Identity in the media industries

Identity broadly refers to questions of "Who am I" and "How should I act" (Alvesson et al., 2008; Cerulo, 1997). In most qualitative research it is seen as a constructivist concept (Ravasi & Canato, 2013). Hence, identity

> can be viewed as our representation of the internalization and incorporation of socially held behavioral expectations. As such, it can have an important impact not only on the way we feel, think, and behave (present), but also on what we aim to achieve (future). It provides us with a frame of reference with which to interpret social situations and potential behaviors and actions

in all domains, as it appears to signify who we are in relation to, and how we differ from, others.

(Leitch & Harrison, 2016, p. 178)

Because identity is multifaceted and multiple, more and more studies suggest that "identity" is better seen as a flow instead of a static fixture (Coupland & Brown, 2012; Gioia & Patvardhan, 2012, Gioia, Patvardhan, Hamilton, & Corley, 2013). Instead of addressing seemingly "enduring aspects" of who or what a person is, the focus shifts towards how people are becoming, what they are doing, and how they are shaping their development (Coupland & Brown, 2012). Identities are in constant motion and more susceptible to rapid external change, depending on the context in which these identities are developed and displayed (Coupland & Brown, 2012; Gioia & Patvardhan, 2012).

This means identities are often not singular, and many entrepreneurs show multiple professional identities that need to be managed (Slay & Smith, 2010). Each identity serves a separate purpose, as many entrepreneurs work in a variety of terrains (Hennekam & Bennett, 2016). Therefore, context plays an important role for the development of individual identities. In the Netherlands 16% of the creative workers fulfil several roles concurrently compared to 7% of the average Dutch worker (Hennekam & Bennett, 2016). And if this context is changing quickly, such as the media landscape, this influences the need for adaptation and change. This might be related to a "blurring of professional stereotypes" because of changing cultural and industry norms (Kasperiuniene & Zydziunaite, 2019). Therefore, belonging to a coherent group and feeling a part of this group, becomes key. Similarly, this creative context might suggest that a continuous reconstruction of multiple professional selves might be needed (Kasperiuniene & Zydziunaite, 2019).

In our current times, entrepreneurial activity is not only about continuous learning and striving to create a new product or service, but also about developing and continuously reforming one's representation as an entrepreneur on social media (Horst & Hitters, 2020; Horst et al., 2019). Therefore, the social identity of the students of journalism drives their entrepreneurial choices and representations. A study by Alsos, Clausen, Hytti, and Solvoll (2016) shows that entrepreneurs can be divided in three categories of identities. These metaphorical conceptions as "Darwinians, Communitarians and Missionaries" describe what entrepreneurs try to achieve and how they act. Essentially, creatives need to balance fundamental differences between economic self-interest, a concern for others, and being free thinkers (Bange et al., 2020). These value tensions are an integral part of who they "are" and how they act (Beech et al., 2012). This highlights that identity is closely related to image, roleplay, and managing social relationships (Alvesson et al., 2008). In this social relationship management, the rise of social media fundamentally transforms how freelance journalists present themselves and how they act on social media (Brems et al., 2017; Gandini, 2015). For example, Gandini (2015) describes that "social media has come to represent a working tool that serves the curation of a professional image and the management of social relationships via the enactment of performative practices of sociality, which exist around a shared notion of reputation as value". Here, "self-branding becomes an investment in social relationships with expected return for the acquisition of a reputation" (Gandini, 2015). How this relates to the entrepreneurial identity work of freelance journalists, we aim to explore in this chapter.

### 10.2.2 Identity work of media entrepreneurs

Following Sveningsson and Alvesson (2003, p. 1165), "identity work refers to people being engaged in forming, repairing, maintaining, strengthening or revising the constructions that are productive of a sense of coherence and distinctiveness". This happens in a constitutive process of shaping this sense of self in tandem with others in their social context and as part of the expectations and understandings of what their social identity pertains (Watson, 2008, p. 129). Identity work includes all the processes, both social and internal, that are being undertaken, such as behavior, social presentation, and online representation, through which identities are shaped (Leitch & Harrison, 2016).

We know from previous research and conceptual developments that identity is enacted in a specific context. Watson (2008) makes a distinction between internal self-identities and external social identities, where these social identities are a connection between what is socially acceptable and what is internally desired for one's identity. That is why organizations influence the identity work of their people, because they function as a "context" which greatly impacts what can be done to stand apart from one's surroundings (Watson, 2008). This suggests that organizational surroundings and similar social media platforms provide resources and structures with and which to construct a personal identity though identity work. For example, Brems et al. (2017) find that journalists on Twitter often struggle with being factual or opinionated, being personal or professional, how to balance broadcasting their message with engagement and how to promote themselves strategically. This shows that journalists shape their communication for their media and as part of their own development as professionals in this social sphere. This means that they need to come to terms with structure and agency (e.g. Brown, 2015; Coupland & Brown, 2012). They need to balance a sense of stability with fluidity, coherence vs fragmentation, positive vs. negative tendencies, and authenticity and adaptation (Brown, 2015). In their identity work, freelance journalists, or most social media users for the matter, will use communicative resources from their contexts and get used to creating a somewhat stable narrative about themselves over time (Beech, Gilmore, Cochrane & Greig, 2012).

This forming and reforming happens through all sorts of social settings and life-events (Nielsen, Norlyk & Christensen, 2018) and is subject to ongoing account-giving, struggling, reflexive questioning, and conflict managing (Beech, et al., 2012; Sveningsson & Alvesson, 2003). For example, the identity work for journalists may include managing tensions between the need to be creative and the need to be commercially successful (Beech et al., 2012; Eikhof & Haunschild, 2007; Manto et al., 2010; Nielsen et al., 2018; Schediwy et al., 2018). This means students of journalism could benefit from workplace exposure to fuel important experiences and understandings that allow them to construct their own entrepreneurial identity. Because of the tensions between artistic/creative values and economic values, creative entrepreneurs often have strong identity needs, which require overcoming ambiguities and shaping processes of identity work (Inversini et al., 2014; Nielsen et al., 2018; Round & Styhre, 2017).

Identity work highlights the discursive aspects of entrepreneurial development. Both the self-identity part and the social identity is connected to and shaped by the discourse around entrepreneurship (Watson, 2009). This self-narrative and social narrative has multiple dimensions and interpretations, depending on the social or professional setting. It is quite possible that what students of journalism know about "Business" or "Entrepreneurship" is structuring how they see themselves and believe they need to present themselves to others (cf. Watson, 2009). Some journalists might not want to be perceived as an entrepreneur, despite current claims from the tech-driven industry (cf. Pardes, 2022). This means entrepreneurial elements might be seen as necessary facets for students of journalism have to display for being conceived as "professional creatives" and "journalists" (Nielsen, Norlyk & Christensen, 2018). This highlights that identity work inherently carries a reflective appreciation of what to share, display and not to be, for example, the image the person does not want to present or be associated with (Duffy & Hund, 2015).

While this carefully curated and often obsessively reflected notion of professional identity is important to keep in mind, identity work in the creative industry is strongly connected with passion and an innate drive to do what you like (Bhansing et al., 2018). Passion can be defined as intense positive feelings by engaging in meaningful roles closely connected to the identity of the entrepreneurs (Cardon, Gregoire, Stevens & Patel, 2013). This passion can be influenced by role models surrounding the potential entrepreneurs and shape identity formation (Bhansing, Hitters, & Wijngaarden, 2018). More broadly, emotions play a big part in identity work (Winkler, 2018).Any work to maintain or create one's identity is inherently emotional labor. This labor affects social identification, emotional attachment, and even detachment (Winkler, 2018). Therefore, how emotions are expressed and connect with certain stories around progress, and success or failure can give insights to the development of an entrepreneurial identity. Without being able to manage these emotions, the building of a new entrepreneurial self can be a draining effort (Winkler, 2018). Emotions and personal drive will most likely impact the way in which young, becoming journalists enact their role identities as freelancers on social media.

What does this post say about me? What might others think of me if I post this? What kind of content am I really interested in, and should I share this with others? In asking these questions, journalism entrepreneurs reflect on their development, how they are presenting themselves to their audiences and potential clients. They will re-consider their what and how and learn that these conceptions are shaped by social perceptions of their stories and mediatized narratives. This underscores that social media is changing the way identity work is being done (Duffy & Hund, 2015; Gandini, 2015; Khamis et al., 2017; Smith & Sanderson, 2015).

## 10.3 Research design

To be able to understand how students of journalism create their entrepreneurial identity and to what practices of identity work they perform, this study employs a qualitative methodology.

### 10.3.1 The research context

Our empirical context is the University of Applied Sciences "Hogeschool" Utrecht, specifically its School of Journalism in Utrecht, the Netherlands. This is a four-year bachelor study with approximately 500 Dutch students. The school is part of the Institute for Media which contains the Communication and Media Design school. Some parts of the curriculum are done together with the two schools, but most of the curriculum is separate.

The first year is split in two semesters where the students focus on writing news stories in one semester and the other semester is focused on creating audiovisual stories. This curriculum is complemented with theory courses on law, ethics, and economics and a series of research related courses. The second year focuses on fast news and uses mainly audiovisual media to teach the students to work closely together on a series of news shows. It teaches the students to write longer stories, mainly in magazines and other print. These main courses are complemented with courses on factchecking, technology, and entrepreneurship. The third and fourth year of the bachelor education at the School of Journalism comprises of four semesters that can be taken in various sequences, with a graduation semester at the end. Students learn about innovation and multimedia production, and complementing courses in art, hard news, or foreign affairs. The other two semesters are to be filled with a minor at any institution the student desires and a "praktijk" – a freelance semester where the students go on an internship (https://my.hu.nl/link/opleidingsinformatie/dNuUtcdH2BHae9Hi5YoY).

Within this setting of the School of Journalism, the students can adapt the program to their own interests and skills to a certain point. All of them get classes in multimedia storytelling skills, research, entrepreneurship, and general knowledge on how society functions. The final two years allow students to specialize and experience internships in various media companies. This leads to a diverse body of knowledge after the four years of the bachelor education for the School of Journalism. Some go out and find a job at a news desk at a regional broadcaster or printed newspaper. Others go to start their own business, either as a freelance copywriter, videographer, audio specialist, or to truly create a new journalistic product. This was a good context to collect data, because most classes stimulate some level of freelance and entrepreneurship.

### 10.3.2 Data collection

The study uses interview material as the primary source of empirical data. The aim of these interviews was to get extensive descriptions of the developing mindset of the relatively young aspiring journalists. The data consists of a total of 14 interviews ranging between 35 to 65 minutes with students from the upper level (2nd year and above), collected between April and June of 2019. The interviews were all recorded and transcribed.

The interviews were conducted in a semi-structured manner using a list of questions that was partially enlarged over time. Furthermore, the interviews were held in English, not Dutch. This caused some loss and confusion of meaning which was moderated by letting the students use Dutch terms and translating these later. Diverse ethical consideration such as respectful conduct and age were included.

### 10.3.3 Data analysis

The method of analysis was thematic content analysis (Braun & Clarke, 2006; Guest et al., 2014). The theory provided numerous concepts which were used to label and sort the collected data. The data analysis was iterative, but broadly progressed through three stages: (1) creation of first-order observations; (2) second-order observations and abstractions, which created a better overview of the collected data; (3) fine-tuning labels and double-checking the coding quality to derive three themes that provide insights and help answer the research question (Locke et al., 2020).

## 10.4 Findings

Our findings will dive deeper into the notion of image building and describe three practices that make this successful. Generally, our analysis shows that there is a shared understanding of the practices related to social media that journalism students think they need for becoming an entrepreneur. Entrepreneurship is seen as a far-away goal for some, but not for all. The shared understanding which emerged from the analysis shows that the students feel that to become an entrepreneur they must be a freelancer first. Pragmatically speaking, an entrepreneur is seen as a person who owns a business, has a plan, a product to push, and usually has some persons working for them. In comparison, a freelancer is seen as a journalist or media producer who is taking on small jobs for different employers and lacks a plan or a specific product and usually works alone.

Within the broader process of becoming a media entrepreneur after transitioning from being a freelancer, the students talk about three core practices they use when performing identity work over social media that are inherent in their "image building". Image building is central because it highlights the communication and interaction with their audiences over digital media (Deckers & Lacy, 2018). "Self-branding" is nurturing audiences' attention and displaying what is needed to attract their attention continuously. This underscores that the student-journalists are enacting their sense of self through communication on various platforms and occasions. It is perpetually in motion and continues like an unfolding narrative in which they describe and discover what they can be. Three core practices concern storytelling, networking, and managing reflections about social media.

Table 10.1 Abbreviated data structure with first- & second-order observations with themes

| First-order observations | Second-order categories (abstracted patterns & grouping) | | Themes of identity work (theoretical abstraction) |
|---|---|---|---|
| Milestones, such as certain courses, the graduation process, first job or first pay check, give students various levels of confidence to go out and be entrepreneurs (9) | Achieving and setting milestones | Achieving milestones and gaining confidence | Practices of identity work (process of being self) |
| Graduation and registering at the Chamber of Commerce is an important milestone (5) | | | |
| Students are looking for milestones to feel confident (3) | | | |
| Students are not very reflective on their entrepreneurial activities (7) | Not being reflective and planning/strategic | | |
| Some students who are almost done with the studies do reflect on their entrepreneurship (2) | | | |
| Students rarely have a plan on strategic parts of entrepreneurship (9) | | | |
| The interview enabled students to reflect on their position regarding entrepreneurship (6) | | | |
| Commercial jobs should not compromise their journalistic position (4) | Balancing value tensions | | |
| Commercial work is easy (or easier) (6) | | | |
| There is a tension between doing commercial and journalistic work (4) | | | |
| Commercial work is sometimes hidden from online profiles (4) | | | |
| Being a journalist entails certain ethical standards | | | |
| Students use storytelling in their communication to represent themselves (5) | Storytelling about their self | Image building | |
| Students claim to have no conscious story about themselves (2) | | | |
| Storytelling skills are helpful in entrepreneurship, networking and self-representation (7) | | | |

| | |
|---|---|
| Networking is seen as very important for getting jobs and contracts (13) | Networking as opportunity building |
| Working extremely hard at a trial job/internship is necessary for getting a foot in the door/getting noticed | |
| Networking is seen as having to become fake | |
| Students have a specific identity or role when performing networking activities | |
| Getting good journalistic jobs as an entrepreneur is hard (2) | |
| Networking is seen to be an energy draining activity (2) | |
| Students show an aversion to having to perform on social media as a whole (5) | Ambivalent relationship with social media |
| Students show a hate for the fakeness and pressure of social media (5) | |
| Social media (Instagram) is needed to build a good image (4) | |
| Students are very active on social media and use Instagram to build an image (3) | |
| Social media profiles should be updated (3) | |
| Students did not have a plan for an online representation of their identity (2) | |
| Some social media, like personal Facebook, is set to private | |
| Social media is cleaned up to show a professional image | |
| Students are very conscious of how they use social media (3) | |

### Practice 1: Storytelling about their self

In the conversations the students mentioned how they use storytelling in their communication to represent themselves. Many have some sort of self-narrative that they update about themselves whenever they introduce themselves to others. Some of the students feel a solid representation of one-self is needed to be able to get jobs or get noticed. An example is given by Iris

> I think you need a good story. first a good solid story or brand or some-thing you can sell. and you sell yourself, so you have to make sure you have a great story.
>
> – Iris, 24 years old, 4th year student

Other students claim they have no conscious story about themselves. That they make up a representation on the spot. This relates to the need for being authentic and highlights the emergent, unplanned nature of the students' identity. This is shown in an example of a student who cannot really explain why or how a story about himself emerges:

> But I'm not really occupied with [my story] lately and when I have a job interview or interview for an internship, we're actually just talking like this. … I'm just myself, so I presented myself in an interview or in a conversation just like I am and it's kind … of hard to explain that.
>
> – Dennis J., 24 years old, 5th year student

In the School of Journalism, the students are taught certain storytelling skills. The students do mention that these skills in storytelling are helpful in their networking and entrepreneurial representations of self. But many feel they do not have a lot of advantages on other media entrepreneurs who have done studies without a lack of focus on storytelling. Still, they talk about being trained to be able to tell a coherent story and find that very useful. Hannah exemplifies this:

> Maybe I do. I have never thought about it, but perhaps that's not a strange idea. I guess while making this documentary you also have to frame people in a certain way or show them who they really are so maybe unconsciously I do look at how I sort of present myself. I guess my skills that I learned here do help with that.
>
> – Hannah, 23 years old, 5th year student

The students seem to underestimate their ability and skills in storytelling and at some point fail to use it to effectively work on their identity. A lot more conscious effort could assist them in building stronger stories about themselves.

## Practice 2: Networking as opportunity building

Networking is of prime importance for getting jobs and contracts. It is essential for becoming an entrepreneur, and few appear to disagree. This becomes remarkably clear in how the students talk about networking:

> TOON: *How important do you think networking is?*
> HANNAH: *I think very important. That's basically how I got most of my jobs until now. Getting in touch with the right people and making sure they know what you do.*
>
> — Hannah, 23 years old, 5th year student

> That is super important. My friends have always told me: "it's not about what you know, it's about who you know". That's incredibly important. One of the reasons I got accepted for the NOS is because my boss knows Suze van Kleef, who is one of the correspondents that I'm actually going to be working with, so that's how I got in there. That's super super important and a perfect example.
>
> — Jeroen, 22 years old, 3rd year student

Not only networking at events or talking to potential employers or peers is seen as important by the student. They also mention that working hard at internships or any trial job is essential in getting noticed. Many feel that the few opportunities they get to working in a big or well-known media company should be exploited to the maximum potential. So, some of the students mention that they work extremely hard just to get noticed. Jeroen explains this perfectly on an opportunity he got to be an intern for one week:

> [The employer said:] "by the end of that week we're going to have a look whether to hire you as a freelancer or have a little bit of patience and do it in a year". So, I worked my ass off that week. I had to start at nine and I was already there around seven-thirty. I had to leave the office around 5 but I left at 10. Like it was insane! It was probably one of the hardest weeks of my life but at the end of the day on Friday she was so impressed by my working skills, my drive and what I wanted to accomplish. I made the shit ton of mistakes, don't get me wrong, I was terrible, but I was enthusiastic. I worked harder than anybody else and I was just so eager and willing to learn. That that was the main reason for her to hire me.
>
> — Jeroen, 22 years old, 3rd year student

But not all aspects of networking are seen as a clear-cut opportunity to get jobs or contacts. The students talk about how their networking feels forced and fake and a lot of work to keep up. Yet others flourish in this social activity and love talking to people and thus maintain their network.

> The funny thing is, it's not something I do on purpose or something. It's just that I like being with people. I like talking to people. I like getting updates of people's lives, of people's work. And it's something that's going pretty smooth. I know people that are like "okay I need to network; I need to send this email". I'm never thinking about that. It's going in a natural way, and I think it's a kind of power I have for my company. Because it's not that I think I need to do this, but I really like to do it.
> – Mila-Marie, 22 years old, 3rd year student

Some even claim to have a specific personality that they show at network meetings, that they act the part of interested and interesting media worker. Lauren mentions having this "fake" persona at the ready:

> I acted a lot and now I noticed that I'm very good at … creating another persona or another narrative, I'm good at that. So, networking I'm good at just pretending I'm this very confident ambitious girl.
> – Lauren, 22 years old, 4th year student

And thus, networking is seen as a draining job by some. The students talk about how they must be mindful all the time in their self-representation because a job or opportunity could be everywhere. They talk about how it is a chore to keep up what everybody around them is working on, or even how their private lives are going. Also, some complaints are heard in the interviews about how networking takes a lot of time outside of regular business hours. A good example of this feeling that networking is energy draining is by Dennis H.:

> Constantly being aware of people in your network, what they are doing right now and if they're successful or not. You have to call them and stay in touch even if you are doing a project for half a year and you're not seeing them. Because people forget … you otherwise. That's what I feel and I'm not really [that kind of guy]. I feel "slijmerig" [slimy] what's the word in English.
> – Dennis H., 23 years old, 6th year student

Networking triggers the students' desire to be authentic. Some of them seem to think a fake persona is needed to effectively get contracts through their network. This shows that at the end, everyone needs to find their own way of networking. Being yourself, being open to think in networks and how opportunities become co-created with others become important. Therefore, conscious networking and positive, co-constructive relating to others are significant for getting ahead in freelancing and entrepreneurship.

## Practice 3: Managing an ambivalent relationship with social media

The analysis showed that these journalism students have a complex relationship with social media. To put it bluntly, they seem to hate it. They talk about how they hate having to perform on social media, how they must show the world all the work they are doing in journalism and entrepreneurship. Not only that, they display a general hate for the fakeness of social media and pressures it puts on them. A few examples:

> There's no added value on social media because people who really like you, you see them on a daily basis, and you see them in the weekends. And the people who are interested in you, they will know how to find [you]. But the Instagram part nowadays is such bullshit, that there are these companies who contact and send emails like … "hey we are looking for influencers do you want to become an influencer?" And I was like: what the fuck? No, I don't want that! I hate social media, yeah! I really do. I don't follow any of the people who has any influential part in there. I don't like that at all.
>
> – Andres, 22-year-old, 3rd year student

> I don't want thousands of followers. I don't want thousands of people commenting on my work. That will only give me stress. I hate social media. So, I'm really not working towards that.
>
> – Georgia, 20 years old, 3rd year student

However, some of the students see that they do need to be visible on social media, especially Instagram, and build a good image there. A good image means to them to show you being active with various jobs and associate yourself with all the brands you work for. Mark exemplifies this:

> Companies really want to know who they're working with and that's an important part, but I think they're more interested in what can I do for them, in what can I make. So, I think with all the video's that I'm posting, on my YouTube channel that is linked with the website and everything, … if people search me for my website they would see okay this guy worked for this this, this is what he is capable of and this is what we can get from him.
>
> – Mark, 24 years old, 4th year student

It is curious, however, that despite saying they hate social media, students are still very active on it. Not only posting but also checking out what their peers and role models are doing on social media. Here again the focus is on Instagram. Facebook seems to be abandoned by the students, Twitter is sometimes mentioned, but not many other outlets. LinkedIn is seen purely as a professional network tool that hosts their resume and requires hardly any attention. However other online representations of the students, like personal websites and the LinkedIn profile, are in dire need of updating, according to how they talk about it. An example:

> I have a website, but it's not really updated, so I have to [do that] soon. But at least there is a website and I have LinkedIn, but … that also says like what I do now. Facebook, I don't use it for work-related things, so that's really private.
>
> – Sophie, 23 years old, 3rd year student

Again, the students display no clear online strategy. Some keep their private profiles hidden, others do not. None seem to have a plan on how to build their image or what to mention on social media. Just being there and show what you are doing seems to be enough for most of them. An example of this casual attitude towards their image is:

> I do have a LinkedIn page that covers most of my work, … and I actually did get a patent on JeroenBoschmedia.com but I never actually launched the website. For example, I don't know, I just think I was [pause] at the time that I was working on that I just, I just postpone it in and postpone it. I think I never really have gotten back to it because I have worked ever since.
>
> – Jeroen, 22 years old, 3rd year student

In a few interviews the cleaning up of their online profiles was discussed. As stated before, some parts of their profiles are set to private. Other students talk about cleaning up some parts of their profile, removing certain party pictures. Mostly the interviewees were already for years very mindful of not posting beer and bikini photos on social media. Many of the students are very aware that the internet does not forget, and they are very conscious and careful in how they use social media. Dennis J. shows an example of this.

> So, I have a bio that describes a little bit what I do when I do journalists work. That is making mostly personal stories and profiles of people. But that's there so if people need me and they Google me, and they find that LinkedIn page then it's there. But I'm not actively using that now to get assignments. A lot of things I have on private, so only my friends can see the content. And yes, I think since a year year-and-a-half I'm more conscious about that, putting things in private spaces online, so not every possible client or employer can see everything. Also, my sources go Googling me and then I think it's good to have quite a professional presentation online. So, when there are talking to you that they take

you seriously and not just thinking "oh that's a guy that is only drinking beer on his socials".

> – Dennis J., 24 years old, 5th year student

Some of the students mention that they want a professional social media presence. But when prompted what a professional social media presence is, they found it very hard to explain. The ambivalent relationship with social media emerges from these interviews. They want to use it to build their image, but lack a clear strategy and a clear end goal. Overall, building your own strategy on how to relate to social media becomes key. Make your own conscious choices. Create sustainable patterns of social media practice. This way the management of ambivalence can become possible.

## 10.5 Discussion and Conclusion

Overall, we find that students perceive the journey of becoming an entrepreneur as one of creating and sustaining a coherent identity as journalists-entrepreneurs-freelancers. They struggle with their perceptions of their profession of journalist, which underscores that they are quite ambivalent on finding their place within the context they perceive. Such ambiguities are endemic in the creative industries. Therefore, the identity work that they perform reflects these uncertainties and contradictions. They lack a fixed plan on constructing their identity because they lack a clear vision of their end goal. This might be representative for the changes in the media landscape at large, with changes practices, habits and forms of work (Singer & Broersma, 2020). We have shown that the learning environment and the day-to-day interactions that take place therein offer students the ability to fuse the building of a sustainable professional and entrepreneurial identity with their creative drive. The ambiguities of commerce and creativity can be explored, blended, and negotiated within the relative safety of the school. We argue that journalism curricula as well as the educational interaction play a crucial role in the development of professional identities.

Our findings suggest that the process of identity work of these journalism students becoming entrepreneurs shows several concrete elements: achieving and setting milestones, balancing value tensions that relate to how they perceive the dichotomy of entrepreneurship-journalism, and continuously performing the conversation about their development through storytelling about themselves and their success, networking through opportunity building, and coming to terms with the need to use social media, however reluctant they may be. This relates to other current research that highlights the importance of interpretive repertoires to embrace technological change (Singer & Broersma, 2020). It also underscores that we need to carefully examine the pedagogy and our understanding of how we best support learning and development of these students (Graybeal & Ferrier, 2021). This could include teaching survival strategies to empower students (Marín-Sanchiz et al., 2021), and reflecting together on what it means to function on and across platforms and harness co-creation on social-media (Horst et al., 2021; Khajeheian, 2021). We also contribute to a nuanced understanding of the conceptualization of Nielsen and Gartner (2017), who show that students can be both: student and entrepreneurs. Their roles may merge towards a more holistic, rich and complex appreciation of who they are becoming. over time. The separation of self and selves becomes a construct that is blurred in the messiness of a mediatized reality.

The *practical relevance* of this research comes from a better understanding of how creative workers like journalists create their entrepreneurial identity and in what way the curriculum of the schools of journalism is relevant in this creation. This is because if we have a better understanding of the way journalists and other creative workers create their identity, the curricula can be improved to give these students a head-start. This head-start could prove to be invaluable in a mediatized world where the creative worker is becoming the backbone of our culture and economy (Chen et al., 2017; Hennekam & Bennett, 2016; Lange, 2017). If these creative workers can be taught to be more effective and purposefully reflective in developing and understanding who they are, they will stand a better chance to be successful as entrepreneurs (Chen et al., 2018). Furthermore, they may be able to address and manage the identity tensions and ambiguities they face and develop with less anxiety in an already turbulent and precarious environment (Nielsen & Gartner, 2017).

Overall, we believe that identity work offers a great conception to guide future research and practice of entrepreneurship, particularly in the media and creative industries, because mediatization, platformization, and technological change will only further increase.

## References

Achtenhagen, L. (2017). Media Entrepreneurship—Taking Stock and Moving Forward. *International Journal on Media Management*, *19*(1), 1–10. https://doi.org/10.1080/142412 77.2017.1298941

Albinsson, S. (2018). Musicians as entrepreneurs or entrepreneurs as musicians? *Creativity and Innovation Management*, *27*(3), 348–357. https://doi.org/10.1111/caim.12254

Alsos, G. A., Clausen, T. H., Hytti, U., & Solvoll, S. (2016). Entrepreneurs' social identity and the preference of causal and effectual behaviours in start-up processes. *Entrepreneurship & Regional Development*, *28*(3–4), 234–258. https://doi.org/10.1080/08 985626.2016.1155742

Alvesson, M., Ashcraft, K. L., & Thomas, R. (2008). Identity matters: Reflections on the construction of identity scholarship in organization studies. *Organization*, *15*(1), 5–28. https://doi.org/10.1177/1350508407084426

Alvesson, M., & Willmott, H. (2002). Identity regulation as organizational control: Producing the appropriate individual. *Journal of Management Studies*, *39*(5), 619–644. https://doi.org/10.1111/1467–6486.00305

Baker, M., & Gielens, L. (2018). *Making employment more inclusive in the Netherlands* (https:// www.oecd-ilibrary.org/content/paper/da8bc5c4-en)

Bange, S., Järventie-Thesleff, R., & Tienari, J. (2020). Boundaries, roles and identities in an online organization. *Journal of Management Inquiry*. https://doi.org/10.1177/1056492 620968913

Beech, N., Gilmore, C., Cochrane, E., & Greig, G. (2012). Identity work as a response to tensions: A re-narration in opera rehearsals. *Scandinavian Journal of Management, 28*(1), 39–47. https://doi.org/10.1016/j.scaman.2011.12.005

Bergamini, M., Van de Velde, W., Van Looy, B., & Visscher, K. (2017). Organizing artistic activities in a recurrent manner: (On the nature of) entrepreneurship in the performing arts. *Creativity and Innovation Management, 27*(3), 319–334. https://doi.org/10.1111/caim.12240

Bhansing, P. V., Hitters, E., & Wijngaarden, Y. (2018). Passion inspires: Motivations of creative entrepreneurs in creative business centres in the Netherlands. *The Journal of Entrepreneurship, 27*(1), 1–24. https://doi.org/10.1177/0971355717738589

Bhansing, P. V., Wijngaarden, Y., & Hitters, E. (2020). Identity work in the context of co-located creative entrepreneurs: How place influences professional identity. *International Journal of Arts Management, 22*(1), 7–23.

Braun, V., & Clarke, V. (2006). Using thematic analysis in psychology. *Qualitative Research in Psychology, 3*(2), 77–101. https://doi.org/10.1191/1478088706qp063oa

Brems, C., Temmerman, M., Graham, T., & Broersma, M. (2017). Personal branding on Twitter. *Digital Journalism, 5*(4), 443–459. https://doi.org/10.1080/21670811.2016.1176534

Broersma, M., & Singer, J. B. (2020). Caught between innovation and tradition: Young journalists as normative change agents in the journalistic field. *Journalism Practice*, 1–18. https://doi.org/10.1080/17512786.2020.1824125

Broersma, M., & Swart, J. (2021). Do novel routines stick after the pandemic? The formation of news habits during COVID-19. *Journalism Studies*, 1–18. https://doi.org/10.1080/1461670X.2021.1932561

Brown, A. D. (2015). Identities and identity work in organizations. *International Journal of Management Reviews, 17*(1), 20–40. https://doi.org/10.1111/ijmr.12035

Brown, A. D. (2017). Identity work and organizational identification. *International Journal of Management Reviews, 19*(3), 296–317. https://doi.org/10.1111/ijmr.12152

Brown, A. D. (2021). Identities in and around organizations: Towards an identity work perspective. *Human Relations*. https://doi.org/10.1177/0018726721993910

Brown, A. D., & Coupland, C. (2015). Identity threats, identity work and elite professionals. *Organization Studies, 36*(10), 1315–1336. https://doi.org/10.1177/0170840615593594

Cardon, M. S., Gregoire, D. A., Stevens, C. E., & Patel, P. C. (2013). Measuring entrepreneurial passion: Conceptual foundations and scale validation. *Journal of Business Venturing, 28*(3), 373–396. https://doi.org/10.1016/j.jbusvent.2012.03.003

Caza, B. B., Vough, H., & Puranik, H. (2018). Identity work in organizations and occupations: Definitions, theories, and pathways forward. *Journal of Organizational Behavior, 39*(7), 889–910. https://doi.org/10.1002/job.2318

Cerulo, K. A. (1997). Identity construction: New issues, New Directions. *Annual Review of Sociology, 23*(1), 385–409. https://doi.org/10.1146/annurev.soc.23.1.385

Chen, M.-H., Chang, Y.-Y., & Pan, J.-Y. (2018). Typology of creative entrepreneurs and entrepreneurial success. *Journal of Enterprising Communities: People and Places in the Global Economy, 12*(5), 632–656. https://doi.org/10.1108/JEC-07-2017-0041

Chen, M.-H., Chang, Y.-Y., Wang, H.-Y., & Chen, M.-H. (2017). Understanding creative entrepreneurs' intention to quit: The role of entrepreneurial motivation, creativity, and opportunity. *Entrepreneurship Research Journal, 7*(3). https://doi.org/10.1515/erj-2016-0001

Coupland, C., & Brown, A. D. (2012). Identities in action: Processes and outcomes. *Scandinavian Journal of Management, 28*(1), 1–4. https://doi.org/10.1016/j.scaman.2011.12.002

Deckers, E., & Lacy, K. (2018). *Branding yourself: How to use social media to invent or reinvent yourself* (3rd ed.). Que Publishing.

Duffy, B. E., & Hund, E. (2015). "Having it all" on social media: Entrepreneurial femininity and self-branding among fashion bloggers. *Social Media + Society*, *1*(2). https://doi.org/10.1177/2056305115604337

Eikhof, D. R., & Haunschild, A. (2007). For art's sake! Artistic and economic logics in creative production. *Journal of Organizational Behavior*, *28*(5), 523–538. https://doi.org/10.1002/job.462

Fachin, F. F., & Langley, A. (2017). Researching organizational concepts processually: The case of identity. *The Sage handbook of qualitative business management research methods: History and traditions*, 308. https://dx.doi.org/10.4135/9781526430212.n19

Ferrier, M. B. (2013). Media entrepreneurship: Curriculum development and faculty perceptions of what students should know. *Journalism & Mass Communication Educator*, *68*(3), 222–241. https://doi.org/10.1177/1077695813494833

Gandini, A. (2015). Digital work: Self-branding and social capital in the freelance knowledge economy. *Marketing Theory*, *16*(1), 123–141. https://doi.org/10.1177/1470593115607942

Gioia, D. A., & Patvardhan, S. D. (2012). Identity as process and flow. In M. Schultz, S. Maguire, A. Langley, & H. Tsoukas (Eds.), *Constructing identity in and around organizations* (Vol. 3, pp. 50–62). Oxford University Press. https://doi.org/10.1093/acprof:oso/9780199640997.001.0001

Gioia, D. A., Patvardhan, S. D., Hamilton, A. L., & Corley, K. G. (2013). Organizational Identity Formation and Change. *Academy of Management Annals*, *7*(1), 123–193. https://doi.org/10.5465/19416520.2013.762225

Graybeal, G. M., & Ferrier, M. B. (2021). Examination of Pedagogy and Instructional Innovation to Create Entrepreneurs in the Media and Technology Fields. *Entrepreneurship Education and Pedagogy*. https://doi.org/10.1177/25151274211033155

Guest, G., MacQueen, K. M., & Namey, E. E. (2014). *Introduction to applied thematic analysis*. Sage. https://dx.doi.org/10.4135/9781483384436

Hennekam, S., & Bennett, D. (2016). Self-management of work in the creative industries in the Netherlands. *International Journal of Arts Management*, *19*(1), 31–41. https://search.proquest.com/docview/1822399848?accountid=13598

Horst, S.-O. (2019). Strategisches Handeln von Start-ups im Kontext der Mediatisierung: Eine empirische Analyse der kommunikativen Praktiken der Markenführung. In C. Kochhan, T. Könecke, & H. Schunk (Eds.), *Marken und Start-ups* (pp. 187–211). Springer. https://doi.org/10.1007/978-3-658-24586-3_10

Horst, S.-O., & Hitters, E. (2020). Digital media entrepreneurship: Implications for strategic identity work and knowledge sharing of beginning entrepreneurs. *Nordic Journal of Media Management*, *1*(1), 23–44. https://doi.org/10.5278/njmm.2597-0445.3612

Horst, S.-O., Järventie-Thesleff, R., & Perez-Latre, F. J. (2019). Entrepreneurial identity development through digital media. *Journal of Media Business Studies*, *17*(2), 87–112. https://doi.org/10.1080/16522354.2019.1689767

Horst, S.-O., & Murschetz, P. C. (2019). Strategic media entrepreneurship: Theory development and problematization. *Journal of Media Management and Entrepreneurship*, *1*(1), 1–26. https://doi.org/10.4018/jmme.2019010101

Horst, S.-O., Salamzadeh, A., Ebrahimi, P., & Kolli, S. (2021). Co-Creation in Provider Side for Developing Innovative Services: How New Technology-Based Firms Benefit from Social Media Platforms. *Nordic Journal of Media Management*, *2*(2), 109–126. https://doi.org/10.5278/njmm.2597-0445.7089

Inversini, M., Manzoni, B., & Salvemini, S. (2014). Daniel boulud: The making of a successful creative individual business model. *International Journal of Arts Management*, *16*(2), 55.

Kasperiuniene, J., & Zydziunaite, V. (2019). A systematic literature review on professional identity construction in social media. *SAGE Open*, *9*(1). https://doi.org/10.1177/2158244019828847

Khajeheian, D. (2017). Media entrepreneurship: A consensual definition. *AD-Minister*, *30*(January–June 2017), 91–113.

Khajeheian, D. (2020). Enterprise as the central focus in media management research. *Nordic Journal of Media Management*, *1*(1), 1–5. https://doi.org/10.5278/njmm.2597-0445.3912

Khajeheian, D. (2021). Platform entrepreneurship. *Nordic Journal of Media Management*, *1*(4). https://journals.aau.dk/index.php/NJMM/article/view/6716

Khamis, S., Ang, L., & Welling, R. (2017). Self-branding, 'micro-celebrity' and the rise of social media influencers. *Celebrity Studies*, *8*(2), 191–208. https://doi.org/10.1080/1939 2397.2016.1218292

Kosterich, A. (2019). Managing news nerds: Strategizing about institutional change in the news industry. *Journal of Media Business Studies*, 1–18. https://doi.org/10.1080/1652235 4.2019.1639890

Lange, B. (2017). Making Your Career in Creative Industries: The Paradox Between Individual Professionalization and Dependence on Social Contexts and Professional Scenes. In C. Chapain & T. Stryjakiewicz (Eds.), *Creative industries in Europe: Drivers of new sectoral and spatial dynamics* (pp. 109–127). Springer International Publishing. https://doi.org/10.1007/978-3-319-56497-5_6

Leitch, C. M., & Harrison, R. T. (2016). Identity, identity formation and identity work in entrepreneurship: conceptual developments and empirical applications. *Entrepreneurship & Regional Development*, *28*(3–4), 177–190. https://doi.org/10.1080/08985626.2016.1155740

Lewis, K. V. (2016). Identity capital: An exploration in the context of youth social entrepreneurship. *Entrepreneurship & Regional Development*, *28*(3–4), 191–205. https://doi.org/10.1080/08985626.2016.1155741

Locke, K., Feldman, M., & Golden-Biddle, K. (2020). Coding practices and iterativity: Beyond templates for analyzing qualitative data. *Organizational Research Methods*. https://doi.org/10.1177/1094428120948600

Manto, G., Constantine, A., Marianne, W. L., & Amy, E. I. (2010). Managing creatives: Paradoxical approaches to identity regulation. *Human Relations*, *63*(6), 781–805. https://doi.org/10.1177/0018726709342929

Marín-Sanchiz, C.-R., Carvajal, M., & González-Esteban, J.-L. (2021). Survival Strategies in Freelance Journalism: An Empowering Toolkit to Improve Professionals' Working Conditions. *Journalism Practice*, 1–24. https://doi.org/10.1080/17512786.2021.1929414

Nielsen, S. L., & Gartner, W. B. (2017). Am I a student and/or entrepreneur? Multiple identities in student entrepreneurship. *Education+ Training*, *59*(2), 135–154.

Nielsen, S. L., Norlyk, B., & Christensen, P. R. (2018). 'Salesman? Hell no!' Identity struggles of nascent design entrepreneurs. *Creativity and Innovation Management*, *27*(3), 358–369. https://doi.org/10.1111/caim.12275

Oliver, D. (2015). Identity work as a strategic practice. In D. Golsorkhi, L. Rouleau, D. Seidl, & E. Vaara (Eds.), *Cambridge handbook of strategy as practice* (pp. 331–344). Cambridge University Press.

Pardes, A. (2022, 24. 01). Everyone Wants to Be an Entrepreneur. *WIRED*. https://www.wired.com/story/everyone-wants-be-entrepreneur

Price Schultz, C. J., & Jones, M. (2017). You can't do that! A case study of rural and urban media entrepreneur experience. *International Journal on Media Management*, *19*(1), 11–28. https://doi.org/10.1080/14241277.2016.1274994

Ravasi, D., & Canato, A. (2013). How do I know who you think you are? A review of research methods on organizational identity. *International Journal of Management Reviews*, *15*(2), 185–204. https://doi.org/10.1111/ijmr.12008

Round, H., & Styhre, A. (2017). Reality bites: Managing identity ambiguity in an advertising agency. *Creativity and Innovation Management*, *26*(2), 202–213. https://doi.org/10.1111/caim.12203

Schediwy, L., Bhansing, P. V., & Loots, E. (2018). Young musicians' career identities: Do bohemian and entrepreneurial career identities compete or cohere? *Creative Industries Journal*, *11*(2), 174–196. https://doi.org/10.1080/17510694.2018.1489197

Schultz, M., Maguire, S., Langley, A., & Tsoukas, H. (2012). Constructing Identity in and around Organizations: Introducing the Second Volume of "Perspectives on Process Organization Studies". In M. Schultz, S. Maguire, A. Langley, & H. Tsoukas (Eds.), *Constructing identity in and around organizations* (pp. 1–18). Oxford University Press.

Sindik, A., & Graybeal, G. M. (2017). Media entrepreneurship programs: Emerging isomorphic patterns. *International Journal on Media Management*, *19*(1), 55–76. https://doi.org/10.1080/14241277.2017.1279617

Singer, J. B., & Broersma, M. (2020). Innovation and entrepreneurship: Journalism students' interpretive repertoires for a changing occupation. *Journalism Practice*, *14*(3), 319–338. https://doi.org/10.1080/17512786.2019.1602478

Slay, H. S., & Smith, D. A. (2010). Professional identity construction: Using narrative to understand the negotiation of professional and stigmatized cultural identities. *Human Relations*, *64*(1), 85–107. https://doi.org/10.1177/0018726710384290

Smith, L. R., & Sanderson, J. (2015). I'm going to instagram it! An analysis of athlete self-presentation on instagram. *Journal of Broadcasting & Electronic Media*, *59*(2), 342–358. https://doi.org/10.1080/08838151.2015.1029125

Sveningsson, S., & Alvesson, M. (2003). Managing managerial identities: Organizational fragmentation, discourse and identity struggle. *Human Relations*, *56*(10), 1163–1193. https://doi.org/10.1177/00187267035610001

Walzer, D. A. (2017). Independent music production: How individuality, technology and creative entrepreneurship influence contemporary music industry practices. *Creative Industries Journal*, *10*(1), 21–39. https://doi.org/10.1080/17510694.2016.1247626

Watson, T. J. (2008). Managing identity: Identity work, personal predicaments and structural circumstances. *Organization*, *15*(1), 121–143. https://doi.org/10.1177/1350508407084488

Watson, T. J. (2009). Narrative, life story and manager identity: A case study in autobiographical identity work. *Human Relations*, *62*(3), 425–452. https://doi.org/10.1177/0018726708101044

Werthes, D., Mauer, R., & Brettel, M. (2018). Cultural and creative entrepreneurs: Understanding the role of entrepreneurial identity. *International Journal of Entrepreneurial Behavior & Research*, *24*(1), 290–314. https://doi.org/10.1108/IJEBR-07-2016-0215

Wijngaarden, Y. (2019). *Places of co-working: Situating innovation in the creative industries* (Vol. 19). Erasmus Research Center for Media, Communincation and Culture.

Will, A., Brüntje, D., & Gossel, B. (2016). Entrepreneurial venturing and media management. In G. F. Lowe & C. Brown (Eds.), *Managing media firms and industries: What's so special about media management?* (pp. 189–206). Springer.

Winkler, I. (2018). Identity work and emotions: A review. *International Journal of Management Reviews*, *20*(1), 120–133. https://doi.org/10.1111/ijmr.12119

Zboralska, E. (2017). No more status quo! Canadian web-series creators' entrepreneurial motives through a contextualized "entrepreneuring as emancipation" framework. *International Journal on Media Management*, *19*(1), 29–53. https://doi.org/10.1080/14241277.2016.1270947

# Index

Printed in the United States
by Baker & Taylor Publisher Services